Radical Democracy in th

After a decade in local office, ᵢ ₋ₘₗᵤₒus peoples' governments in the Andes fulfilling their promise to provide a more participatory, accountable, and deliberative form of democracy? Using current debates in democratic theory as a framework, Donna Lee Van Cott examines 10 indigenous-party-controlled municipalities in Bolivia and Ecuador. In contrast to studies emphasizing the role of individuals and civil society, the findings underscore the contributions of leadership and political parties to promoting participatory–deliberative institutions. In addition, they suggest that democratic quality is more likely to improve where local actors initiate and design institutions. Van Cott concludes that indigenous parties' innovations have improved democratic quality in some respects, but that authoritarian norms associated with Andean cultures and political organizations have limited their positive impact.

Donna Lee Van Cott is associate professor of political science at the University of Connecticut. She is author of *From Movements to Parties in Latin America: The Evolution of Ethnic Politics* (2005), winner of the 2006 Best Book on Comparative Politics Award, American Political Science Association, Organized Section on Race, Ethnicity and Politics, and a 2006 Choice Outstanding Academic Title. She also is author of *The Friendly Liquidation of the Past: The Politics of Diversity in Latin America* (2000) and editor of *Indigenous Peoples and Democracy in Latin America* (1994). Van Cott has published articles on ethnic and Andean politics in such journals as *Comparative Political Studies, Journal of Democracy, Studies in Comparative International Development, América Latina Hoy, Democratization, Latin American Research Review,* and *Latin American Politics and Society.* She has held fellowships from the Fulbright Foundation and the Helen Kellogg Institute for International Peace, University of Notre Dame.

Radical Democracy in the Andes

DONNA LEE VAN COTT
University of Connecticut

CAMBRIDGE
UNIVERSITY PRESS

University Printing House, Cambridge CB2 8BS, United Kingdom

One Liberty Plaza, 20th Floor, New York, NY 10006, USA

477 Williamstown Road, Port Melbourne, VIC 3207, Australia

314-321, 3rd Floor, Plot 3, Splendor Forum, Jasola District Centre, New Delhi - 110025, India

79 Anson Road, #06-04/06, Singapore 079906

Cambridge University Press is part of the University of Cambridge.

It furthers the University's mission by disseminating knowledge in the pursuit of education, learning and research at the highest international levels of excellence.

www.cambridge.org
Information on this title: www.cambridge.org/9780521734172

© Donna Lee Van Cott 2008

First published 2008

A catalogue record for this publication is available from the British Library

Library of Congress Cataloging in Publication data

Van Cott, Donna Lee.
Radical democracy in the Andes / Donna Lee Van Cott.
   p.   cm.
Includes bibliographical references and index.
ISBN 978-0-521-51558-0 (hardback) – ISBN 978-0-521-73417-2 (pbk.)
1. Andes Region – Politics and government.   2. Democracy – Andes Region.   3. Political participation – Andes Region   4. Politics, Practical – Andes Region.   I. Title.
JL866.v36   2009
320.984 – dc22   2008014781

ISBN 978-0-521-51558-0 Hardback
ISBN 978-0-521-73417-2 Paperback

Contents

Acknowledgments

I have many professional and intellectual debts to acknowledge. I owe the staff of the Helen Kellogg Institute for International Studies – particularly director Scott Mainwaring, Sharon Sheirling, and Judy Bartlett – an enormous debt for their generosity and friendship during a residential fellowship at Notre Dame in 2005. I also profited immensely from the comments, advice, and encouragement that Kellogg and Kroc Fellows Michael Coppedge, Joyce Dalsheim, Robert Fishman, Jan Hoffman French, Kenneth Greene, Frances Hagopian, and Guillermo O'Donnell generously provided as I began the first phase of writing. The opportunity to initiate this ambitious project in the company of Kellogg Institute political scientists who I had idolized for years inspired me to expand the boundaries of my previous research. The David Rockefeller Center for Latin American and Caribbean Studies at Harvard University provided a library scholarship in July 2006 that enabled me to complete a good portion of the research and writing. Jorge I. Domínguez, Merilee Grindle, and Maria Regan ensured that my working environment in Cambridge was pleasant and productive. Working in the proximity of Professor Domínguez, who has been my mentor for more than a decade, increased my productivity by osmosis. Jamy and Jimmy Madeja made my stay on Beacon Hill a dream come true. I also wish to thank Tulane University's Graduate School for partial funding of my 2005 research, the Department of Political Science at the University of Connecticut for a course release that enabled me to complete the manuscript, and my wonderful colleagues at UConn for their encouragement and friendship.

In Ecuador, Fernando García, Jorge León, and Simón Pachano generously provided advice and patiently listened to my initial ideas. In

Guaranda, Manuel Alban helped arrange interviews and provided a warm welcome. In Bolivia, Eduardo Córdova Eguivar, Abraham Borda, and Daniel Moreno Morales helped me to arrange interviews and obtain access to research materials. Their assistance was crucial to the success of that research trip. Once again the librarians at the Universidad de la Cordillera in La Paz were extremely helpful. I also must thank the dozens of social movement and political party leaders, social scientists, NGO professionals, and government officials who agreed to sit for interviews.

I received generous, insightful comments from my friends and colleagues Angelica Bernal, Stephen Dyson, Lisa Heaton, José Antonio Lucero, Michael Morrell, Pablo Regalsky, Roberta Rice, and Brian Wampler. Generous comments and encouragement from Todd Eisenstadt, Shannan Mattiace, and David Samuels were particularly helpful toward the end of the writing. I am indebted to Rachel Gisselquist for access to primary documents in Bolivia, to Lisa Heaton for help in obtaining Bolivian legislation, and to Roberta Rice for sharing her extensive contacts in both countries. My graduate assistant at Connecticut, Maria Fernanda Enriquez, was a great help in getting the final manuscript into production. Portions of the theoretical arguments were developed at private workshops. For their suggestions and encouragement I want to thank participants in the workshop "Deliberative Politics and Institutional Design in Multicultural Democracies," which Will Kymlicka and Dan Munro hosted at Queens University, Kingston, Ontario, in May 2007, as well as participants in the workshop "Transnational Linkages and Institutional Transfers," which Peter Evans, Will Kymlicka, and Ron Levi organized in Toronto in October 2007, under the auspices of the Canadian Institute for Advanced Research.

Finally, I wish to thank my patient and supportive editor at Cambridge University Press, Eric Crahan, as well as two anonymous reviewers, who provided enthusiastic encouragement as well as generous, challenging, and constructive comments. These contributions immensely improved the quality of the final product.

A primitive version of the book's argument was published as Kellogg Institute for International Studies Working Paper #333 in 2006. A brief passage from Robert Albro's "Bolivia's 'Evo Phenomenon': From Identity to What?" is reproduced by permission of the American Anthropological Association from the _Journal of Latin American and Caribbean Anthropology_, 11 (2), 2006. The epigraph to Chapter 3 is taken from _From Max_

Weber: Essays in Sociology, edited by H. H. Gerth and C. Wright Mills, 1973, p. 128, and is reproduced by permission of Oxford University Press. Material from Judith Tendler, *Good Government in the Tropics*, 1997, p. 18. The Johns Hopkins University Press, is reprinted with permission of The Johns Hopkins University Press.

List of Acronyms

AC	Agrupaciones Ciudadanas (Citizens' Groups)
ACOBOL	Asociación de Concejalas de Bolivia (Bolivian Association of Female Councillors)
ADN	Acción Democrática Nacional (National Democratic Action)
AIIECH	Asociación de Iglesias Indígenas Evangélicos de Chimborazo (Chimborazo Association of Indigenous Evangelical Churches)
ANC	Asamblea Nacional Constituyente (National Constituent Assembly)
ASP	Asamblea de la Soberanía de los Pueblos (Assembly for the Sovereignty of the Peoples)
CEDOC	Confederación Ecuatoriana de Organizaciones Clasistas (Ecuadorian Confederation of Classist Organizations)
CEJIS	Centro de Estudios Jurídicos e Investigación Social (Center for Juridical Studies and Social Investigation)
CIDOB	Confederación Indígena del Oriente Boliviano, later Confederación Indígena del Oriente y Amazonía de Bolivia (Indigenous Confederation of the Bolivian East, Indigenous Confederation of the East and Amazon of Bolivia)
CINEP	Centro de Investigación y Educación Popular (Center for Popular Research and Education)

CIPCA	Centro de Investigacíon y Promoción del Campesinado (Center for Investigation and Promotion of the Peasantry)
CMS	Coordinadora de Movimientos Sociales (Coordinator of Social Movements)
CNE	Corte Nacional Electoral (National Electoral Court)
COB	Central Obrero Boliviano (Bolivian Workers Central)
CODENPE	Consejo de Desarrollo de las Nacionalidades y Pueblos del Ecuador (Council for the Development of the Nationalities and Peoples of Ecuador)
CONAIE	Confederación de Nacionalidades Indígenas del Ecuador (Confederation of Indigenous Nationalities of Ecuador)
CONAMAQ	Consejo de Ayllus y Markas del Qullasuyu (Council of Ayllus and Markas of Qullasuyu
CONDEPA	Conciencia de Patria (Conscience of the Fatherland)
CONFENIAE	Confederación de Nacionalidades Indígenas de la Amazonía Ecuatoriana (Confederation of Indigenous Nationalities of the Ecuadorian Amazon)
CONPOCIIECH	Confederación de los Pueblos, Organizaciones, e Iglesias Indígenas Evangélicos de Chimborazo (Confederation of Indigenous Peoples, Organizations, and Evangelical Churches of Chimborazo)
CPESC	Coordinadora de Pueblos Etnicas de Santa Cruz (Coordinator of Ethnic Peoples of Santa Cruz)
CSCB	Confederación Sindical de Colonos Bolivianos (Syndical Confederation of Bolivian Colonists)
CSUTCB	Confederación Sindical Unica de Trabajadores Campesinos de Bolivia (Single Syndical Confederation of Peasant Workers of Bolivia)
DP	Democracia Popular (Popular Democracy)
ECUARUNARI	Ecuador Runacunapac Riccharimui (Awakening of the Ecuadorian Indian)
FADI	Frente Amplio de la Izquierda (Broad Leftist Front)
FECAB–RUNARI	Federación de Campesinos de Bolívar (Federation of Peasants of Bolívar)

FECAMTROP	Federación de Mujeres Campesinas del Trópico (Federation of Women Peasants of the Tropics)
FEI	Federación Ecuatoriana de Indios (Ecuadorian Federation of Indians)
FEINE	Federación Ecuatoriana de Iglesias Indígenas Evangélicas (Ecuadorian Federation of Indigenous Evangelical Churches)
FEJUVE	Federación de Juntas Vecinales (Federation of Neighborhood Juntas)
FENOCIN	Federación Nacional de Organizaciones Campesinas, Indígenas, y Negras (National Federation of Peasant, Indigenous, and Black Organizations)
FETCH	Federación Especial del Trópico de Chimoré (Special Federation of the Tropics of Chimoré)
FETCTC	Federación Especial de Trabajadores Campesinos del Trópico de Cochabamba (Special Federation of Peasant Workers of the Tropics of Cochabamba)
FEYCH	Federación Especial de los Yungas del Chapare (Special Federation of the Yungas of the Chapare)
FICI	Federación Indígena y Campesina de Imbabura (Indigenous and Campesino Federation of Imbabura)
FORMIA	Fortalecimiento a Municipios Indígenas Alternativas (Strengthening of Indigenous Alternative Municipalities)
FSCCT	Federación Sindical de Colonizadores de Carrasco Tropical (Syndical Confederation of Colonists of Tropical Carrasco)
FSUTCC	Federación Sindical Unica de Trabajadores Campesinos de Cochabamba (Single Syndical Federation of Campesino Workers of Cochabamba)
ICCI	Instituto Científico de Culturas Indígenas (Scientific Institute of Indigenous Cultures)
ID	Izquierda Democrática (Democratic Left)
IPSP	Instrumento Político para la Soberanía de los Pueblos (Political Instrument for the Sovereignty of the Peoples)
IU	Izquierda Unida (United Left)

LPP	Ley de Participación Popular (Law of Popular Participation)
MACOJMA	Markas, Ayllus y Comunidades Originarias de Jesús de Machaca (Markas, Ayllus and Original Communities of Jesús de Machaca)
MAS	Movimiento al Socialismo (Movement Toward Socialism)
MBL	Movimiento Bolivia Libre (Free Bolivia Movement)
MIAJ	Movimiento Indígena Amauta Jatari (Amauta Jatari Indigenous Movement)
MIAY	Movimiento Indígena Amauta Yuyay (Amauta Yuyay Indigenous Movement)
MICH	Movimiento Indígena de Chimborazo (Chimborazo Indigenous Movement)
MIP	Movimiento Indígena Pachakuti (Pachakuti Indigenous Movement)
MIR	Movimiento de Izquierda Revolucionario (Revolutionary Leftist Movement)
MNR	Movimiento Nacional Revolucionario (National Revolutionary Movement)
MPD	Movimiento Popular Democrático (Popular Democratic Movement)
MRTKL	Movimiento Revolucionario Tupaj Katari de Liberación (Tupaj Katari Revolutionary Liberation Movement)
MSM	Movimiento Sin Miedo (Movement of the Fearless)
MST	Movimiento Sin Tierra (Movement of the Landless)
MUPP–NP	Movimiento de Unidad Plurinacional Pachakutik–Nuevo País (Pachakutik United Plurinational Movement–New Country)
NFR	Nueva Fuerza Republicana (New Republican Force)
NGO	nongovernmental organization
OSG	Organización de Segundo Grado (Second-Level Organization)
OTB	Organización Territorial de Base (Territorial Base Organization)
PB	participatory budgeting
PCB	Partido Comunista de Bolivia (Bolivian Communist Party)
PDC	Partido Demócrata Cristiano (Christian Democratic Party)

PDM	Plan de Desarrollo Municipal (Municipal Development Plan)
PI	Pueblo Indígena (Indigenous People)
POA	Plan Operativa Anual (Annual Operating Plan)
PODEMOS	Poder Democrático Social (Democratic Social Power)
PRE	Partido Roldosista Ecuatoriano (Ecuadorian Roldosista Party)
PRODEPINE	Programa Nacional para el Desarrollo de los Pueblos Indígenas y Negros (National Program for the Development of the Indigenous and Black Peoples)
PRONASOL	Programa Nacional de Solidaridad (National Solidarity Program)
PS	Patria Solidaria (Fatherland in Solidarity)
PSE	Partido Socialista Ecuatoriano (Ecuadorian Socialist Party)
PSP	Partido Sociedad Patriótica (Patriotic Society Party)
PT	Partido Trabalhista (Brasiliera) (Workers' Party)
PUAMA	Pueblo Unido Multiétnico de Amazonas (United Multiethnic People of Amazonas)
SAFCO	Sistema de Administración Financiera y Control Gubermental (Financial Administration and Governmental Control System)
SIISE	Sistema Integrado de Indicadores Sociales del Ecuador (Integrated System of Social Indicators of Ecuador)
TSE	Tribunal Supremo Electoral (Supreme Electoral Tribunal)
UCIG/UOCIG	Unión de Organizaciones Campesinas e Indígenas de Guamote (Union of Campesino and Indigenous Organizations of Guamote)
UCS	Unión Cívica de Solidaridad (Civic Union of Solidarity)
UN	Unidad Nacional (National Unity)
UNDP	United Nations Development Program
UNORCAC	Unión de Organizaciones Campesinas e Indígenas de Cotacachi (Union of Peasant and Indigenous Organizations of Cotacachi)
USAID	U.S. Agency for International Development

Introduction: The Political and Cultural Origins of Democratic Institutional Innovation

In the 1990s, as South America's party systems began to undergo serious crises, indigenous peoples formed electorally viable political parties for the first time. In Bolivia, Colombia, Ecuador, Guyana, and Venezuela, candidates emphasizing an ethnically indigenous identity and representing parties affiliated with indigenous social movement organizations gained control of local and intermediate governments, as well as a foothold in national legislatures. They became most successful in Bolivia and Ecuador, where today they dominate dozens of local governments and control significant blocs in Congress. In 2005 and 2002, respectively, indigenous parties elected the country's president.[1]

It is no accident that the new indigenous parties emerged at a time when public confidence in parties had plummeted. The failure of parties to reduce poverty and inequality, to protect citizens from crime and violence, to promote economic development, and to protect human rights two decades after the end of military rule generated declines in public support for parties and for democracy itself (Drake and Hershberg 2006: 10; Hagopian 2005: 320; O'Donnell 2004: 46–51; UNDP 2004: 62).[2] Latin American citizens view traditional political parties as corrupt, self-serving, incapable of addressing complex economic and social problems or protecting citizens rights and the rule of law, and unresponsive to increasing demands for action (Hagopian 2005: 321; Mainwaring and

---

[1] On indigenous peoples' formation of political parties see Birnir (2004, 2007), Collins (2000, 2001), Pallares (2002), Rice (2006), Van Cott (2000, 2003, 2005), and Yashar (2005, 2006).

[2] Public confidence in parties in Latin America fell to 11% in 2003, down from 20% in 1996 (UNDP 2004: 38).

Hagopian 2005: 2; O'Donnell 2004). Voters are searching for representation alternatives that offer real solutions, as opposed to patriotic platitudes. Many are attracted to indigenous peoples' parties because they seem to provide an alternative. Amid the "disorientation of the post-communist ideological vacuum" (Merkl 2007: 340) indigenous parties offer a passionate critique of neoliberalism, political corruption, and foreign economic exploitation alongside an alternative vision of government accountability, economic justice, social solidarity, collective identity, and national sovereignty – albeit one that often lacks practical details.

The implications for democratic quality of the recent decline of Latin America's traditional parties have received significant scholarly attention (e.g., Coppedge 1998; Mainwaring 1999; Mainwaring and Scully 1995; K. Roberts 2002). But we have yet to learn much about the impact of the new indigenous parties on the quality of democracy. They have fulfilled their promise to indigenous constituents to improve descriptive representation by electing representatives who share the same ethnic and cultural characteristics (Mansbridge 2000: 100–1). Their rise to local, regional, and national office has transformed relations of power and challenged status quo views of the nation, the role of the state, and democracy. Their origin in social movements and representation of a "onetime despised minority" constitute a transformation of state–society relations.[3]

But indigenous parties promised more. For example, the Ecuadorian indigenous-movement-based party, Pachakutik Movement of Plurinational Unity (Pachakutik), promised to facilitate "the metamorphosis from utopia to reality" through the creation of "Alternative Local Governments" (Coordinadora de Gobiernos Locales Alternativos 2004: 3). Pachakutik candidates promised voters that they would provide a more participatory, intercultural model of democracy. And they proposed that this model serve as a model for the world. As one of Pachakutik's coordinators explained to me:

We believe that we were the first, the pioneers. Now there are other experiences in Ecuador, but we were the pioneers with respect to what is a participatory, democratic government, and we defined various areas. This is not done as an experiment but rather as a real exercise of power in order to demonstrate to the country and to the world what is possible, that it is possible to have other

---

[3] Peter Merkl incorrectly identifies labor movements as the only "onetime despised minority" that has converted itself from a minority to a majority "party of government" (2007: 334–5). Bolivia's MAS achieved this in 2005 after only 10 years in existence – much swifter than labor movements, which typically took decades to reach that goal.

types of democracy where the society is taken into consideration. (My translation; interview, Benito Suarez, Quito, 21 June 2005.)

Similarly, at its 2003 Fifth Congress, the Bolivian indigenous-movement-based party Movement toward Socialism (Movimiento al Socialismo, or MAS) approved the following principles, among others:

> To postulate a true participatory democracy of consensus, respect and recognition of the diverse social organizations, where the Communities and the people find their liberation from all forms of poverty, misery and discrimination without being subordinated or exploited....
>
> To consider Bolivia to be a multinational and pluricultural State integrated by living and existing together in mutual respect....
>
> The Movement toward Socialism expresses its profound commitment to the development of a Communitarian Democracy, of consensus and Participation, of social and economic content. This democracy must contain political mechanisms that constitute channels for links between government and all popular sectors. (My translation; Movimiento al Socialismo 2004a: 19–22.)

We are most likely to perceive the impact of indigenous-party governance at the local level in municipalities where parties have controlled some governments for a decade. Thus I focus on indigenous parties' experiences promoting institutional innovation in local government. As Hiskey and Seligson observe, local institutions are crucial for the construction of system support in ailing democracies (2003: 85). Promising local experiments in institutional design have the potential to inspire and provide useful models for democratic reforms with geographically broader impact. Local government reform is particularly important in democratizing poor countries because they typically are governed by weak states with a limited presence and a limited ability to provide services and protect rights throughout their territory. Thus I ask, after 10 years in local office, are indigenous parties fulfilling their promise to deepen democracy? If so, under what political conditions can an indigenous party serve as catalyst, designer, and executor of democratic innovation? Are indigenous-party-led governments offering anything more innovative than participatory budgeting overlaid with cultural motifs? Are "successful antisystem parties" (see Merkl 2007: 335) more suited than system-sustaining parties to comprehensive democratic reform? What value do indigenous political parties add to procedures that have been implemented elsewhere? More broadly, what does the experience of institutional reform in the rural Andes teach us about the prospects for improving democratic quality in democratizing ethnically diverse regions? I focus on political and cultural variables that have received little attention from the literature on democratic reform in local government. That literature has tended to foreground the organization and actions of civil society as a catalyst for institutional change (Wampler 2008). Instead, I focus on two key actors that have received insufficient attention: mayors and political parties. I make three central arguments.

First, I argue that the political dynamics of decentralization and institutional design profoundly affect the quality of democratic institutional innovations and that these innovations promote higher-quality democracy when their institutional settings are flexible and the impetus for their adoption comes from municipal actors – chiefly mayors and civil-society organizations. Scholars typically distinguish between decentralization processes characterized by a "top-down" dynamic, in which national-level leaders initiate decentralization and design and impose uniform subnational institutions throughout the territory, and a "bottom-up" dynamic, in which the impetus for transferring political and administrative powers and the design of subnational institutions comes from the local or regional level (Eaton 2004: 8; Montero and Samuels 2004: 10–11; O'Neill 2004: 41). Between these extremes we find a balance of inputs from national, state, and local actors.

Ecuador and Brazil exhibit a mixture of the top-down and bottom-up approaches. Central-government elites in Ecuador facilitated decentralization by providing legal mechanisms that enable local governments to petition for responsibilities in specific policy sectors and by transferring national revenues to municipalities. But local governments must initiate this process, and they have considerable flexibility with respect to institutional design. This is unusual because it is the norm for national politicians to design subnational institutions (Eaton 2004: 32). In Brazil, as well, after the transition to civilian-elected rule in the 1980s, a coalition of reformers representing government and civil society promoted decentralization from the top down but gave local governments the freedom to develop their own organic laws and decision-making processes (Baiocchi 2005: 8).

Bolivia and Mexico exemplify a markedly more top-down approach. In the mid-1990s President Gonzalo Sánchez de Lozada imposed a rigid, universal model on 327 diverse municipalities. Since then, only modest refinements have been made in response to citizen complaints. Municipalities in 1995 were required to take responsibility for health and education provision and to adhere to a variety of complex restrictions regarding the allocation of resources. Bolivia's rigid, top-down dynamic, and the fact that Sánchez de Lozada designed the 1994 Law of Popular Participation (Ley de Participación Popular, or LPP) in part to improve his party's future electoral chances (O'Neill 2004) evokes the Mexican decentralization process. Mexico's central-state-led decentralization evolved slowly and tentatively between 1980 and 2005. The process accelerated and deepened in the 1990s after the central government imposed the National Solidarity Program (Programa Nacional de Solidaridad, or PRONASOL). After 1997, the ruling party lost control of Congress, greatly increasing the amount of resources for local governments (Grindle 2007: 18, 164). The Bolivian cases demonstrate that it is difficult for a national government to impose a universal, rigid institutional design on diverse municipalities with distinct relations of power, political cultures, and geography, for the same reasons that foreign governments have largely failed to export democratic institutions abroad. Citizens are less likely to identify with imposed institutions or to defend them from counterreform. And imported institutions are less likely to address the particular governance problems of a locality without the input of local actors. My findings confirm Eaton's: The content of decentralizing reforms owes much to the identity (state/civil society) and location (national/subnational) of the actors who initiate the transfer of powers and resources and who design the subnational institutions (Eaton 2004: 8). Other things being equal, top-down imposition of participatory spaces is unlikely to result in deepening democracy. Rather, as Wampler discovered in Brazil, there must be a rough balance between state and society with respect to the impulse to transfer power and authority (2008).

Owing to the distinct dynamics of decentralization and institutional design, compared with the Bolivian cases, all of the Ecuadorian cases demonstrate more democratic outcomes in terms of the quality of participation and deliberation. This finding calls into question the degree to which the Bolivian reform has served as a model for the development community, whereas the more flexible, piecemeal Ecuadorian approach has received relatively little attention or praise. A comparison of the two national experiences demonstrates that a strong national commitment to decentralization and the provision of a reliable revenue stream to local governments may more effectively shift resources to poor communities, but it does not necessarily improve the quality of local democracy.

My second argument underscores an inconvenient truth: Leadership matters. It matters more than scholars would like to admit. Many dismiss leadership as a residual category for unexplainable outcomes. Others disregard leadership because it is a difficult concept to operationalize. As

Tendler argues, foregrounding leadership emphasizes the singularity of particular individuals. If leadership depends on luck, then it cannot be replicated in other settings and, thus, is not worth studying (Tendler 1997: 18). Because the objective of participatory and deliberative institutions is to maximize the role of ordinary citizens while reducing the importance of power hierarchies, some utopian political philosophers deem leaders to be irrelevant (Budge 2000: 206).

But empirical research demonstrates that leaders play an important role in determining substantive outcomes and decision-making procedures, particularly in local government (e.g., Andersson and Van Laerhoven 2007; Grindle 2007; Humphreys, Masters, and Sandbu 2006; Wampler 2004, 2008). Leadership is crucial in a context of weak and emerging democratic institutions and scant state authority because leaders can compensate for these institutional weaknesses by activating feelings of personal loyalty and trust. In the cases I studied indigenous political parties provided beneficial institutional reform in municipalities in which they were able to attract, elect, and maintain continuously in office mayors who could establish personal bonds of loyalty and trust with voters. These mayors also had to perform five crucial functions: (1) communicate effectively across ethnic lines; (2) provide sufficient political continuity for innovations to become institutionalized by staying in office for several terms; (3) attract financial resources from NGOs and international donors that augment tiny municipal budgets; (4) maintain the support and cohesion of key civil-society organizations; and (5) establish a degree of autonomy from them. My findings are significant because indigenous communities are considered "hard cases" for demonstrating the importance of individual agency, given the emphasis by anthropologists and philosophers on the communitarian–collectivist nature of indigenous culture. Indigenous politicians themselves tout the distinctive consensual–communitarian nature of indigenous decision making, as seen in the quotation in the preceding text.

Third, I demonstrate that institutionalized parties improve citizen participation – even at the local level. Political scientists have long understood the importance of political parties and civil society to the quality of democratic institutions.[4] But many scholars envision participatory and

---

[4] With regard to Latin America, see, e.g., Alcántara and Freidenberg (2001); Coppedge (1998); Dahl (1971); Foweraker, Landman, and Harvey (2003); Hagopian and Mainwaring (2005); Levitsky (2001); Levitzky and Cameron (2001); Mainwaring (1999); Mainwaring and Scully (1995); O'Donnell (1997); Roberts and Wibbels (1999).

deliberative institutional designs to be a replacement for parties, while giving society a larger role in governance. They share citizens' low regard for parties and view civil society in idealistic terms (Baiocchi 2005: 149; Budge 2000). I argue that, in the context of relatively new and weak local institutions, political parties play a crucial role as partners to innovative mayors by providing the institutional source for the recruitment and production of leaders and serving as their most important base of support. Moreover, where the formal and informal rules of political competition are new and uncertain, political organizations act as a counterbalance to charismatic executive leadership, which in Latin America has a tendency to overrun legislative and judicial institutions and to obstruct the creation of strong parties or democratic institutions that might limit their prerogatives (Kitschelt 2000: 855). And parties have the potential, still unrealized in Bolivia and Ecuador, to act as transmission belts for the diffusion of local innovations horizontally – as occurred in Brazil with the dissemination by the Workers' Party (Partido Trabalhista, or PT) of the Porto Alegre model to other PT cities (Baiocchi 2005: 12; Goldfrank 2007b; Wampler 2007) – and vertically to higher levels of government.

Indigenous peoples' parties are well suited to promoting institutional innovation. They are "organic parties" – electoral vehicles that civil-society organizations formed to advance their interests from inside the political system (Panebianco 1988; Roberts 1998). The cultural institutions and social-movement organizations in which indigenous parties are rooted provide institutional cohesion during the reform process, embody normative content that inspires constituents to participate in time-consuming activities and patiently await substantive results, and infuse public institutions with meaningful cultural symbols that convey legitimacy and authority on government while fledgling institutions earn public trust. Their rootedness in social movements makes them ideal partners for innovating mayors because they are less vulnerable to professional incentives and bureaucratic rigidity and more receptive to institutional designs that place society at the center of public decision making. In the Andes in the last decade, promoting such changes has been critical to indigenous parties' strategy to transform themselves from idealistic electoral longshots to governing parties.

A focus on political organizations enables us to examine the "environmental complexity" (Panebianco 1988: 210) in which institutional innovations are demanded, designed, and deployed. I argue that radical democratic reform is more likely to occur in environments in which relations of power are shifting and uncertain and new actors struggle to enter and reshape political institutions. Under conditions of complexity and uncertainty new system entrants are more likely to affect political outcomes and declining elites may be more likely to agree to new arrangements in order to retain a place in the political order. Like Panebianco, I focus on the "organizational order" and the relationship between political organizations and the context in which they compete for power and resources (1988). Organizational orders evolve over time; they result in and are affected by institutional innovations. The opening of local political space provided an unprecedented opportunity for indigenous social movements to enter formal politics and to pursue long-standing self-government goals.

NORMATIVE AND EMPIRICAL APPROACHES TO EVALUATING DEMOCRATIC QUALITY

My theoretical framework engages the rich debate in normative theory that proposes alternative – sometimes utopian – norms and processes that aim to significantly improve the quality of democratic life. These alternatives usually are grouped under the heading "radical democracy."[5] For its adherents, radical democracy evokes a "distinctive form of democracy" through which a free and dynamic civil society and formal representational institutions "are transformed by their connections with participatory–deliberative arrangements for solving problems" (Cohen and Fung 2004: 32). Although there is considerable variety among the proposals, most emphasize institutions that promote the following: public debate on public policy issues; opportunities for civil-society organizations and individual citizens to deliberate on public policy choices and participate in the monitoring of government activities; the creation of quasi-state institutions representing identity groups as a complement to territorially based representative institutions; measures to ensure that disadvantaged individuals and groups have the resources necessary to participate on a basis of greater equality with more advantaged groups; and the promotion of a more lively and free civil society (Saward 2000b: 219–20).

---

[5] Among the most influential, seminal works in this vast literature are Barber (1984); Cohen and Arato (1992); Cohen and Rogers (1995a); Dryzek (1990); Fung and Wright (2003a, 2003b); Habermas (1984); Mansbridge (1983); Mouffe and Laclau (1985); and Offe (1984).

I use the term radical democracy in the sense that contemporary political philosophers do to connote the expansive scope of the democratic reforms proposed, rather than an association with Marxist revolution (Cohen and Rogers 1995a: 11, 239, 262; Fung and Wright 2003b: 22). This vision of radically democratic change focuses on values and culture and on deepening democracy by making it more participatory and deliberative (Cohen and Fung 2004: 23–4; Nylen 2003: 147). It is distinct from the socialist vision's emphasis on redistribution and class relations, although the two projects are philosophically and practically compatible, and both are concerned with promoting social justice. In fact, the radical democracy literature developed as much in opposition to class-based analyses as to liberal-democratic proposals for incremental reform and represents a deliberate departure from Marxist–Leninist thinking (Nylen 2003: 146). Although they accept the important role that representative–competitive politics plays in democratic life, radical democrats critique this style of politics for failing to promote important democratic values, such as responsibility, equality, and autonomy (Cohen and Fung 2004: 24–6). Whereas Marxists urge political actors to redistribute productive assets to create the equality necessary for democracy, radical democrats call for the institution of more participatory–deliberative mechanisms that give citizens a direct role in public decision making. These mechanisms better promote equality by giving more authority to poor and marginalized groups (ibid.).

Radical democrats challenge us to expect more from modern political institutions. For example, political theorist Mark E. Warren is "impressed with the possibility that even today democracy might be rethought and even radicalized within the vast array of participatory spaces that large-scale, complex, and differentiated societies now offer combined with the multiple means of making collective decisions that now exist" (2001: 13). Sociologist Gianpaolo Baiocchi classifies Porto Alegre's participatory budgeting experiment as a "radical democratic vision of popular municipal control" that PT administrators viewed as "part of a broader transformative project" (2003: 68). The greatest impact of the renowned Porto Alegre case, he argues, has been its inspiration of projects elsewhere that seek to "radically democratize democracy," rather than the promotion of socialist models (Baiocchi 2005: 154–5). In contrast to Marx, who argued that economic change must precede political change, radical democrats assume that it is possible for government and social institutions to effect major social and political changes, which may have redistributive effects.

Institutional innovators in my cases shared this assumption. Notwithstanding their economic marginalization – the average poverty rates for
my five municipal cases in Bolivia and Ecuador were 88.84% and 87.58%
in 2001, respectively, significantly higher than the national averages of
58.6% and 61.3% – indigenous parties seized political institutions and
altered the values and processes of local governments (Censo Nacional
de Población y Vivienda 2001; SIISE 2003). But only in a few cases and
in limited ways has there been any change in the underlying economic
relations because local contexts are embedded in larger, stickier, national
and international systems. In most cases the paltry sums available for
local investment have been reallocated toward more needy, once-ignored
groups, but they are insufficient to alleviate poverty. Whether the reader
finds such projects and their results to be "radical" is beside the point;
the innovators and their supporters sought radical change. For example,
the Pachakutik platform in the province of Bolívar explicitly identifies
radical democracy as a guiding principle, defining it as follows:

> Where the people effectively exercise social control and make decisions about
> their history, present and future, guaranteeing, thus, real participation of civil
> society in the decision, management, and conduct of the most important aspects
> of their own lives. (My translation; Arévalo and Chela Amangandí 2001: 21.)

The normative philosophical literature on radical democracy has limitations. It tends to be abstract and usually fails to offer concrete models
applicable to real-world cases (Johnson 1998: 175–6; Fung and Wright
2003a; James 2004: 15). Rare, real-world examples usually are taken
from advanced industrialized societies (e.g., Cohen and Rogers 1995a,
2003; James 2004: 3; Warren 2001[6]), and philosophers often ignore
divided societies, writing them off as impossible cases (James 2004: 15).
This is unfortunate because ethnically divided developing countries are
more in need than institutionalized democracies of innovative solutions
for democratic stagnation or reversal. Moreover, Western democracies
might learn from developing-country examples, just as developing countries have learned from Western models (Armony and Schamis 2005:
126). If innovative institutional designs can succeed under adverse conditions should we perhaps raise our aspirations for political life in established democracies?

Whereas normative political theory has often failed to test abstract
theories against existing conditions, comparative empirical approaches

---

[6] Fung and Wright (2003b) and Avritzer (2002) are notable exceptions.

are equally deficient because they are trapped in paradigms that have failed to explain why democracies are performing so poorly (Hagopian 2005: 336). Despite the extensive scholarship that comparativists have produced on democratic quality, the literature lacks a consensus on an appropriate definition of democracy or the appropriate criteria for the assessment and measurement of its quality (Armony and Schamis 2005: 115; Vargas Cullel 2004: 107). Definitions of democracy tend to exaggerate the importance of elections while its measures tend to overrepresent levels of contestation and to omit indicators measuring informal barriers to participation (Coppedge et al. 2008: 13; Munck and Verkuilen 2002).[7] The criteria used most commonly to measure or assess the quality of democracy are the two dimensions that Robert Dahl identified more than 35 years ago: *contestation*, or the ability of contenders to compete in a fair electoral contest in which the outcome is uncertain; and *participation*, or the extent to which competition is extended to the entire adult population (1971). In fact, Coppedge et al. discovered that the most common indicators of democracy primarily measure levels of contestation and participation (2008). Such measures fail to capture information about diverse modes of participation beyond voting, to assess the participation of civil society organizations in public life, or to reveal and assess patterns of domination based on group membership. By emphasizing the participatory elements of democratic quality, this study helps to redress that imbalance and to bring Dahl's dimensions into the 21st century.

Practitioners typically use the insights of the comparative politics literature on democratic quality to promote incremental institutional reforms, such as adjusting the formula for turning votes into seats or the relative power of executives and legislatures. They choose from a small toolbox of familiar instruments. However, given the profound problems of Latin American democracy – particularly in the ethnically divided, politically unstable, impoverished Andean countries (Arnson 2001; Drake and Hershberg 2006; Mainwaring, Bejarano, and Pizarro 2006; Mauceri and Burt 2004) – improvements in democratic quality cannot rely solely on existing institutional designs and processes copied from distinct contexts. Timid, gradual reforms will not assuage growing citizen discontent,

---

[7] Munck and Verkuilen observe that these measures tend to use multiple indicators to measure the same democratic attribute, distorting the importance of particular attributes relative to others, and they tend to use additive methods for calculating summary scores of democratic quality without theoretical justification, ignoring the possibility that some attributes might be more important than others or may amplify or counteract their effects (2002).

particularly when they are accompanied by meager development budgets. We must look instead to *radical* alternatives that challenge the prevailing values and institutions that have consistently failed to provide conditions for meaningful citizenship. We must look more closely at the connections between citizens and institutions of representation to understand better why the latter are failing (Hagopian 2005: 336; K. Roberts 1998). And we must expand our vision of democratization in developing regions like Latin America to encompass new possibilities that may originate in non-Western culture – as the founders of the United States looked to the Great Binding Law of the Haudenosaunee for inspiration.[8] It is particularly important to look at local experiences that can act as laboratories for state–society partnerships and institutional reform (Bebbington, Delamaza, and Villar 2005: 8).

Fung (2007: 443–4) argues that an artificial boundary has emerged between normative political theory and empirical political science that impoverishes both and impedes the advancement of democratic theory. The result is a disconnect between explanations of democratic success and failure and the effort to imagine what a better democracy would and could look like. Fung urges scholars of democracy to constantly adjust our conceptions of democracy to ensure that the institutions we prescribe do not yield consequences that are inimicable to the values that underpin them but, rather, promote them (2007: 444).

This goal to reunite normative democratic theory and positive comparative politics inspired my approach. I address the limitations of the normative radical democracy literature by testing its insights against comparative empirical research. I observed 10 municipalities in two countries in which indigenous-movement-based political parties attempted to realize some or all of the goals that radical democrats articulate by establishing participatory–deliberative institutions. I follow the cases from 1995, when the earliest indigenous parties were formed, through 2005, when field research concluded. I explain how distinct dynamics of decentralization, the performance of mayors, and the role of political parties help explain variation in the design and impact of radically democratic institutional innovation.

---

[8] The Haudenosaunee formed their confederation hundreds of years before the arrival of Europeans in what is today upstate New York and Québec. It ultimately incorporated six indigenous nations and consisted of a system of democratic ideals and processes that influenced the founding structures of the United States, such as bicameral government, direct democracy mechanisms like the recall, referendum, and legislative initiative, and a system of checks and balances. See Grinde (1992) and Wilkins (2007).

INDIGENOUS VISIONS OF DEMOCRACY AND RADICAL DEMOCRATIC THEORY

The visions of local democracy that distinct indigenous movements throughout the Andes express share remarkable similarities. Andean indigenous movements over the past 25 years have developed a common ideology of intercultural, participatory, deliberative, and transparent government that infuses indigenous parties' vision of governance. What vision of democracy are indigenous peoples' parties pursuing? Based on our understanding of this vision how might we expect indigenous political parties and movements to adapt Western participatory–deliberative designs developed for modern cities to rural, economically stagnant settings?

Indigenous parties in the Andes, like radical democrats, reject the sharp distinction between the public sphere of government decision making and administration and the private sphere of family and voluntary organizations that the Western, liberal model of representative democracy delineates. These spheres traditionally have been fused in indigenous communities, where the same leaders may perform administrative, economic, law enforcement, and spiritual roles, and where families are the basic unit of politics. Each family is responsible for service to the community and adult men and women perform distinct roles in the public and private spheres, respectively. Thus public and private are linked through the married couple. Indigenous political cultures typically embody the features that Mansbridge attributes to "unitary democracy": a preference for making decisions through consensus rather than voting; direct participation of all community members in face-to-face interactions, as opposed to representation; an assumption of common rather than conflicting interests; and an ethic of equal respect. These features, in Mansbridge's words, "encourage members to identify with one another and with the group as a whole" and foster a strong sense of identification with the group's common interests (1983: 3–5).

In Andean indigenous communities there is a tradition that communities hold leaders closely accountable, that leaders "serve obeying." As Andrade explains, indigenous parties transferred this tradition to local government and thereby facilitated greater community control over elected authorities and greater transparency with respect to budgeting and spending. The alternative governments they sponsor obey the demands of organized social sectors, such as churches, indigenous organizations, neighborhood groups, and unions, and convene with public officials in various fora (2003: 123). Scholars of governance typically identify

holding public officials accountable as among the most important elements of good governance (e.g. Ackerman 2004). Long-standing norms
of social control and conformity and new mechanisms that incorporate
civil society into decision-making spheres enable indigenous parties to do
this well.

Most Latin American indigenous communities have legitimate structures of self-government and their own customary methods of justice,
dispute resolution, leadership rotation, and collective decision making.
As Segundo Andrango, the Quichua coordinator of a U.S. Agency for
International Development- (USAID-) funded NGO project in Ecuador,
told me:

> There is a long tradition that the people govern themselves in these territories,
> these families. There they resolve their conflicts, they make accords and decisions.
> That is to say, there is a strong political participation and also exercise of democ-
> racy and governability, which doesn't happen in an urban–mestizo neighborhood
> of Western culture, where all are individuals. They [urban people] are neighbors
> but they are not citizens. This is the strength of [Ecuadorian indigenous parties]
> Pachakutik and Amauta Jatari, this structure from below. (My translation; inter-
> view, Quito, July 8, 2005.)

Self-governing structures are widely considered legitimate because of their
long-standing use and their effective defense of indigenous cultures.

As my case studies demonstrate, however, the full potential of institutional innovations has not been achieved in part because Andean indigenous cultures, and the contemporary political organizations that represent them, present a number of serious challenges for democracy. In
some cases civil society and government structures are excessively fused,
preventing each from questioning undemocratic tendencies in the other.
After centuries of exploitation, indigenous organizations often seek to
monopolize governing power and to disenfranchise the nonindigenous.
Diverse organizations struggling for the exclusive right to represent the
indigenous population engage in bitter factional disputes that bring institutional change to a standstill and may even result in violence. Norms
of social conformism and unexamined inequalities within indigenous cultures prevent women and other disadvantaged groups from exercising
full citizenship.

According to the indigenous ex-mayor of Guamote, the innovations
that indigenous parties have instituted recuperate "ancestral" indigenous
cultural traditions (cited in Ayo 1999: 66). Such statements must be
examined critically, owing to the tendency of some indigenous leaders
and their advocates to essentialize, romanticize, and reinvent cultural

histories for external consumption, and the uniquely *indigenous* nature of indigenous parties' institutional innovations should not be exaggerated. Nevertheless, indigenous peoples are emphasizing aspects of their own cultures and offering them as improvements upon Western governance models as they adapt Western institutions like participatory budgeting and gender quotas to local conditions.

How do indigenous visions of democracy engage contemporary debates in the West concerning radical democracy and democratic quality? Like indigenous parties, radical democrats seek to expand the procedural definition of democracy that most political scientists employ (e.g., Dahl 1971; Schmitter and Karl 1991; Schumpeter 1996). They seek not only to dramatically improve the quality of contestation, participation, and the protection of civil liberties, but also to improve in substantive ways the nature of civic life and the lives of citizens. This implies both the greater equalization of power and resources within a society and the uplifting of human beings as autonomous moral actors. Like indigenous parties, radical democrats are committed to expanding the sphere of democracy beyond the state and rooting it more in social life (see, e.g., Cohen and Rogers 1995b: 239, 262; Hirst 1994: 12; Warren 2001).

The relevant scholarship on radical democracy can be divided loosely into work on participatory democracy, associative democracy, and deliberative democracy, although overlap exists among those categories and the categories themselves are fraught with significant internal debates and divergences. *Participatory democrats* seek to expand opportunities for common citizens to take part in a variety of government decision-making processes, particularly at the local level at which it is more feasible for individuals to play an active role. Expanding participation requires that structural changes be made to government institutions that put citizens in contact with each other and with government representatives (Barber 1984; Fung 2007: 450). Thus they share with Andean indigenous movements the goal of making existing representative institutions, in which citizens participate mainly by voting, more open to opportunities for collective decision making involving individuals and civil-society organizations, particularly those representing disadvantaged and excluded groups. Although liberal political theorists usually define participation in terms of individuals, Andean indigenous organizations pursue collective citizenship rights – alongside liberal individual rights, such as voting and free speech – and consider the autonomous participation of legitimately chosen representatives of their community organizations to constitute effective participation (Yashar 2005). Such organizations have a high level of legitimacy and accountability to members and are crucial to the maintenance of ethnic identity and group cohesion.

Associative democrats propose that internally democratic voluntary associations govern public life (Perczynski 2000: 163). They owe a debt to Alexis de Tocqueville, who observed that the ability and propensity of Americans to form a dense web of voluntary associations contributed significantly to the success of the American democratic experiment by organizing collective action, facilitating trust-building horizontal attachments, and linking state and society (Warren 2001: 39, 42–3). Associative democrats emphasize the failure of the state in advanced democracies to satisfy human needs, resolve political conflicts and social problems, and participate in global cooperative activities (Hirst 1994: 9; Warren 2001: 6). To fill this vacuum, they call upon civil society to perform some of these roles. Associations are particularly important for excluded and oppressed groups, which lack sufficient financial resources or votes to exert political power. Associations may constitute their only or most "critical resource" for preserving their collective identity and advancing their rights (Warren 2001: 81). The insights of associative democrats are important to an analysis of indigenous parties in Latin America because most are the electoral vehicles of social-movement organizations that link dozens or hundreds of community associations. They also share associative democrats' goal of facilitating society's collective self-government. Indeed, in many rural areas, and in the teeming migrant-receiving shantytowns that encircle the region's major cities, indigenous-community organizations provide law and order and regulate economic and social life (Van Cott 2006a).

Associative democrats and development professionals argue that civil society associations contribute "social capital," which fosters trust and solidarity that may extend beyond them to society as a whole. High levels of trust and solidarity improve the quality and efficiency of democratic governance, reduce its elitist tendencies, and enable marginalized groups to resolve the collective action problem (Cohen and Rogers 1995a: 44; Fox 1996; Nylen 2003: 149; Putnam 1993; Warren 2001: 74). Comparative studies of development outcomes demonstrate that indigenous peoples' communities have high levels of social capital that enable them to overcome institutional and economic obstacles that plague nonindigenous communities (Ackerman 2004; Andersson and Van Laerhoven 2007: 1095; Blair 2000: 28; Fox 1996; Grindle 2007). Indigenous communities have ample stores of social capital because they are organized around strong collective identities forged through mutual suffering and self-defense. Their collective identities are rooted in a particular territory and reinforced by local self-governing systems and a tradition of community cooperation in pursuit of collective goals (Baéz et al. 1999: 50–2). In the Andes, this has generated a stock of "Andean social capital" that is based on norms of "reciprocity, complementarity, and redistribution" (my translation; ibid.: 51). Participation in assemblies that might seem burdensome to urban citizens who lack strong bonds of mutual solidarity and responsibility are to indigenous citizens valued opportunities to enjoy the company of family and friends and to reinforce valued identities and relationships. As Mansbridge explains, in unitary democracies based on friendship, "the costs of participation, of which some make so much, do not feel heavy" (1983: 9). Friendship and kinship provide a "'natural' or 'organic'" basis for democracy (ibid.).

Associative democrats Cohen and Rogers argue that, under conditions that they specify, associations improve democratic quality by making the system of interest representation more diverse and differentiated and thereby allowing the maximum expression of interests that parties and formal institutions poorly represent (1995a: 29). In some cases they serve as instances of "alternative governance," in which associations take on some of the problem-solving functions of government and participate in the design and implementation of public policy (1995a: 44). Many indigenous organizations perform this role. For example, Ecuador's 25-year old Union of Campesino and Indigenous Organizations of Cotacachi (Unión de Organizaciones Campesino e Indígenas de Cotacachi, or UNORCAC) functions like a "little municipality" by providing services to its members, maintaining its own technical management team of approximately 20 people, and serving as an operating arm for NGOs and international donors (Ortiz Crespo 2004: 104–6).[9]

As Warren cautions, associations are just as likely to promote illiberal values and practices that impair the quality of democracy as they are to improve it (2001: 18). Many associations are advocacy groups that formed to promote narrow interests and not to create "alternative venues of governance" in which opposing ideas gain equal attention (2001: 27). Divided societies present particularly difficult conditions for associative democracy because civil-society associations are likely to include

---

[9] In 2002 it managed a budget of approximately $500,000 (Ortiz Crespo 2004: 102).

particular identities while excluding others. As Warren succinctly concludes, "Under these circumstances, every conflict or threat cues an entire universe of meaningful social attachments, which will tend to provoke (rigidly principled) war rather than deliberation, negotiation, and bargaining" (2001:15). Developing societies face further challenges because socioeconomic inequality and a weak rule of law tend to exacerbate existing unequal power relations and the creation of voluntary associations may intensify inequalities and social tensions (Armony 2004: 4).

Moreover, Andrew Szasz observes that social movements often employ methods that weaken democratic institutions by normalizing or legitimizing extrainstitutional and sometimes extralegal, even violent, direct actions (1995: 150). Groups based on a "feeling of belongingness" are threatened by any manifestation of internal disunity, especially if they consider themselves to be in a state of war against nongroup members. Such groups do not tolerate dissent because they cannot afford to weaken the group unity they believe underpins their survival or to give adversaries the perception of weakness (Simmel 1955; see also, Warren 2001: 36). This explains the tendency of some indigenous communities to use coercion within social-movement organizations and their electoral partners. Bolivian indigenous parties sometimes use intimidation and violence to resolve internal conflicts, to prevent women from exercising the powers of elective office, and to confront long-standing political opponents. Therefore we must not idealize indigenous cultures. The democratic potential of indigenous-community social capital varies according to local historical conditions, leaving some areas with more horizontal, democratic, equitable relations whereas others are more marked by the opposite (Baéz et al. 1999: 50–2; Fox 1996: 1093). Moreover, some community members – such as women, less-educated members, members of less-dominant or less-numerous indigenous subgroups, and those considered outsiders – have difficulty speaking in community fora because they are silenced or they lack the self-confidence to speak publicly.[10]

Deliberative democrats share concerns with associative democrats because associations operate through face-to-face communication. But

---

[10] Gender discrimination in local politics is not unique to indigenous cultures: Andersson and Van Laerhoven report that in 2002 "more than 95% of all mayors in rural municipalities in Brazil, Chile, Mexico, and Peru are male" (2007: 1107). Blair found that women are poorly represented on local councils around the world except where there are gender quotas, and even where they are elected they may be marginalized or their husbands may govern through them (2000: 24).

deliberative democracy requires a particular type of communication: reasoned argument among equal individuals who are predisposed toward cooperation, respect for others, and the possibility of being persuaded (Dryzek 2005: 220; Elster 1998: 8; James 2004: 6). Deliberative democracy is a type of participatory democracy that stresses the use of reasoned arguments to structure citizen interactions in public policy making. Jurgen Habermas revived the fifth-century B.C.E. Athenian democratic ideal for a modern audience with his work on communicative action theory, arguing that democracy should be more than the aggregation of interests: It should create conditions for the transformation of individual interests into the common good (Elster 1998: 1; Habermas 1984). Deliberative democrats argue that democratic quality improves when public policy decisions are made collectively and publicly following reasoned arguments, which are made by and to those affected. Deliberation increases the availability and facilitates the exchange of information; forces citizens to make reasoned arguments that appeal to others; legitimizes collective decision making as people feel that their own views were heard and recognize that collective decisions reflect the majority's will; and facilitates implementation, compliance, and monitoring, because citizens feel greater ownership of decisions. Consequently, deliberation improves the quality of citizens (Elster 1998: 8–11; Fearon 1998: 50). Debates concerning the parameters of deliberative democratic institutions have been a central focus of political philosophy since 1990 (Saward 2000a: 5).

Virtually all indigenous communities in the Andes (and elsewhere in the Americas) have a tradition of regularly scheduled and occasional deliberative assemblies, at which leaders are chosen, important decisions are made, and cultural identities and community solidarity are built and maintained (Baéz et al. 1999; Ortiz Crespo 2004: 70).[11] Unlike radical democrats, indigenous peoples perceive deliberation to be more than a means toward a just end or a tool for citizen education. Deliberations – in which the community establishes its rules and community members provide their reasons – facilitate the exercise of indigenous visions of self-determination. In the face of external misunderstanding and abuse, indigenous communities find sanctuary in deliberative assemblies that are deeply rooted in historical and contemporary cultural symbols. This activity goes to the core of indigenous peoples' political aspirations in the Andes.

---

[11] On the use of *usos y costumbres* (customary self-governing norms) in Mexican municipalities, see Eisenstadt (2008), Grindle (2007: 131).

Indigenous community assemblies are auspicious spaces for deliberation because wealth and power inequalities are relatively small, providing one of the most important background conditions for fruitful deliberation (Fung 2005: 398). Moreover, indigenous cultures are disposed to deliberate, since they promote consensus-seeking as a means to strengthen community identity and solidarity against the threat of external oppression. The regular habit of meeting together and working together to solve problems gives indigenous organizations and movements – and the local governments they sponsor – an advantage over mestizo organizations and governments, which are less able to convoke regular and intensive member participation. In the Andes, decisions typically are made in assemblies in which all actors have an opportunity to express their position, although in many cases those speaking are mainly male. Deliberations go on at length until the majority opinion becomes clear. In Cotacachi's annual budget-planning assemblies, for example, decisions are more often taken by consensus than by vote (Ortiz Crespo 2004: 158). According to Assembly President Patricia Espinosa, this is appropriate for ethnically divided societies because the goal is to overcome, rather than to emphasize or exacerbate, communal conflicts. She views assemblies to be spaces devoted to "listening to diverse opinions and tolerating discrepancies, and to a practice of dialogue and reconciliation" (my translation; cited in Ortiz Crespo 2004: 160). Similarly, in Mexico, Fox found that indigenous communities make important decisions by consensus and hold their leaders accountable (1996: 1093).

Pressure within indigenous communities to conform to the group's interests, as community elites shape and define them, is troubling for deliberative democrats because it restricts individual autonomy. Nevertheless, from the point of view of Andean indigenous cultures, the benefits of prioritizing consensus rather than autonomy outweigh the risks. Systems of social control ensure that communities support decisions that thus enjoy greater legitimacy. The high legitimacy of government decisions, strengthened by their embeddedness in cultural institutions, facilitates more-effective implementation. As the La Paz Director of the Association of Municipalities explains,

Sometimes there are problems of conflicts among authorities, but they have achieved the incorporation of ancestral cultures into public administration to some extent in the moments of municipal planning, their authorities participate in the convocation of the people, they take part in deciding what projects to prioritize, the management of community resources. If someone commits an error they are punished using *usos y costumbres* [customary practices], so this permits the culture to be immersed in the government. This form of administration is empowering to both in a complementary way. (My translation; interview, Filemon Choque, Association of Municipalities, Department of La Paz, July 26, 2005.)

Deliberative democrats offer little hope for the institutional innovations that indigenous parties are undertaking because the necessary conditions they stipulate are not available in ethnically divided, economically unequal societies, in which rival groups may not be open to persuasion or willing to compromise identity- or resource-based demands (Dryzek 2005: 219–20). As Dryzek observes, members of disadvantaged groups "may feel insulted by the very idea that questions going to their core be deliberated." They seek "'cathartic' communication that unifies the group and demands respect from others" (2005: 220). Kymlicka concurs that deliberative democracy is particularly challenging for societies fractured by communal identity conflicts because they tend to lack the common basis of understanding, trust, and mutual interest that fuel effective deliberation. Although it is possible to find "genuinely participatory democratic fora and procedures" that transcend social cleavages, deliberation requires a common language because political debates tend to occur within language groups (Kymlicka 1999: 119). These challenges are daunting. But subordinate cultures that have developed a habit of deliberation and consensus-seeking may draw on this social capital to offset them (Fearon 1998: 58).

In addition, indigenous cultures in the Andes can use social and cultural capital to compensate for the scarce economic resources available to their local governments owing to the scant tax base in impoverished municipalities. Indigenous communities throughout Latin America have a tradition of contributing unpaid labor for community projects and public works. In the Andes this practice usually is called the *minga* (Baéz et al. 1999: 52; Ortiz Crespo 2004: 62, 96; interview, Abraham Borda, Strategies for International Development, July 26, 2005). Such labor is generally supplied without resistance provided that the leaders convoking the minga are considered legitimate and all members participate according to their gender and physical capabilities, including community leaders. In some cases community authorities may impose sanctions – monetary fines or extra work – on community members shirking minga duties (Barona 2003). For example, Lucero reports that in the Ecuadorian community in which he lived those refusing to perform the minga risked a deduction in access to water (Lucero 2008). The availability of collective, unpaid labor is a valuable resource for indigenous-party mayors.[12]

In sum, we can discern an ideal–typical model of indigenous-party-directed institutional innovation that encompasses an emphasis on direct participation (as opposed to representation), usually through regular, frequent, open assemblies where public spending preferences are freely aired and jointly prioritized. Voluntary associations are incorporated into the spheres of government decision making, oversight, and implementation through the construction of working groups or committees comprising municipal government officials and representatives of civil society and development NGOs. The values and processes that radically democratic projects promote constitute a strategy for securing ends even more valuable to indigenous peoples than democracy: equality, autonomy, and self-government. But the indigenous vision puts greater emphasis on collective (as opposed to individual) participation through family units embedded in larger kinship relations, which are rooted in shared cultural identity, and (at least rhetorically) on promoting cross-cultural communication and cooperation in divided, highly unequal societies, in which many radical democrats do not believe democratic innovation is feasible.

In contrast to Avritzer's idea of "participatory publics," which emphasizes face-to-face interactions among individuals and the maintenance of separate spheres for public discussion and the state (2002: 39), indigenous parties emphasize collective representation and participation in a fused public sphere populated by state and private authorities. Like a growing set of scholars of democratic governance (e.g. Ackerman 2004; Avritzer 2002; Evans 1997; Fung and Wright 2003b), indigenous parties prefer to insert civil society organizations and voluntary associations directly into public policy-making spheres – what Ackerman calls "co-governance" (2004) and Evans calls "state–society synergy" (1997). They share Avritzer's emphasis on constructing stronger public spaces for deliberation, giving social movements privileged access to this space, and fusing Western institutional traditions with nonwestern cultural specificities (Avritzer 2002: 40–4, 56). Although the specific features of Andean indigenous communities may not be replicated elsewhere, they provide

---

[12] Baéz et al. observe that in Ecuador approximately 80%–90% of community members participate in the execution of public works projects (1999: 52). Although voluntary collective labor in South America typically is associated with indigenous cultures, and it can be difficult to induce mestizo citizens to participate in such efforts, in Porto Alegre the PT organized *mutiroes* – voluntary labor performed on weekends – in urban neighborhoods in the early years of the participatory budgeting experience (Bruce 2004: 42).

thought-provoking lessons for transferring Western political institutions to non-Western cultures and infusing them with cultural symbols that are meaningful to citizens.

RESEARCH DESIGN

Prior to field research, I did not know to what extent indigenous parties were fulfilling their promises. Thus I set out inductively to learn as much as I could by observing a wide variety of cases, while using insights from the radical democracy literature and prior knowledge of indigenous politics to ask informed questions. I reasoned that institutional innovations are most likely to occur and endure where indigenous parties enjoyed relatively high levels of electoral support and governing experience. So I chose to investigate the two Latin American countries scoring highest on these measures: Bolivia and Ecuador. Indigenous political parties formed in both countries at around the same time (1995 and 1996, respectively) and expanded and consolidated their electoral reach at roughly the same rate – entering municipal government in 1995/1996, winning national legislative offices in 1997/1996, and electing their country's president in 2005/2002, respectively.[13] Thus both countries provide a 10-year history of ethnic party governance. Both have had an indigenous peoples' movement-based political party with a consistent presence at the national level since 1997 and 1996, respectively, as well as a rival indigenous party with a more circumscribed regional base. As noted earlier, the choice of predominantly indigenous parties and movements presents a "hard case" for testing whether leadership affects the development of radically democratic institutional reform. At the same time, focusing on *indigenous-party-movement* dynamics enables us to explore cases in which collective actors have defined programmatic goals and there are clear links between parties and sponsoring civil-society associations.

Bolivia and Ecuador share many other relevant similarities. Both countries' indigenous populations are large and diverse. An estimated 62.5% of Bolivia's 8 million people are indigenous, and the government recognizes 37 distinct ethnic groups. Most Bolivian Indians are Aymara (25%) or Quechua (31%) and are settled in the western highland departments. In the last decade, many have left their rural communities and migrated

---

[13] Pachakutik was part of the winning coalition that elected President Lucio Gutiérrez in 2002, although it left the alliance in 2003; the MAS elected its leader, Evo Morales, in 2005.

to highland cities or lowland areas. The remaining 286,726 Indians live mainly in the eastern lowland departments (Censo Nacional de Población y Vivienda 2001). Estimates of Ecuador's indigenous population vary widely, ranging from 6.6% (from a 2001 census undertaken by the government's statistical agency, Sistema Integrado de Indicadores Sociales del Ecuador (SIISE) (SIISE 2003) to 45% of the country's approximately 12 million people (estimated by the country's main indigenous organizations and sympathetic anthropologists). This variation is partly attributable to the agency involved and how indigeneity is measured or reported. Indigenous population concentrations in excess of 25% of the total can be found in 7 of 22 provinces. The Quichua are by far the largest language group, with an estimated 1.3 million in the highlands. Many Quichua migrated to the lowlands in search of land, where they also are the most numerous group (approximately 90,000 members). There are 17 distinct subgroupings or "pueblos" within the Quichua group. In the Amazon region, apart from the Quichua, there are 12 indigenous "nationalities" (Pallares 2002: 6).

Both Bolivia and Ecuador have struggled with the challenge of national economic, political, and social integration owing to the physical barriers to communication and transportation that high mountain ranges and dense Amazon forests present. These geographic enclaves facilitated the relative isolation of many indigenous cultures until the 20th century. As a result, both countries have a significant population that retains and expresses a distinct identity, alternately expressed as *originario*, *indígena*, or *campesino*. The two central Andean countries also have been experiencing similar political problems: the extreme fragmentation of party systems; the decline of once-important political parties; increasing tensions between the highland region of each country, where indigenous movements are militant and politically powerful, and lowland regions, where mestizo and white elites are more dominant; and social unrest owing to the imposition of neoliberal structural adjustment policies on an increasingly dissatisfied and impoverished population (Drake and Hershberg 2006; Mainwaring, Bejarano, and Pizarro Leongómez 2006).

The year 2000 marked the start of political crises in both countries. After months of discontent, indigenous organizations led massive demonstrations that brought down the Ecuadorian president in January 2001; popular pressure unseated another in April 2005. In Bolivia massive demonstrations in April and September 2000 launched a period of heightened social mobilization and unrest that led to the ouster of a Bolivian president in 2003 and 2005. In both countries a severe crisis of authority opened space for the emergence of not just new political actors but also new styles and sources of authority. In both countries declining public support for democracy coincided with the emergence of viable ethnic parties. In Bolivia, 64% of respondents agreed with the statement, "Democracy is preferable to any other kind of government" in 1996, but only 50% agreed in 2003. In Ecuador, affirmative responses to the same question fell from 52% to 46% during the same period (Mainwaring and Pérez-Liñan 2005: 50). Bolivia and Ecuador consistently score in the bottom quarter of Latin American countries in surveys measuring trust in government and satisfaction with and support for democracy (Hagopian 2005: 334).

Comparing these two countries also is illuminating because their decentralization drives were so different. In Ecuador the national government dictates no set model of decentralization or institutional reform but, rather, provides a legal framework for municipalities to petition for the transfer of responsibilities and resources in specific policy sectors. In Bolivia, in contrast, the national government imposed a rigid, standardized scheme that requires the installation of particular institutions and closely monitors local governments for conformity to complex norms. Thus, comparing Ecuador and Bolivia enables us to assess the outcomes of a top-down, compulsory, rigidly codified decentralization regime compared with a regime with a more bottom-up, voluntary, and flexible approach. The two countries also differ significantly in terms of the percentage of public expenditures that local government represents. Bolivia ranks with five larger, wealthier economies in which more than 20% of public expenditures occurred at the local or state level, whereas Ecuador ranks in the middle group of countries, spending between 10% and 20% at the subnational level.[14]

A qualitative, comparative research design was employed based on 10 municipalities, 5 in each country. Focusing on multiple municipalities within two similar countries provides significant leverage for theoretical generalization. As Snyder argues, subnational comparative research designs facilitate the control of relevant contextual variables and the

---

[14] The Inter-American Development Bank (2002: 4) cites data from 1997 prior to the implementation of Ecuador's Law of 15%. Ecuador is listed in the "less than 10%" category with 7.5%, together with nine poorer and smaller countries.

accurate coding of cases, while accounting for within-country variations in the progress and impact of larger political and macroeconomic forces (2001: 93). The municipalities chosen provide a wide range of outcomes rather than a representative sample of municipalities in each country. As Panebianco did in his landmark 1988 study of Western European parties, I chose some municipalities for "reasons of convenience," such as the availability of data, interview subjects, and ethnographic monographs, and the relative accessibility and safety of research sites (1988: 164).

Each indigenous-party-governed administration is considered within the context of a municipal case. The use of multiple cases with diverse outcomes and contexts provided optimal conditions for the development of theoretical propositions through successive direct replications (Strauss and Corbin 1999: 23, 111; Yin 2003: 43–7). Fieldwork began in June 2005 in Ecuador, where I started to formulate propositions with respect to the legal and political conditions promoting beneficial democratic innovation. I refined these propositions as I collected data on five municipal cases. Propositions that evolved during fieldwork in Ecuador were transported to Bolivia and tested against a distinct national context for municipal innovation during research there in July and August. As preparation of the case studies proceeded I refined my initial propositions continually, moving between the case study data and the developing theory.

Choosing fewer cases would have enabled me to collect more detailed information on each one and to increase confidence in my explanations. However, because the conditions in each municipality were distinct, making theoretical generalizations based on a smaller number of cases would have limited the contexts to which the resulting theory would apply, as well as the range of outcomes studied. Moreover, given my initial uncertainty with respect to the relevant contextual conditions, and the likelihood that multiple conditions interacting with each other in complex ways would explain variation in outcomes, including a larger number of cases made it easier to identify important conditions. Developing the theory while drawing from a wide variety of experiences increased the robustness of my theoretical model as a tool for explaining radically democratic institutional innovation in a particular class of cases: small-to-medium-sized local governments in ethnically divided, starkly unequal developing countries (Strauss and Corbin 1999: 109; Yin 2003: 46–52). Indeed, the findings held up consistently across the 10 diverse cases.

In Ecuador and Bolivia the average municipal population is 61,700 and 26,800, respectively (Inter-American Development Bank 2002: 8–9). In the five municipalities selected for study in Bolivia the population ranges from 6981 to 70,503; in Ecuador, the population ranges from 35,210 to 90,188. My choice to focus on smaller- and medium-sized cities marks a break in a literature that, with few exceptions, and until recently, has focused most attention on large urban areas (Grindle 2007: 13). Comparative studies of institutional reform in smaller municipalities emerged only after 2000 (e.g., Andersson and Van Laerhoven 2007; Bartholdson, Rudquist, and Widmark 2002; Bebbington et al. 2005; Blair 2000; Grindle 2007). Focusing on smaller municipalities is appropriate because the majority of Latin American local governments are small: 90% of local governments attend to populations of 50,000 or less; 53% of municipalities have populations under 10,000, and approximately one-third have fewer than 5000 inhabitants. Municipalities with small-to-medium-sized populations face unique and daunting challenges that low levels of human and financial capital, stagnant or declining economic development, the greater expense of providing services to rural areas, and weaker governance and legal institutions pose (Inter-American Development Bank 2002: 8–9). Thus focusing on small-to-medium-sized local governments enables us to target cases that are in particular need of attention and are comparable with relatively more localities outside the case sample (Andersson and Van Laerhoven 2007: 1095–96).

Like other scholars who aim to present successful models as a means to encourage the adaptation of their promising features (e.g., Ackerman 2004; Blair 2000; Tendler 1997), I selected cases that are "purposeful and illustrative, not scientific or inclusive" (Blair 2000: 22). I chose a small number of subnational regions in each country in order to further enhance my control over "cultural, historical, and ecological conditions" (Snyder 2001: 96). I chose departments/provinces where indigenous parties were most likely to succeed in initiating and instituting democratic innovations. La Paz, Bolivia, and Chimborazo, Ecuador, were the first subnational regions selected because the dominant indigenous party competed successfully in local elections there between 1995 and 2005 and both regions are the strongholds of the weaker, more geographically circumscribed indigenous party. This choice enabled me to observe how indigenous parties address the challenge of competitors for the same constituency within their "hunting ground" (Panebianco 1988: 209). Choosing these two regions also illuminates variations within and across indigenous parties within a relatively homogenous political space.

Both subnational regions possess high proportions of indigenous populations: the highest in the country in Ecuador (49.3%) and the second-highest in La Paz (77.5%). I included Cochabamba, another majority-indigenous Bolivian department (74.31%), because it is the bastion of Bolivia's most successful indigenous party, MAS, and the region where it has the longest experience controlling local government. From La Paz and Cochabamba I chose five municipalities where indigenous parties were likely to be successful in pursuing their goals based on the proportional size of their population, the strength of allied civil society organizations, and the party's historic strength. Within La Paz I chose Achacachi and Ayo Ayo, where the Pachakuti Indigenous Movement (Movimiento Indígena Pachakuti, or MIP) elected mayors in 2004. In Cochabamba I chose three MAS-controlled local governments in the coca-growing Chapare region: Villa Tunari, Chimoré, and Puerto Villaroel. These municipalities were expected to provide the most favorable conditions for democratic institutional innovation.

Given the paucity of published case studies – many of my secondary sources are unpublished bachelor's and graduate-level theses and studies that development professionals produced for donors – it was impossible to identify the most-successful cases prior to beginning field research. In fact, the results in most of these cases were less favorable than expected, owing to the top-down imposition of a rigid decentralization model, as well as authoritarian tendencies within indigenous organizations that impeded the inclusion of diverse voices in deliberative spaces and distorted the dynamics of imported participatory budgeting models. Although there are several examples of successful implementation of the 1994 LPP, my initial decision to focus on municipalities controlled by indigenous political parties precluded their inclusion in the research design. At the conclusion of field research, I was not aware of any cases that might have provided more promising results.

Ecuador is a smaller country than Bolivia, and its subnational regions contain fewer municipalities (see Table 1.1). Therefore I chose *two* Ecuadorian provinces in addition to Chimborazo in order to expand the case sample. Bolívar and Imbabura both have relatively large indigenous populations (28.4% and 39.6%, respectively), and Pachakutik has had electoral success in both provinces. The five Ecuadorian cases include the earliest and most-acclaimed cases of indigenous institutional innovation (Cotacachi [Imbabura] and Guamote [Chimborazo]) as well as understudied success stories (Guaranda [Bolívar]; Otavalo [Imbabura]). I also included as a basis for comparison Colta (Chimborazo), the Ecuadorian canton where the evangelical indigenous party Amauta Jatari has had the most electoral support.

TABLE 1.1 *Geographic Scope of Research*

Country	Bolivia	Ecuador
Total municipalities (2004)	327	219
Subnational regions compared	Department of La Paz Total population: 2,350,466 Percent indigenous: 77.5 Municipalities: 75 Indigenous parties in local government: MAS, MIP[a]	Province of Chimborazo Total population: 403,185 Percent indigenous: 49.3 Municipalities: 10 Indigenous parties in local government: MUPP MIAJ/MIAY[b]
	Department of Cochabamba Total population: 1,455,711 Percent indigenous: 74.4 Municipalities: 45 Indigenous parties in local government: MAS, MIP	Province of Bolívar Total population: 168,874 Percent indigenous: 28.4 Municipalities: 7 Indigenous parties in local government: MUPP
		Province of Imbabura Total population: 345,781 Percent indigenous: 39.6 Municipalities: 6 Indigenous parties in local government: MUPP

[a] MIP: Movimiento Indígena Pachakuti (Pachakuti Indigenous Movement).
[b] MUPP: Movimiento de Unidad Plurinacional Pachakutik (Pachakutik United Plurinational Movement); MIAJ: Movimiento Indígena Amauta Jatari (Amauta Jatari Indigenous Movement); MIAY: Movimiento Indígena Amauta Yuyay (Amauta Yuyay Indigenous Movement).
Sources: Censo Nacional de Población y Vivienda (2001. La Paz: República de Bolivia); Instituto Nacional de Estadística y Censos, 2001, www.inec.gov.ec; SIISE Version 3.5 (2003).

Data were collected from diverse sources. I conducted 53 unstructured interviews with subjects offering diverse perspectives on institutional innovation: leaders, members, and elected officials of indigenous parties; representatives of nonindigenous parties and government agencies; social scientists; and staff of NGOs and foreign governments working with indigenous communities. I consulted published and unpublished ethnographic studies and gathered documents produced by municipal governments and those evaluating them for national governments or NGOs. Archival records were relatively less important because some rural municipal officials keep poor records, record events incorrectly (deliberately or inadvertently), or block strangers' access to records owing to the severe legal, political, and financial consequences that the discovery of errors might unleash. I also compiled collections of local, regional, and national newspaper articles for the last decade concerning the activities of indigenous parties in both countries.

EVALUATING THE RESULTS

The quality of democratic participation and deliberation and the empowerment of marginalized groups are difficult to measure. The quality of democracy in the Andes is poor by any social science measure, the experiments studied are at most 10 years old, and the social and economic conditions are extremely adverse. Thus our expectations for the results of these efforts should be modest. Rather than setting some artificial threshold of "success," I seek to determine if the institutional innovations have resulted in "better local governance" than existed prior to the reforms. I ask whether indigenous parties' institutional innovations improved the quality of democracy and empowered citizens.[15] I determine that innovative institutions have been established if they survive the transition from the founding administration to another (under the same mayor or not) and these institutions are formally open to the participation of all citizens – individually, or collectively through membership in voluntary associations. This admittedly low standard constitutes an impressive achievement given the constraints on such reforms in the environment studied: high inequality and poverty, and long-standing interethnic hostility and mistrust. After only one decade in use, it would be unfair to expect transformative results from new institutions.

Low standards are common to studies of institutional reform.[16] As Abers avers, "[a]ny positive transformation will have contradictions,

[15] Grindle uses this measure in her study of decentralization in Mexico (2007:1). Ron Levi, Will Kymlicka, and Peter Evans employ a similar approach in a collaborative study of the process of "transnational construction of institutions aimed at expanding rights and enhancing capacities" (2007).

[16] For example, Tendler sets a low standard for success in her study of municipal reform in Ceará, Brazil, arguing that this more realistically reflects development outcomes (1997: 17). Fishman, in his study of the quality of public life in Spain, discerns whether or not a political society "affords citizens an engaging public arena within which they may contemplate, discuss if they wish, and ultimately choose among competing views, alternatives, and proposals," rather than measuring substantive improvements in public

imperfections, and failures. The temptation is often either to focus on the inadequacies or to ignore them altogether" (2000: 18). Thus she urges us to "appreciate modest gains, understanding them as windows of insight into better possibilities" (2000: 19). Similarly, David Booth urges scholars and practitioners to abandon overly optimistic expectations for political development, as well as impossibly high standards for "successful" development outcomes, both of which obscure the real possibility of beneficial, albeit slow and partial, improvements in the quality of democracy and development (Booth with Piron 2004: 3). As Humphreys et al. (2006: 586–7) argue, even when measurable improvements in economic and social development do not emerge from deliberative fora, normative and instrumental benefits may occur. Based on the work of Amartya Sen, they observe that merely providing a space for citizens to freely air their views and preferences is a valuable and *constitutive* end in itself. Instrumental benefits, such as the wider public acceptance and ownership of public policies, may be equally beneficial to democratic development by generating public support for painful but beneficial reforms and by making governments, particularly in developing countries, take seriously citizens' concerns.

Much of the literature evaluating the impact of decentralization and local institutional innovation measures success in terms of substantive impact on the quality of life in terms of measurable socioeconomic indicators, such as literacy and poverty. It is important to remember that such impacts may take a generation or more to produce measurable results, and even where dramatic increases in public investment in poor neighborhoods occur, the larger negative macroeconomic environment may offset material gains. In fact, Bebbington et al. found that poverty was not reduced in any of the 18 Latin American settings studied in which "Public Spaces of Local Planning" were instituted (2005: 25; see also Blair 2000: 21). Grindle discovered that even the noblest efforts of Mexico's local political leaders could not overcome declining sources of employment, outmigration, and the difficulty of competing in a globalizing market (2007: 183). Notwithstanding these disappointing material results, the people affected by radically democratic institutions value highly the intangible benefits of greater participation in public deliberations, such

policy or social justice (2004: 3). Finally, Nylen determines that participatory budgeting improves democracy because it expands access to state decision-making spaces for marginalized groups (2003: 150–1).

as self-esteem, solidarity, improved citizenship skills, dignity, and feelings
of satisfaction that are difficult to measure (Bebbington et al. 2005: 24).
The empowerment of local people – particularly excluded groups, such
as women and ethnic minorities – provides considerable benefits, such as
raising aspirations, igniting interest in politics, and providing leadership
experience (Blair 2000: 25–6; Wampler 2008: 32). In short, pursuing and
studying radical democratic reform is worthwhile.

ORGANIZATION OF THE BOOK

In the following three chapters I develop my arguments with respect to
decentralization dynamics, leadership, and the role of political parties in
institutional reform. In Chapter 2 I describe and contrast the legal and
political context for municipal reform in Ecuador and Bolivia, showing
how decentralization differed in each country with respect to the initiative
of national versus local actors. I show how indigenous social movements
took advantage of the opening that decentralization presented to enter
formal politics in unprecedented numbers. In Chapter 3 I disaggregate
the concept of leadership into six specific qualities associated with the
creation of institutional innovations and show how these qualities were
present or absent in the cases studied. A Weberian framework is used
to illuminate how mayors construct and maintain political authority. In
Chapter 4 I explore the role of indigenous political parties in promoting
democratic institutional innovation. I examine the challenges that social-
movement-based parties face when they compete for office and enter
government, with particular emphasis on the problem of maintaining
movement support and cohesion. In Chapters 5 and 6 I present empirical
data on municipal reform in Ecuador and Bolivia, respectively, in order
to illustrate the theoretical arguments in the preceding three chapters. I
emphasize national and regional similarities as well as variation at the
municipal level. I situate my explanations within the political context
surrounding the design and implementation of institutional reforms and,
in some cases, their collapse.

    In Chapter 7 I construct a model to demonstrate how my three facilita-
tive conditions – a flexible, bottom-up dynamic of municipal decentralization, innovative mayors, and cohesive political parties with strong roots
in grassroots civil society organizations – work together in a mutually
reinforcing way. I show how these conditions may produce diverse outcomes when placed in distinct political contexts. I conclude that the most
favorable political context consists of the presence of moderate political

pluralism together with the absence of a single ethnic group that constitutes an overwhelming majority of the population. Finally, I present the implications of my findings for radical democratic theory as well as practical implications for local governments in countries where excluded minorities are seizing political power for the first time.

2

The Legal and Political Context for Institutional Reform in Bolivia and Ecuador

Decentralization and democratization in Bolivia and Ecuador occurred in the context of regional and global trends that shifted powers from central to local governments and expanded citizen participation in public decision making.[1] These trends converged with the return to civilian-elected rule in Latin America in the late 1970s and accelerated and deepened over the next decade. Latin America in subsequent decades produced some of the most admired decentralization experiences (Eaton 2004: 36). Development professionals embraced the writings of political theorists extolling the "normative, substantive and instrumental benefits of participation" (Humphreys et al. 2006: 585–6). By the 1990s virtually all major development players – multilateral and bilateral donors and civil society groups – had embraced a preference for governance methods that facilitate the autonomous involvement of stakeholders in the choice, design, implementation, and monitoring of development programs. Thus, when Andean indigenous governments sought new ways to link social-movement organizations with public decision-making bodies in the 1990s, they received enthusiastic support from many development actors.

Before we investigate the variations in institutional innovation in particular municipalities, it is important to understand the enormous impact of the larger legal, political, and economic contexts in each country. We must remember that the most important decisions that affect local living conditions are made in distant national, and even international,

---

[1] An introduction to the vast literature on decentralization in Latin America would include Eaton (2004), Garman, Haggard, and Willis (2001), Grindle (2000, 2007: 4–9), Montero and Samuels (2004), O'Neill (2005), and Willis, Garman, and Haggard (1999).

34

capitols (Bebbington 2005: 5; Grindle 2007: 182–3). In the first section I describe the development of decentralization in Ecuador and Bolivia. I then describe the subsequent emergence of indigenous electoral vehicles and indigenous-party-dominated governments and the expansion of their bases of support. I show that indigenous social movements took advantage of opportunities for entering government that the decentralization of political and administrative power provided in a context of declining public support for traditional parties.

EARLY DECENTRALIZATION IN ECUADOR

Compared with other Latin American countries, Ecuador was an early decentralizer. The country established direct municipal elections at the time of the return to civilian-elected rule in 1979. Decentralization deepened and accelerated in the 1980s and 1990s, and new cantons (the local territorial unit) were formed. Beginning with roughly 100 in 1978, the number rose to 219 by 2000, and 220 by 2006 (Faust and Harbers 2007). Above the cantons are 22 provinces, which have directly elected prefects and provincial counselors. Cantons are divided into several parishes, each of which has a parish junta. There were 1149 rural and urban parishes in 2004, which have been directly elected since 2000 (Sánchez 2004: 88). The canton's government is called the municipality, and it has a directly elected mayor and municipal council. In rural areas municipal councils typically comprise seven to eight councilors (Cameron 2000: 2). Based on the presence of indigenous voters, former Pachakutik leader Miguel Lluco estimated in 1999 that indigenous or campesino (indigenous) mayors were likely to be elected in approximately 36 of the country's municipalities (Cameron 2000:4).

The rural, highland municipalities that new indigenous political parties now control are characterized by high rates of outmigration to large farms in Ecuador, neighboring countries, as well as the United States and Spain. Foreign remittances constituted 7% of the Ecuadorian GDP in 2006 (Machado Puertas 2007: 131). This constant outmigration results from persistent poverty that dozens of development agencies working for generations have yet to reduce. It has made foreign remittances the second-most-important source of Ecuadorian income, behind petroleum. Thus mayors confront populations that in many cases have been denuded of men of working age and of the women that often follow them (Santana 2004: 239). Citizens who view their future as linked to economic opportunities outside the municipality are less likely to devote time and resources to local development initiatives, regardless of their empowering, participatory nature.

Ecuador's decentralization dynamic is unique in a region where national governments typically design subnational institutions (Eaton 2004: 32). Municipal governments had little power to innovate with respect to institutional design until the 1997 Law of Decentralization of the State and Social Participation and the 1997 Law of 15%, which shifted significant resources and responsibilities to municipal government. The former contained provisions promoting social participation in public management in order to secure a more equitable distribution of public resources. The latter directed 15% of Ecuadorian state revenues to Ecuador's sectional governments, with 70% allocated to municipalities and the remainder to provincial councils, according to territorial extension, population, and the percentage of population with unmet basic needs (Lalander 2005: 157; Sánchez 2004: 83; UNDP 2006: 19). The 1998 Constitution augmented municipal responsibilities and resources by giving municipalities and provinces the right to petition for the transfer of central-government responsibilities, but it did not provide a blueprint for taking on the new powers and there is great diversity with respect to policy areas that particular municipalities seek to take on. Only one new policy area may be decentralized at a time. Approximately two-thirds of Ecuador's municipalities have requested responsibility for a policy area, with a majority requesting responsibility for environment and tourism (Faust and Harbers 2007: 9–13).[2] According to Faust and Harbers' survey, mayors representing Pachakutik are 30% more likely than non-Pachakutik mayors to demand the transfer of administrative responsibilities and resources, a correlation that held even when they controlled for poverty (2007: 18).

The 2000 Law of Rural Parish Juntas brought local government closer to rural communities and gave them an opportunity to participate in community-level decision making with respect to public investment. Parish juntas are required to convoke assemblies to make decisions regarding planning and spending priorities, to provide annual reports to

---

[2] Article 226 reads, "The competencies of the central government may be decentralized, except with respect to defense and national security, the direction of foreign policy and international relations, the economic and tax policy of the State, the management of external debt, and those that the Constitution and international conventions expressly exclude. By virtue of decentralization, competencies may not be transferred without the transfer of equivalent resources, nor can resources be transferred without corresponding competencies. Decentralization will be obligatory when a sectional entity requests it and has the operating capacity to assume it" (my translation).

these assemblies with respect to their activities, to write a development plan for the parish, and to promote the organization of neighborhood committees to work on sectoral issues. Each junta comprises five members elected to four-year terms by registered voters in their district. The law also requires that 30% of members must be female (UNDP 2006: 20).

The Ecuadorian government in 2001 presented its First National Plan for Decentralization and promulgated a decree implementing the Special Law of Decentralization. According to the United Nations Development Program (UNDP), among the decentralization plan's objectives were the "deepening of democracy," the promotion of citizen participation, and the "transformation of the relationship between political representation and social participation" (my translation; 2006: 20). In addition to promoting greater social participation, the new legislation is designed to accommodate ethnic and cultural diversity, as required under the 1998 Constitution. Article 6 of the law requires that "[s]ocial participation will be sustained in the principles of democracy, social and gender equity, pluralism, respect and recognition of the values of indigenous and black peoples and other ethnic groups" (my translation; reproduced in UNDP 2006: 88). Article 42 addresses measures to accommodate the traditional organizations of indigenous and black peoples – for example, coordinating planning for groups that transcend municipal boundaries.

After municipal governments complained that the national government was ignoring their petitions, in 2004 a new Law of the Municipal Regime required the national government to transfer responsibilities if they have not responded to petitions within 90 days. Municipalities still must struggle for access to adequate resources to carry out new responsibilities, a problem that has caused conflicts, particularly when a mayor's political opponents control higher levels of government. If the resources are not transferred, subnational governments are stuck with the responsibilities, making petitions potentially risky. Moreover, mayors complain that national governments often do not remit the 15% of state resources legally accruing to municipalities, or do not do so on time. Ministries resist their constitutional duty to transfer functions at the request of municipalities, engaging them in lengthy political battles (Cameron 2003b: 341; Lalander 2005: 176). In addition, to protect their prerogatives, public-sector unions typically oppose transfers, igniting conflicts between local unions and municipalities (Faust and Harbers 2007: 10).

Ecuador's municipal regime is vague and flexible with respect to the budgetary process. The 2001 Law of Decentralization does not specify mechanisms for promoting citizen participation in decision making or oversight, which allows for innovation by local governments as well as greater variation in experiences. Similarly, the 2004 Law of the Municipal Regime specifies that "the administrative structure will be adapted to the unique characteristics of each municipality, with the goal of ensuring an adequate provision of municipal services" (my translation; Article 26, reproduced in UNDP 2006: 87). Thus participatory budgeting and citizen oversight institutions exist in Ecuador only where local authorities have taken the initiative to establish them, whereas (in theory) they exist in all Bolivian municipalities (Grindle 2000; Radcliffe 2001; Sánchez 2004: 84). Only 35% of Ecuadorian municipalities have created local development plans (Ojeda Segovia 2004: 109), and only 24% are considered "innovative" (UNDP 2006: 4).

The relatively early onset of decentralization in Ecuador, as well as the greater difficulty of working in other Andean countries owing to protracted violence or sparse populations, led many development NGOs and multilateral development agencies to choose the Ecuadorian sierra as a laboratory for development investment in the 1980s and 1990s (Bretón 2001: 57). International aid to indigenous organizations and issues affecting them increased in the late 1980s as mature organizations gained the capacity to absorb and manage it (Cameron 2003b: 342). Municipalities controlled by center–left governments with predominantly indigenous populations were particularly attractive to foreign NGOs and development agencies (Radcliffe 2001: 7). The new flexible framework created after 1997 attracted additional NGO interest in supporting municipal democratization and development. Development professionals also were attracted to Ecuador because they were convinced that one of the necessary ingredients for successful economic development – social capital – was in abundant supply in Ecuador's highland indigenous communities (ibid.; Ospina 2005: 1–2). In fact, Bretón finds a 76.9% correlation in the Ecuadorian sierra between the concentration of development NGOs and the size of the rural population living in indigenous areas (Bretón 2001: 141). Five of the 13 cantons with both high indigenous populations and high density of NGOs are examined in this book. Although NGOs also are attracted by high rates of poverty, and there is a strong correlation between indigenous ethnicity and poverty, the statistical correlation between NGO activity and indigenous communities is higher than that between NGO presence and poverty (Bretón 2001: 129–30).

Indigenous communities are inclined to form civil society organizations for a variety of purposes – rights advocacy organizations, economic cooperatives, labor unions, cultural institutions, as well as self-government institutions derived from cultural practices. However, a significant number are formed at the instigation of NGOs, which require the formation of associations of a particular size and scale before disbursing development assistance. They require cooperative, organized partners on the ground. Secondary-level organizations (Organizaciónes de Segundo Grado, or OSGs) are civil society organizations that aggregate a number of local grassroots organizations that work at a geographic level somewhere between the size of a municipality and a province. Based on his intensive study of the relationship between development NGOs and indigenous communities' formation of OSGs, Bretón is convinced that NGO density in indigenous regions is a direct result of governmental and NGO institutions forming subsidiary civil society organizations (2001: 151). He concludes that the tendency of NGOs to foster new indigenous organizations is attributable to a paternalist attitude on the part of development institutions and their desire to create "new subjects of development" that internalize NGO norms (ibid.: 152).

LATE DECENTRALIZATION IN BOLIVIA

Decentralization started later in Bolivia, which was a highly centralized state in the early 1990s. In 1994 the government of Gonzalo Sánchez de Lozada designed and imposed by means of an absolute congressional majority a Law of Popular Participation (Ley de Participación Popular, or LPP). The LPP created an original scheme for municipal government emphasizing participatory planning, national–local revenue sharing, and the incorporation of civil society organizations into the formal scheme of government oversight (Gray Molina 2003; Grindle 2000; Van Cott 2000). Prior to the LPP, municipal government functioned only in urban areas, and few municipalities beyond the major urban centers and departmental capitals had any resources of their own to invest in economic or social development. The LPP created 311 municipalities out of preexisting provincial sections. After territorial subunits within them demanded autonomy for economic, social, cultural, and/or political reasons, the number increased to 327. Each municipal council has a minimum of five members; for every 50,000 persons after the first 50,000, two councillors are added, to a maximum established by law. Above the municipal level are the provinces (there are 112), which have little practical meaning or autonomy beyond coordination of lower-level activity, and above these are nine departmental governments. The 1995 Law of Administrative Decentralization facilitated the transfer of national government functions to the nine departmental governors (appointed by the president until 2005), but revenues still flow directly to municipalities (Molina Monasterios 1997).

Compared with Ecuador, Bolivia has far more majority-indigenous municipalities and thus greater potential for the expansion of indigenous parties and governance practices. Based on 2001 census data, Aramayo estimated that, in 219 of the 314 municipalities existing at the time, more than 60% of the population over 15 years of age self-identified as indigenous; in 186 municipalities (59% of the total) more than 80% of the population over 15 identified themselves as indigenous (Aramayo 2003: 40–1). The exact size and indigenous proportion of such municipalities are difficult to estimate accurately owing to a tradition of seasonal migration between the countryside and the city and between highland and lowland areas. Bolivia's National Statistical Institute estimates that 15.73% of all Indians have migrated outside their area of origin (Arnold 2004: 96). The urban–rural cycle of migration is a modern practice, in which members of the family (usually men) spend part of the work week in the city and return to their rural community for the rest of the week, or return for community festivals and other important occasions (Miranda 2003: 77–9). As in Ecuador, in Bolivia outmigration diminishes the ability of local rural leaders to count on regular participation from citizens in political institutions.

The LPP distributed resources from the National General Treasury to newly created municipalities that encompass urban centers as well as surrounding rural areas, with resources distributed primarily according to population. The money distributed, 20% of the annual treasury, is called coparticipation money. Subsequently other sources of funds were added: international aid targeted to poverty reduction through the Heavily Indebted Poor Countries II initiative (totaling more than $1.3 billion)[3]; national funds made available in 2000 through the Special Account of the 2000 National Dialogue; and, potentially of greatest importance, a Direct Tax on Hydrocarbons instituted with the new hydrocarbon regime that the Morales government negotiated in 2006. These supplemental national development funds may be difficult for smaller municipalities to

---

[3] In 2000 Bolivia was among the first countries to participate in the World Bank/International Monetary Fund poverty reduction program, which provides debt relief in exchange for participation in a Poverty Reduction Strategy Process that engages civil society actors. See Bartholdson, Rudquist, and Widmark (2002), Booth with Piron (2004), and Morrison and Singer (2007).

gain access to because they require an expensive, sophisticated planning process as well as a 20% counterpart contribution from the municipality (Córdova Eguivar 2004: 191). Thus, although Bolivia's decentralization scheme has problems, it is far more generous with respect to the distribution of funds than Ecuador's. Ecuador's mayors, however, typically are dealing with less-substantial deficits with respect to meeting basic human needs and have more capacity to absorb development aid owing, in part, to higher literacy.[4] Under the LPP, municipal governments acquired responsibility for promoting social and economic development, building and maintaining public infrastructure, and administering the provision of health and education. Incoming Bolivian mayors and municipal councils have an advantage over their counterparts in Ecuador: They have more flexibility in firing staff from previous administrations, and, indeed, it is not uncommon for new administrations to dismiss the entire previous administration's staff (*El Diario* 2005; *Gente* 2005; Lizárraga and Villarroel 1998: 29).

The most unusual aspect of the LPP was the establishment of vigilance committees in each municipality. These comprise representatives of territorially based civil society organizations – campesino communities, indigenous communities, and urban neighborhoods – collectively called community associations as of 1999. By 2002, approximately 16,000 such organizations had been recognized and linked to the participatory planning process (Gray Molina 2003: 351). This scheme increased significantly the formal representation of civil society organizations but excluded nonterritorial, functional organizations, such as businesses, women's organizations, and producers' groups. Sánchez de Lozada saw this as the only way to ensure that elites and centrally organized unions and business organizations would not capture the process. Vigilance committees have the right to review public records relating to municipal budgets and contracts and to monitor the implementation of public works. Committee members do not receive any salary and did not originally receive state resources to fund their activities. This arrangement caused problems for vigilance committee members representing poor constituents, particularly those that must travel significant distances to

---

[4] The Bolivian government estimates that the new contracts will bring in more than US$1.3 billion annually (*La Razón* 2006c). The formula for distributing hydrocarbon revenues is determined by whether the municipality is located in the department that produces the hydrocarbons; coparticipation funds are distributed by population (*La Razón* 2006a).

participate in committee activities. To partially remedy the problem, the 1999 Municipalities Law established a "social control fund" to cover transportation and other administrative costs that vigilance committee members incur, but it upholds the prohibition on receiving a salary.[5] In practice, it is difficult for many vigilance committees to perform their functions owing to a lack of resources and the political opposition of the local government.

The LPP mandated that municipal governments undertake a participatory planning process that incorporates representatives of the vigilance committees as well as common citizens through participation in periodically scheduled assemblies. Vigilance committees are supposed to participate in the elaboration of required five-year municipal development plans (Planes de Desarrollo Municipal, or PDMs). The government-prescribed process consists of stages in which the municipality undertakes a self-diagnostic, articulates its population's needs and demands, and prioritizes the fulfillment of those needs with respect to the budget. In practice, owing to the lack of education and public-sector experience in most municipal governments, a patchwork of NGOs and international aid agencies typically oversees the process and each devises its own methodology for interpreting the LPP. In theory, community association representatives participate in planning activities, as do a variety of functional organizations and higher-tier social-movement organizations. They are allowed to submit their own proposals to the vigilance committees but may not vote. The vigilance committees then submit their proposals to the municipal council for approval. In practice there may be little participation on the part of community associations or vigilance committees if political conditions are adverse or NGOs effectively dominate the process (Ayo 2004; De la Fuente 2001). In some cases NGOs will completely take over, allowing only nominal participation or preventing some groups from participating autonomously (Kohl 2001: 81–9). The NGOs themselves can generate political conflict and tensions because they are often allied with political movements or parties, have differing development philosophies, and have relationships with different community organizations and political actors (Kohl 2001: 85). Moreover, NGO representatives sometimes compete for political positions, and thus NGOs are seen as political actors

---

[5] The amount of resources provided remains small: only 1% of coparticipation money flows to municipalities with less than 10,000 inhabitants; 0.75% of coparticipation funds up to 25,000 inhabitants, decreasing a quarter percentage as the number of inhabitants increases from 25,000 to 100,000, and above.

who use development resources to amass and exert political power (Kohl 2001: 107).

The municipal council is responsible for ensuring that the five-year plan is prepared in a participatory fashion and for developing more detailed annual operating plans (Planes Operativos Anuales, or POAs) that implement plan priorities. The POAs must be developed according to a participatory methodology, and the vigilance committee must approve these each year. Community associations are supposed to participate directly in the planning process and participate through their representatives on the vigilance committee in monitoring the projects' progress. The budget for each year's plan is based on the municipality's projected share of the national pool of revenue, which fluctuates annually. The program and budget must specify the municipal government's development objectives, the amount allocated for each project, the expected goods and services to be produced, and expected year-end results (Kohl 2001: 81). In the absence of vigilance committee approval, funds will not be disbursed to municipalities and existing funds may be frozen. Any single member of the vigilance committee can prevent the approval of the plan because the committees operate by consensus. Committee members report objections to the department-level Popular Participation office and, if they are not satisfied with the response, to the Ministry of Hacienda (Kohl 2001: 82).[6]

The ability of municipalities to plan is restricted by extreme levels of local government instability. In Bolivia, mayors are directly elected if they finish first with more than 50% of the vote among other candidates for municipal council. Otherwise, municipal councillors entering office choose a mayor from among themselves. After serving one year, mayors may be removed by a majority vote of the council no more than once a year. Thus, as political alliances change, mayors may be unseated between elections and municipal personnel replaced (Hiskey and Seligson 2003; O'Neill 2004: 38; Rojas Ortuste 1998). Such actions make it more difficult for municipalities to carry out participatory, consensus-driven planning activities and to execute them faithfully (Ministerio de Desarrollo Municipal 2002: 103). Between 1995 and 1999 half the Bolivian population lived in a municipality whose mayor had been replaced. In 57 municipalities, between three and eight changes of mayor occurred during this four-year period. Forty percent of municipalities changed their

---

[6] Between 1997 and 1999, vigilance committees issued 46 complaints, and 21 of these resulted in the Ministry freezing the flow of resources (Ministerio de Desarrollo Sustenible y Planificación 2000).

mayor every year between 1995 and 1999, primarily through the censure vote (Ministerio de Desarrollo Sustenible y Planificación 2000).

In ways somewhat similar to Ecuador's 2001 Decentralization Plan, the 1999 Law of Municipalities further articulated the ethnic nature of municipalities, stating that "the Municipality expresses the ethnic and cultural diversity of the Public" (Article 3, II). Municipalities are created to "contribute to the satisfaction of the collective need and guarantee the integration and participation of citizens in planning and sustainable human development" (Article 5, I) and "to maintain, promote, defend, and diffuse the cultural, historical, moral, and civic values of the population and of the ethnic groups of the Municipality" (Article 5, II) (my translation). The 1999 reforms also sought to address the problem of the revolving door at the mayor's office. It initially reduced the number of mayors ousted, such that only 19% of municipalities changed their mayor between 2000 and 2001. But in 2000, 26% of mayors were removed (Ministerio de Desarrollo Municipal 2002: 103), and in 2002 and 2003 the percentage increased to 33% (Albó and Quispe 2004: 130). The ouster of mayors continues to be more likely in Cochabamba and La Paz departments, where eight and four mayors were removed, respectively, in 2006 (*La Razón* 2006b).

During the year 2000 the Banzer government organized a National Dialogue to discuss a variety of issues causing social tensions. Among the most important was reforming the Constitution to expand the regime of indigenous peoples' rights. Many indigenous groups demanded the creation of "indigenous municipalities," which would have all of the rights and resources of a regular municipality while allowing indigenous-majority communities greater flexibility in designing their own governing, decision-making, participation, and accounting practices. Although many intellectuals and activists argued that this would effectively fuse the best of Western law and indigenous culture, others warned of the "ethnocide" that might occur as "pure" indigenous practices became infused with Western norms. The proposed law created an "indigenous municipality," defined as a political unit in which 85% of the population belong to a socioculturally distinct community, whose municipal territorial boundaries have been adjusted to accommodate the cultural identity of its citizens (my translation; Medina 2003a: 21). However, by the time Congress passed the law in 2001, this audacious proposal had been watered down to a "mission to promote negotiated processes of adjustment, integration, and fusion of territorial entities, based on the principle of necessity and public utility, adjusting socioculturally homogeneous territories to the municipal regime of the Bolivian State" (my translation; ibid.: 22; Bustillo 2003: 33). Implementation was left to the discretion of the Ministry of Sustainable Development and Planning. The first five Indigenous Municipalities were established in 2002.

Municipalities received greater responsibility for reducing poverty under the 2001 Dialogue Law and a sizable increase in funds with which to do so. Thus National Dialogue funds provide more adequate funding for the poorest, rural municipalities to provide substantive improvements in social welfare and thereby construct support for new institutions (Booth with Piron 2004: 25). Seventy percent of poverty alleviation funds are now allocated to the poorest municipalities, and the country's nine departments share equally the remaining 30%, distributing funds within the department by population (Bartholdson et al. 2002: 23). Previously, owing to pressure from larger, richer departments during the development of the law, population was a more important criterion than need. The funds tripled the amount available to poor municipalities, which also received preferential access to national Social Investment Funds. As a result, municipalities now manage approximately 40% of public investment (Booth with Piron 2004: 25). Recall, however, that this extra money did not begin to flow until the end of the period studied (1995–2005).

Law 2150, which concerns political and administrative units of the Bolivian territory, was created to take into account Bolivia's existing forms of social and political organization, rooted in diverse cultures and traditions, while adapting them to a universal municipal regime (Miranda 2003: 76). Thus, it expanded the potential for differentiation in municipal institutions and for the penetration of a rigid state design by diverse cultural practices. The difficulty lies in adjusting a relatively rigid municipal regime to the vast diversity of forms of indigenous cultural organization and their dynamic manifestations in newly established migrant communities in both urban and rural municipal spaces. Moreover, many indigenous communities are heterogeneous and there is no single, authoritative traditional form of self-government (Miranda 2003: 78–9). Despite the new flexibility, the challenge of fitting ethnic organization to the municipal legal structure remains greater in Bolivia than in Ecuador because there is less room in the law for institutional flexibility. Criteria for budgeting and decision making are imposed by law and enforced by the central government (Movimiento al Socialismo 2004b: 1).

The rigidity of these administrative criteria in the LPP generated conflicts with local cultures and inhibited the adoption and implementation of the law. The LPP requires introducing the Western concepts of planning and saving into societies and economies where they did not previously exist. For example, Galindo writes that the concept of saving is completely absent in lowland Bolivia, where indigenous communities annually decide what they will sell, what the community needs to consume, and what must be traded for other goods that they need. Once these needs are determined, the amount of the excess determines how many days the annual party will last, during which all of the excess will be consumed. Some indigenous cultures believe that each new year is an opportunity for rebirth and must be started fresh. This makes it difficult for their traditional leaders to appropriate the idea of devising a five-year plan or investing municipal resources in long-term projects. In the Chapare, subsistence farmers save income only in the form of coca paste, which is hidden and tapped in emergencies. They do not want to save too much, because there is a risk that it will be taken by the drug police (Galindo Soza 2003: 118). Implementing the complicated new methodology for participatory planning and budgeting encountered numerous additional obstacles. Eleven years later only "the majority" of municipalities actually produce them, and the extent to which the planning process is truly participatory is open to question (*La Razón* 2006d).[7]

Although, compared with Ecuadorian law, Bolivian law provides a more rigid, mandatory municipal structure, there is room for the incorporation of traditional authorities and customs in decision-making processes. As José Blanes observes, some mayors have adapted the Popular Participation framework and initiated creative innovations that allow communities to stretch the scarce resources provided by "coparticipation" revenues, and many of these are rooted in the strong socioterritorial identification that communities share (2003: 200). Traditional communities are redefining the law's goals and using it to enhance the authority of their traditional leaders and self-governing practices (Blanes 2003: 202). Following years of complaints from indigenous and other civil society groups, a 2004 constitutional reform, codified in Law 2771 (July 6, 2004) allowed citizens' groups (*agrupaciones ciudadanos*, or ACs) and indigenous peoples (*pueblos índigenas*, or PIs) to participate in local elections without registering as political parties, breaking the partisan monopoly on local political power.[8] In the Department of La Paz alone, 60 ACs

---

[7] To address the problem, the Morales government instituted a system of *Directrices* to provide greater technical and legal assistance to each municipality (*La Razón* 2006d).

[8] Indigenous organizations and their supporters want the reforms to go further to incorporate legal recognition of the use of customary decision making and leadership-selection practices (Arnold 2004: 61; López 2003; Medina 2003a: 19). Some of these suggestions were incorporated into the 2007 Constitution, which awaited national referenda in 2008.

and PIs participated in the 2004 municipal elections. Forty-one PIs won office in 60 municipalities and elected 105 municipal councillors (*Enlared Municipal* 2005).

Indigenous political parties and registered indigenous peoples in the highlands are likely to incorporate local ethnic traditions into governance – for example, creating a role for traditional authorities in local decision making or having traditional authorities serve a dual role as official representatives on vigilance committees (interview, Filemon Choque, July 26, 2005; Blanes 2000). Some communities are rejecting the role of political parties in the selection of local authorities while appropriating mechanisms to maximize their ability to benefit from the new Popular Participation regime. This is the case in the rural Aymara municipality of Jesús de Machaca, described in Chapter 6.

Other indigenous communities are experimenting with the creation of new institutions designed to reduce the political conflict that electoral competition generates. For example, in Irupana, a 60% indigenous municipality in La Paz, following the 1995 elections local government officials, with the help of the local campesino federation and the development NGO Qhana, created a Development Committee to represent the interests of all three sectors and to coordinate development activities within the municipality. The new institution – one not anticipated by the LPP – was part of a larger response to the problem of internal political conflicts generated by the institution of municipal elections in 1995. According to the municipal council president, councillors decided to identify collectively with the community and to set aside partisanship (Zubieta 2000: 36). In a report on the local development experience in Irupana, Zubieta reports that, in addition to government officials, the largest civil society organizations are represented on the Committee, as are representatives of the Catholic Church and development NGOs. The Development Committee meets to share information on the various activities sponsored by the organizations represented and to investigate possibilities for mutual assistance. It also sponsors public assemblies on economic and social policy issues and on economic development projects and coordinates the process of public meetings that contributes to the development of the PDM. During the first administration following implementation of the law, it was the Development Committee that wrote the five-year plan, based on the diagnostic and priority-setting workshops it sponsored (Zubieta 2000). Thus, beyond what was stipulated in the LPP with respect to planning and social control, the Committee provides a deliberative space that links government, civil society, and representatives of external actors. Examples like this contradict the general tendency of national governments since 1994 to impose a uniform model. They occur where indigenous cultural and political institutions are particularly strong.

Despite problems with implementation, Bolivia's LPP gained immediate international acclaim and has been copied by numerous other countries. More than a decade later, the innovative institutional experiment continues to garner international praise and attention (Blair 2000: 32; Sogliano H. and Cusicanqui M. 2006; Van Cott 2000: 203).

INDIGENOUS POLITICAL PARTIES

The timing of decentralization processes in Ecuador and Bolivia varies with respect to their relationship to the emergence and expansion of indigenous political parties. In Ecuador, decentralization had progressed for more than a decade before a national indigenous movement formed a political party in 1996. The political surge of the indigenous movement thereafter intensified pressure to deepen decentralization as Pachakutik-controlled municipalities demanded greater autonomy and resources. The decisive participation of the movement in the 1998 constitutional reform, and its resulting recognition of indigenous peoples' rights, gave the regime a decidedly more culturally sensitive and accommodating character. In Bolivia, in contrast, all attempts to form viable indigenous political parties had failed until the sudden onset of political and administrative decentralization and municipal elections in 1995. Subsequently, leaders of dynamic and deeply rooted indigenous social movements ran for office with existing mestizo parties or formed new electoral vehicles. Thus, in both countries, indigenous-movement parties benefited from the opening that political elites provided when they established decentralizing policies. Once the movements had gained a political foothold, they effectively pressed for greater autonomy and resources for municipal governments and greater flexibility in adapting local governance to indigenous norms.

Indigenous Parties in Ecuador

The most important indigenous political party in Ecuador is the Pachakutik United Plurinational Movement [9] (Pachakutik). The Confederation of Indigenous Nationalities of Ecuador (Confederación de Nacionalidades

---

[9] Pachakuti was a legendary ruler of the Andean pre-Colombian civilization of Tawantinsuyu. The word evokes a new awakening or beginning of a new era.

TABLE 2.1. *Electoral Results for Pachakutik and Amauta Jatari/Amauta Yuyay*

Year	Pachakutik Mayors Elected[a]/ Municipal Councilors Elected	Amauta Jatari/Amauta Yuyay Mayors Elected/Municipal Councillors Elected
1996	11/45	Did not compete
1998	27/35	0
2000	25/84	1
2002	0[b]/73	0/3
2004	20/no data	3/no data

[a] In all five years there were 215 mayors. The number of municipal councillors varied. It was 791 in 1996, 880 in 2000, and 677 in 2002. Data not available for other years.

[b] There were only two mayoral elections in 2002.

Sources: Tribunal Supremo Electoral, www.tse.gov.ec/resultados, Quito: Ecuador, 1996, 2002; Scott Beck and Kenneth Mijeski, "Barricades and Ballots: Ecuador's Indians and the Pachakutik Political Movement," *Ecuadorian Studies* 1 (Sep. 2001). http://www.yachana. org/ecuatorianistas/journal/journal.html; Luis Macas, "Reflexiones sobre el sujeto comunitario, la democracia y el Estado. Entrevista realizada por Daniel Mato en Quito, el 25/07/2003"; editada y revisada por Luis Macas y Pablo Dávalos, en marzo de 2005. Colección Entrevistas a Intelectuales Indígenas, No. 3. Caracas: Programa Globalización, Cultura y Transformaciones Sociales, CIPOST, FaCES, Universidad Central de Venezuela, 2005. Disponible en: http://www.globalcult.org.ve/entrevistas.html. 2002); Luis Fernando Sarango Macas, "Movimiento indígena Frente a los Estados Nacionales. El Caso de Ecuador," in Magdalena Gómez, coordinator, *Derecho Indígena* (Mexico City: Instituto Nacional Indigenista, 1997), 318–9.

Indígenas del Ecuador, or CONAIE) formed Pachakutik in 1996 in association with a variety of weaker popular movements.[10] In its first contest in 1996, Pachakutik won 8 of 82 National Congress seats, becoming the fourth-largest bloc in a highly fragmented parliament. It also won 68 seats in local elections, roughly 7 of every 10 races it entered. The new party elected mayors in eight different provinces, demonstrating the strength of the indigenous movement in the highlands and Amazon, as well as a successful strategy of alliance formation with leftist parties (Beck and Mijeski 2000; Tribunal Supremo Electoral 1996). (See Table 2.1.)

The 1998 Constitution codified significant advances in the recognition of indigenous peoples' right to self-government. The convergence in time of rising indigenous political power and the transfer of greater municipal autonomy and resources enabled Pachakutik to advance rapidly

[10] On the development of the Ecuadorian indigenous movement and the creation of Pachakutik, see Andolina (1999), Lucero (2008), Pallares (2002), Selverston-Scher (2001), Van Cott (2005: 106–11), and Yashar (2005).

the indigenous movement's long-standing goal of local self–government. After Pachakutik already had consolidated a political base, the municipality increased in importance as a source of political power and economic resources. The party's geographic coverage expanded after the 2000 regional elections, which netted Pachakutik 5 of 22 provincial prefectures, 25 of 215 mayors, and 60% of the seats on parish advisory councils.

In 2002 Pachakutik entered the national government as a partner in a coalition with the Patriotic Society Party (Partido Sociedad Patriótica, or PSP) of former coup leader Lucio Gutiérrez. After winning 20.43% of the vote, Gutiérrez was elected president in a runoff with 54.79% of the vote. Bitter divisions quickly emerged between President Gutiérrez and Pachakutik party leaders and government officials after the president promoted conservative economic policies and established an independent base of power. The alliance ended in August 2003, after which the president set out to cripple CONAIE and Pachakutik. Gutiérrez provided political and financial backing to Pachakutik's main rival, the evangelical indigenous party Amauta Yuyay, which took advantage of these extra resources as well as widespread disillusionment with Pachakutik in the 2004 elections. Pachakutik's share of mayors and prefects declined to 20 and 3, respectively (Febres Cordero 2004; José Delgado, interviewed in Proyecto Formia 2004: 53; Ronquillo 2003; confidential interviews, Riobamba, June 2005). Pachakutik continued to suffer the repercussions of the Gutiérrez alliance in the 2006 national elections, owing to internal conflicts, defections from the party, and voter disillusionment (Pachano 2006: 2). Pachakutik's presidential candidate – long-time CONAIE leader and former national legislator Luis Macas – finished sixth, with only 2.19% of the vote. The party elected six deputies to Congress (four fewer than in 2002), including one each representing Bolívar and Chimborazo (Machado Puertas 2007: 134–7).

The evangelical indigenous movement has been challenging CONAIE and Pachakutik's political support among highland indigenous communities since the 1990s. North American missionaries began proselytizing in Ecuador in the late 19th century, and evangelical churches gained numerous adherents among the highland indigenous population in the 1980s and 1990s. Missionaries who gained influence in the sierra were conservative and endeavored to prevent indigenous communities from participating in the increasingly radical political activity that CONAIE and the progressive Catholic Church promoted. Instead, they preached obedience to the government and encouraged the demobilization of political protest. However, indigenous evangelicals increasingly rejected the view that worldly political activity and civil disobedience were inherently sinful and that indigenous cultural practices were pagan. Local evangelical indigenous organizations chose to participate in a number of the massive protests that CONAIE led in the 1990s and early 2000s.

Evangelical indigenous militants increasingly resented their political marginalization and their lack of access to the government resources and political positions that CONAIE affiliates enjoyed. The Ecuadorian Federation of Indigenous Evangelical Churches (Federación Ecuatoriana de Iglesias Indígenas Evangélicas, or FEINE), formed in 1980, established the Amauta Jatari Indigenous Movement (Amauta Jatari) in 1998 to compete against Pachakutik in local elections (Andrade 2003: 125). Amauta candidates mobilized the FEINE network of 17 provincial organizations and hundreds of churches and targeted voters through Bible-study classes and radio programming (Andrade 2005: 54–5).

Amauta Jatari fared poorly in its first two electoral outings (1998, 2000). After failing to elect its candidates in a minimum of 10 Ecuadorian provinces in 2002 (it finished last with less than 1% of the vote), the party lost its legal registration and had to reregister as Amauta Yuyay (Andrade 2003: 125; author interview, Vicente Chucho, June 29, 2005). In keeping with the evangelical indigenous faith of its members, in office Amauta Yuyay emphasizes seeking guidance from the Bible, while sharing many of the same cultural and economic interests as indigenous communities aligned with CONAIE and Pachakutik. The twist is that Amauta characterizes indigenous cultures as "works of God" and service in government as service to God. The party claims a higher standard of morality and incorruptibility based on its religious mission (Andrade 2005: 57).

Indigenous Parties in Bolivia

The coca growers of Cochabamba, in conjunction with segments of the indigenous–campesino movement, formed the Assembly for the Sovereignty of the Peoples (Asamblea de la Soberanía de los Pueblos, or ASP) in March 1995. They did so in order to facilitate their direct participation in the first-ever municipal elections without having to depend upon political parties that had deceived and abandoned them in the past. Intense discussions about forming the party began in 1994 during meetings of the Special Federation of the Tropics, the principal coca growers organization, and the Bolivian Workers Central (Central Obrero Boliviano, or COB). Campesinos promoting the creation of the party explicitly warned

TABLE 2.2. *Electoral Results for ASP, IPSP, and MIP*

Year	ASP (IU, PCB) Mayors/Municipal Councillors Elected	IPSP (MAS) Mayors/Municipal Councillors Elected	MIP Mayors/Municipal Councillors Elected
1995	10/54, 3.0% of votes	Competed with ASP	Did not compete
1999	4/23,	10/80, 3.3% of votes	Did not compete
2004	Did not compete	22+[a]/453, 18.5% of votes	10[a]/63, 2.4% of votes

[a] Data with respect to the number of mayors are difficult to estimate outside of the minority of municipalities where one party won an absolute majority and thus the right to name the mayor. The MAS won absolute majorities in 22 municipalities and thus at least that many mayors, but it won majorities in a total of 47 Bolivian municipalities, so the number may be higher.
Sources: "Los resultados no muestran tendencias a nivel nacional," *La Razón*, December 16, 2004 (online); estimate of MIP mayors comes from "MAS arrasó con alcaldías cochabambinas," *Los Tiempos*, December 9, 2004, 4.

that the party must serve as a "political instrument" of the movement and that it would never have greater power than the movement or the ability to dominate the movements' component organizations. Party decisions would be made within the existing campesino and coca growers' decision-making structures. After the National Electoral Court rejected the ASP's application materials on technical grounds, ASP leaders made a deal with the Bolivian Communist Party (Partido Comunista de Bolivia, or PCB) to present its candidates on that party's list. The PCB, in turn, had borrowed the legal registration of the United Left (Izquierda Unida, or IU), an alliance of small leftist parties. The PCB placed its own candidates in races in Beni, Potosí, and La Paz, leaving the remaining departments to the coca growers (Albó 1997; Córdova Eguivar 2004: 68–70; CSUTCB 1996: 68–9).

The institution of direct municipal elections throughout the country in 1995 transformed Bolivian democracy by sweeping 464 indigenous and campesino municipal councillors (predominantly men) into local offices. Nearly one-third of municipal councillors elected in 1995 identified themselves as indigenous or campesino; in 73 of the country's then-311 municipalities, they constituted a majority (Albó 1997: 7–26; Gray Molina and Molina Saucedo 1997: 9). Indigenous candidates entered office representing diverse political parties. The ASP-IU won 3.4% of the national vote, electing 10 mayors and 54 municipal councillors. These were primarily concentrated in Cochabamba, where the party won 17.5% of the vote and placed 49 of its municipal councillors primarily in the coca-growing Chapare (CSUTCB 1996: 17, cited in Colanzi 2006: 20; www.cne.org.bo). (See Table 2.2.)

At a national assembly Morales' rival Alejo Véliz was chosen to lead the ASP-IU 1997 national electoral list as its presidential candidate. The party won 3.7% of the vote nationwide and gained four single-member-district (uninominal) seats in the 130-seat lower chamber. Coca growers' leader Evo Morales won the highest proportion of the vote of any uninominal deputy in the country (60%). Véliz's supporters claim that Morales and his faction instructed their followers to vote for the Revolutionary Leftist Movement (Movimiento de Izquierda Revolucionario, or MIR) list in order to deny Véliz a seat in Congress. This allegation is supported by electoral results in Cochabamba, where the majority in the Chapare supported the uninominal candidacies of leaders like Morales and Roman Loayza but rejected the Véliz contingent (Herbas and Lizárraga 2001: 44). Resentments surrounding the issue generated a serious division within the campesino movement and within its new political instrument. In 1998 Alejo Véliz seized control of the ASP and Morales left to form his own party, the Political Instrument for the Sovereignty of the Peoples (Instrumento Político para la Soberanía de los Pueblos, or IPSP) (*Los Tiempos* 1999b).

The IPSP was formed during the January 1999 Congress of the Single Syndical Federation of Campesino Workers of Cochabamba (Federación Sindical Unica de Trabajadores Campesinos de Cochabamba, or FSUTCC). At that meeting the Cochabamba coca growers' federations allied themselves with Morales' vehicle. Owing to problems with its registration, the IPSP adopted the legal registration of the MAS, which its owner offered without conditions (Córdova 2004: 92; Herbas and Lizárraga 2001: 44; *La Razón* 1998; *Los Tiempos* 1999a). In 1999 Morales' IPSP-MAS elected 80 municipal councillors in six departments, 4.7% of those available, demonstrating the rapid expansion of the party beyond the Chapare. It finished first in 11 municipalities, mostly in Cochabamba, where it won 8.2% of the vote, compared with the 3.27% of the vote it won nationally (Colanzi 2006: 22; Van Cott 2005: 86–7).

In 2002 the coca growers' party burst onto the national scene, taking advantage of the collapse in support for traditional parties and widespread dissatisfaction with the democratic regime. The MAS expanded its support beyond the rural highlands and Chapare to include urban and middle-class voters. It finished a surprising second in the national elections with 20.94% of the vote, less than 2% behind winner Gonzalo Sánchez de Lozada (www.cne.gov.bo). The MAS became the largest opposition bloc and returned Morales to Congress. Thus began a tumultuous three-year period in which Morales and rural indigenous–campesino leader Felipe Quispe – both elected to Congress in

2002 – contributed to the popular overthrow of Sánchez de Lozada in 2003 and to the forced resignation of his vice president Carlos Mesa in 2005.

In the December 2004 municipal elections the MAS was the clear victor. The party expanded its coverage in both rural and urban areas. With the Bolivian political party system on the verge of collapse, MAS finished far ahead of any other political party or newly registered social movement, winning 453 municipal council seats, 25.1% of those available, with a national vote of 18.48%. The most popular parties for the 1999 municipal elections[11] – the MNR (20%), the MIR (15%), and ADN (12%) – had been the dominant parties nationally for almost 20 years. They saw their popularity decline after 1999 and were all but eliminated in the 2004 elections when none of them exceeded 5% of the vote. The MAS won the most majorities on municipal councils in the country (47), 22 of which were absolute majorities. After the MAS, citizens' groupings obtained the next–highest number of majorities (21) (www.cne.org.bo).

As expected, MAS finished first in Cochabamba, electing 51.7% of the total municipal council seats available, 34 of 45 mayors. In the Chapare, the MAS victory was overwhelming: The party took all nine seats in Villa Tunari, all five in Pojo and Bulo Bulo, four of five in Chimoré, five of seven in Tiraque, and six of seven in Puerto Villarroel. The party even finished second behind a new citizens' group (Citizens United) in the urban-mestizo departmental capital, winning 31.11% of the vote (*Los Tiempos* 2004: 4). In La Paz, the MAS finished second behind the regional party Movement of the Fearless (Movimiento Sin Miedo, or MSM) and elected 22.4% of municipal council seats. The MAS also became the second force in the capital. MAS gained power in 21 of 79 La Paz municipalities, finishing first slightly ahead of diverse citizens groups and indigenous peoples. According to Rafael Archondo, and other analysts, the MAS' victory would have been even more overwhelming had it not been for the emergence of citizens groupings and indigenous peoples, many of whom had affiliated with the party in prior elections but preferred to compete autonomously in 2004 (Archondo n.d.b: 2–3).

The new Law of Citizens Groupings and Indigenous Peoples led to the proliferation of civil society-based vehicles throughout the country. As a result, in 2004 collectively, civil society-based vehicles finished second behind the MAS but before the traditional parties. According to the

[11] MNR: Movimiento Nacional Revolucionario (National Revolutionary Movement); ADN: Acción Democrática Nacional (National Democratic Action).

National Electoral Court (Corte Nacional Electoral, or CNE), 343 separate citizens groupings participated (www.cne.org.bo). Officially registered "indigenous peoples" won 104 municipal council seats, 29 of which (27.9%) went to women, owing to the requirement that 50% of each citizen's group and indigenous people fill half of the positions on their candidate lists with female candidates. This constitutes a stricter gender quota than that imposed on political parties, which have been required since 1997 to register lists of candidates that are 30% female. Seventy-one MAS municipal councillors elected (15.7% of the total) were women. Registered indigenous peoples won majorities in 11 municipalities, including five absolute majorities.[12]

In the western highlands, since 2002 the MAS has had to compete with the MIP, a political party formed by Evo Morales' rival for control of the highland campesino movement, Felipe Quispe. Quispe's career as an indigenous–campesino leader appeared to be over after his incarceration for involvement in an armed guerrilla movement during the 1980s. It was resuscitated when he was chosen as a "unity" candidate for president of the Single Syndical Confederation of Peasant Workers of Bolivia (Confederación Sindical Unica de Trabajadores Campesinos de Bolivia, or CSUTCB) during the 1998 conflict between Véliz and Morales. He was elected secretary-general and used this position to build a personal following (Córdova 2004: 93). Notwithstanding Quispe's ties to the CSUTCB, the MIP is more a personalist vehicle for Quispe than the electoral expression of a social-movement organization. It is a classic charismatic party in that the leader determines party goals, chooses all militants and candidates, mediates all disputes, oversees all communications, distributes all incentives, and prevents the institutionalization of structures or leadership beyond his personal control (Panebianco 1988: 143–5). Quispe's authoritarian behavior and failure to attract votes beyond a militant, indigenous base in La Paz has caused the party's influence to decline since its impressive debut in the 2002 national election. That year Quispe won 6.09%

[12] Because they were required to include women as 50% of their list, it is not surprising that PIs and ACs finished first and fourth, respectively, in terms of election of female municipal councillors (27.9% and 23.7%). Apart from these new, special actors, in competition with other political parties, the two indigenous political parties did not perform well on this measure. The MAS ranked fifth out of 17 parties, whereas the MIP ranked 10th. The political parties most inclusive of women in 2004 were the MNR, ADN, and the Free Bolivia Movement (Movimiento Bolivia Libre, or MBL), whose municipal councillors included 25%, 24.3%, and 17.6% women, respectively. Underrepresentation of women in public roles has been a chronic problem for indigenous movements and parties in Bolivia.

of the vote and he entered the Chamber of Deputies with five other MIP deputies. He later resigned from Congress in anger, which contributed to his declining appeal among voters.

In 2004, MIP elected 45 municipal councilors in La Paz, 8 in Cochabamba, and 10 in Potosí. The appeal of a radical indigenous autonomy agenda to rural La Paz voters is demonstrated by the fact that the MIP was the third-most-successful party in La Paz (*Los Tiempos* n. d.). It won majorities in four municipalities, one of which was absolute. But its national reach is limited. Because Quispe's base is the most traditional sector of the indigenous population, where traditional authorities still hold considerable power, it is likely that the 2004 law allowing indigenous peoples to compete in elections without forming a party hurt the MIP's electoral prospects in the same way that it hurt the MAS. In rural areas many allyus (traditional self-governing, kinship communities) affiliated with Quispe's political movement took advantage of the new law. In the 2005 national elections the MIP attracted only 2.16% of the vote. Under Bolivian law, having missed the 3% threshold in two consecutive elections, Quispe must reregister the party to compete again (interviews, La Paz, July 2005; CNE www.cne.org.bo; *La Razón* 2004b).

The results of the 2005 national elections stunned observers, who expected a close vote. Instead, Morales and the MAS seized 53.74% of the vote, a comfortable margin above the number required for victory, as well as 84 seats in Congress (12 of 27 in the senate and 72 of 130 in the lower chamber). With control of the presidency and a dominant congressional voice, the MAS won 54% of seats in the 2006 Constituent Assembly. The second-most-popular party, PODEMOS (Poder Democrático Social, or Social Democratic Power), a new vehicle representing traditional elites, whose parties were now defunct, finished far behind with 24% (www.cne.org.bo; CNE 2005; International Crisis Group 2006). The MAS significantly extended its geographic coverage by making alliances with diverse civil society and social-movement organizations (*La Razón* 2006a). But these alliances came at a high cost because they required promises of jobs to each alliance partner. Observers remarked on the impossibility of satisfying so many promises. Moreover, a scandal erupted in early 2007 when the press reported that MAS leaders had been selling jobs. The party now faces a serious dilemma that Panebianco poses: Distributing an excessive amount of *selective* incentives will reduce the credibility of the party "as an instrument dedicated to the realization of its 'cause,'" which reduces the organization's "capacity to distribute collective incentives." On the other hand, shifting the balance toward *collective* incentives threatens "organizational continuity" by reducing the level of selective incentives that the party can offer to its militants (1988: 10). The rapid expansion of the MAS has brought it to national power, but it threatens the party's internal cohesion and identity (ibid.: 42–3).

CONCLUSION

Indigenous movements in Bolivia and Ecuador took advantage of legal and political changes to take control of dozens of local governments. In some cases they were the primary initiators of legal reform and key actors in its ultimate design. In Ecuador, decentralization resulted in a flexible, voluntary regime that enables grassroots movements – in conjunction with indigenous mayors – to obtain access to new responsibilities and resources and to design institutions to increase popular participation in public policy making. In Bolivia, decentralization reflected a distinct agenda. President Sánchez de Lozada used a brief moment of political hegemony to impose a rigid, universal, mandatory structure of municipal decentralization. Over time, however, this regime has been made more flexible as indigenous organizations successfully lobbied for greater cultural autonomy. In Chapters 5 and 6 I show how efforts by indigenous parties to take advantage of these opportunities varied within each country, notwithstanding identical legal and political constraints.

3

Mayoral Leadership and Democratic Institutional Innovation

> Certainly all historical experience confirms the truth – that man would not
> have attained the possible unless time and again he reached out for the
> impossible. But to do that a man must be a leader, and not only a leader
> but a hero as well, in a very sober sense of the word.
>
> Max Weber, "Politics as a Vocation"
> Gerth and Mills (1946a: 128)

Durable radical democratic institutional innovations have this in common: an exceptional mayor to initiate the innovation, to guide it through its initial, rocky stages, and to ensure that it survives the innovating mayor's departure. Mayoral leadership was particularly important in Ecuador because mayors there have broader scope to initiate and design new institutions. In the most acclaimed Ecuadorian cases (Cotacachi and Otavalo) the innovating mayor is still in office after multiple terms. In contrast, there are several once-acclaimed cases (Guamote and Guaranda) in which a mayor oversaw the design and implementation of promising institutional innovations but then left office and the new government was unwilling or unable to sustain the institution – even though the replacement mayor was from the same party. The close correlation between the presence of the initiating mayor and sustained democratic institutional innovation underscores the importance of particular leaders to any explanation of the conditions for beneficial reform.

To a social scientist seeking generalizable conditions that could point us toward replicable solutions for troubled, conflictual democracies, the apparent need for highly qualified leaders is frustrating. We all can agree that "effective and willing leadership tends to be scarce," particularly in local politics (Fishman 2004: 16). But many political scientists studying

58

democratization avoid the study of leadership (Bernhard 1998: 2) and denigrate it as a residual category for the unexplained portion of an outcome. Others recognize leadership's importance but set it aside because it a difficult variable to predict or influence. As Judith Tendler observed with respect to Brazil, emphasizing the causal impact of leadership necessarily foregrounds the qualities of individuals and "the singularity of certain experiences" that are unlikely to occur elsewhere. This confounds the goal of policymakers to identify and replicate successful models. Since we cannot seem to produce effective leaders, studying leadership provides no "guide for action" (Tendler 1997: 18).

Yet numerous studies of leadership in government, the military, business, and organizations conclude that leadership influences organizational outcomes. Leaders are particularly important to the development of new institutions, especially in a context of weak or nonexistent countervailing institutions, are crucial to efforts to effect institutional change, and are a likely source of organizational innovation (Bass 1997: 11–15; Campbell 2003; Domínguez 1997; Grindle 2007: 87, 92–3). In fact, as Bass observes, many scholars consider leadership to be decisive in determining institutional outcomes (1997: 12). This is even the case in deliberative settings where the influence of leaders is designed to be reduced.[1] My findings concerning the importance of mayoral leadership confirm those of scholars studying comprehensive municipal institutional reform elsewhere in Latin America (e.g. Andersson and van Laerhoven 2007; Baiocchi 2005; Bebbington et al. 2005: 13, 20–1; Campbell and Fuhr 2004; Grindle 2007; Tendler 1997: 11, 17–19; Velásquez 2005: 17; Wampler 2004).

The scholarly and professional literature on leadership typically focuses on two sources of variation – personal attributes of leaders and the situation or context in which the leader operates – as well as interactions between the two (Vroom 1997: 278–9). This literature suffers from three main limitations. First, many definitions are essentially circular: Effective leaders are those who lead effectively; where successful outcomes occur, there must have been good leadership. Second, the literature emphasizes

---

[1] A recent study of an experiment in national deliberations on budget issues in Africa found that leaders of discussion groups had a strong and significant impact on the views expressed and recorded for the group, notwithstanding apparently "ideal conditions" for deliberation" (Humphreys et al. 2006: 584). They concluded that "leaders matter profoundly," and that a few participants determine the outcome of deliberations involving thousands of participants by using misrepresentation and, intentionally or not, causing group members to censor themselves to appear more consonant with the leader's views (ibid.: 604, 617–8).

innate, personal qualities of individuals who are conceived to be naturally occurring and incapable of being inculcated or "cloned" (Campbell and Fuhr 2004: 6–7). For example, Robin Hambleton enumerates specific personal characteristics of leaders associated with positive outcomes: "vision, strength, stamina, energy, and commitment" (2004: 5). This is useful because we can break down the diffuse, complex concept of leadership into observable qualities. But these qualities are difficult to measure and to compare systematically across cases. It would be more useful to operationalize leadership qualities in terms of actions that leaders take or skills that they possess rather than their personal traits.

A third limitation is that scholars of leadership work in a variety of disciplines and study diverse legal, political, cultural, and institutional settings. Qualities associated with beneficial outcomes in one setting may not easily be transferred to another (Hambleton 2004: 5; Lowndes and Leach 2004: 562–3; Vroom 1997). Even within studies of local political leadership there are important contextual variations that affect the impact of distinct leadership styles and make it difficult to generalize from them. For example, most studies of municipal innovation and leadership illuminate the experience of large, urban municipalities (e.g., Campbell 2003; Campbell and Fuhr 2004; Goldfrank 2006; Tendler 1997), making it difficult to apply their findings to rural contexts. For example, in their study of urban development since the 1990s, Campbell and Fuhr tell us that successful Latin American mayors are likely to have professional qualifications, to be able to hire highly qualified and educated professional staff, and to have access to relatively abundant financial transfers from the central government, as well as the capacity to generate their own income from local sources (2004: 14–16). But in smaller, impoverished Andean towns, mayors have few professional qualifications and may even lack government experience, they have difficulty attracting qualified staff, municipalities receive far lower transfers from the center, and mayors have limited ability to tax impoverished constituents. Thus the qualities associated with successful urban mayors may not be transferable to rural towns, particularly predominantly indigenous towns. Executive authority in indigenous cultures tends to emphasize the adjudication of disputes and the personalized resolution of problems with leaders playing a decisive role, in contrast with the Western model, in which leaders apply written, predetermined standards in a consistent fashion across time and space.[2]

---

[2] See Wilkins (2007: 132) on the "adjudicating and mediating" emphasis of aboriginal government in North America and its contrast with "the predominantly legislative approach that Europeans introduced into Indian Country."

Any study of leadership therefore must manage the tension between the need to account for transferable leadership qualities and strategies and the need to situate actors within a particular context that provides incentives for action (or inaction) and institutional constraints and that is, in turn, situated within a larger political context and political culture.

Even within Latin America, mayors vary significantly in terms of the legal authority they possess to establish new institutions and allocate spending. The success of participatory budgeting (PB) experiences in Brazil is largely owing to the high degree of autonomy from municipal legislators that Brazilian mayors enjoy and the ample financial assets (almost 15% of public funds) they control (Wampler 2008; Goldfrank 2007b). In contrast, Bolivian and Ecuadorian mayors typically must negotiate with deadlocked councils or those that opposition parties control.

In a recent study of local governance reform in Mexico, Grindle avoids the pitfalls inherent to studying individual leaders by conceptualizing public leadership collectively as "state entrepreneurship" and foregrounding behaviors and strategic choices: "In this view, the state, in the guise of reform leaders and their teams, identifies particular problems and promotes policy, programmatic, or organizational solutions to them, even in the absence of party support or future electoral opportunities and incentives" (2007: 11). Grindle's approach is part of a recent trend to conceptualize leaders as strategic actors within challenging contexts[3] (2007: 87) and is appropriate for cases in which a set of players in public office was the primary agent of reform. However, because in the Andes, fewer political colleagues or technical specialists were available to guide mayors, and civil society activists and NGO representatives had a greater influence on institutional design than government staff, a more singular focus on mayors is more appropriate. Here, mayors are the dominant figures in the dominant coalition that exercises power within local party organizations. Where a mayor exercises considerable legal and political authority, he or she is the fulcrum of local power relationships and "controls crucial zones of uncertainty" (Panebianco 1988:37) that determine the fate of institutional innovation.

Anirudh Krishna also found local leaders to be crucial to the construction of social capital in rural villages in India. Effective, entrepreneurial village leaders help communities to solve collective action problems by

---

[3] Bebbington and Carroll use surveys to measure the organizational capacity of federations of poor communities with respect to seven criteria, including leadership. Leadership is among the seven dimensions of capacity surveyed, but the authors do not define leadership or indicate how it is derived from survey questions (2000).

taking the initiative to form new organizations, to establish and maintain rules governing behavior, and to maintain social capital once it has been formed. They use their visibility and prestige to convince villagers that joint action is worthwhile. Thus, "village leaders have absorbed the set-up costs associated with building social capital" (Krishna 2007: 954). Krishna discovered that local leaders are not equally effective in promoting the development and maintenance of social capital, however. Local government officials and caste leaders – perhaps because they are associated with political cultures that tend to erode social capital – are not effective, but new, younger, educated leaders are (2007: 943, 952). Although Krishna identified additional factors that promote the formation and growth of social capital, he emphasizes the capacity of "effective agency" to overcome structural barriers like inequality, which otherwise obstruct social capital growth (2007: 954).

In sum, many of the limitations of the leadership scholarship are inherent to the subject matter, whereas others can be remedied through more careful operationalization of the concept. My objective here is modest: I seek to identify and operationalize the specific qualities of leaders in rural indigenous-party-governed Andean municipalities that foster democratic institutional innovations; to identify how personal qualities interact with conditions external to leaders to facilitate the fulfillment of leadership goals; and to explain why these qualities and conditions tend to promote institutional innovations that improve the quality of democratic governance. I combine a consideration of ways in which leaders establish their authority, which I derive from Max Weber's widely used trichotomy, with an examination of the particular strategies that facilitate leadership of local-level, radically democratic institutional reforms.

SIX QUALITIES THAT FACILITATE LEADERSHIP

Six characteristics of leadership are associated with the creation of durable institutional innovations that increase the deliberative, participatory, and transparent nature of democratic governance: (1) considerable personal charisma; (2) the ability to be reelected; (3) the support of civil society groups that elected them; (4) a continuous, visible presence in the community and frequent interaction with constituents; (5) the capacity and will to communicate and negotiate effectively across ethnic divides and with external actors, especially donors; and (6) a degree of autonomy from their organizational benefactors. The first, fourth, and fifth qualities are attributable to the personal inclinations and capacities of individual mayors. The remainder denote the interaction of personal qualities with conditions in the political environment that enable mayors to effectively pursue institutional innovation.[4] All six may not be necessary for beneficial democratic institutional reform, but the greater the number and intensity of characteristics present in mayors, the greater the capacity they have to realize their vision of reform and to ensure that it survives their term in office.

To achieve qualitative improvements in democracy in terms of citizen participation, feelings of solidarity and trust, and empowerment of marginalized sectors, factors 3–6 must be present and working together to maximize the accountability of mayors and the inclusion of diverse actors in the design and implementation of new decision-making processes and mechanisms that enable civil society to hold government leaders accountable. Factor 3 (the support of the mayor's base constituency in the indigenous-popular movement), apart from increasing the effectiveness of the mayor as he/she confronts inevitable political opposition to change, ensures that excluded sectors help to design institutions that are truly participatory and open. Factors 4–6 ensure that additional sectors of local society beyond his/her base have access to the mayor and that opposed perspectives are accommodated in the design and implementation of new institutions. Only institutions that a majority can support will be sustainable beyond the mayor's term. These factors are interdependent: Mayors may cultivate trust and negotiate effectively beyond their ethnic and class base only if they enjoy sufficient autonomy from that base.

Charismatic Authority

Charisma is an innate quality and its inclusion constitutes a divergence from my goal to focus on leaders' behaviors and skills. The fact that so many informants used this specific term to describe exceptional mayors and to explain their ability to introduce radical democratic institutions while overcoming political opposition convinced me that it was worth mentioning, with the necessary qualifications. Although charisma is impossible to replicate, it is important to observe its effects where it is present. Because it is impossible to measure charisma precisely, and I was not able to personally observe it in all cases, I defer to the judgment of informants to indicate its likely presence.

---

[4] I thank an anonymous reader for pointing out this distinction.

Weber introduced the concept of charismatic authority as one of three
ideal types of political authority. He defines this as:

a certain quality of an individual personality, by virtue of which he is set apart
from ordinary men and treated as endowed with supernatural, superhuman, or
at least specifically exceptional powers or qualities. These are such as are not
accessible to the ordinary person, but are regarded as of divine origin or as exem-
plary and on the basis of them the individual concerned is treated as a leader.
(Weber 1947: 358–9.)

Given the fact that leaders to whom "supernatural" or "divine" gifts are
attributed are very few, I focus on the less-demanding end of the charisma
spectrum: persons with "exceptional powers or qualities" relative to other
individuals. In some cases the term charisma may denote the ability to
develop an excellent rapport with diverse individuals and groups in a
short period of time through sheer force of personality.[5]

Charismatic leaders exert authority over others by virtue of the senti-
ments of loyalty and admiration that they inculcate. They typically emerge
during extraordinary times when their extraordinary powers are viewed
as the only solution to extraordinary crises because they are deemed capable of challenging existing, incompetent sources of authority (Eisenstadt
1968: xxiii–xxiv). Although distancing himself from Weber's definition,
Panebianco defines "situational charisma" as something that emerges
during "a state of acute social *stress* that gets the people ready to perceive
as extraordinarily qualified and to follow with enthusiastic loyalty a leadership offering salvation from distress"[6] (1988: 52). Charismatic leaders
take advantage of the emotion and excitement accompanying extraordinary events "by destroying existing norms and transforming old values"
(Bernhard 1998: 2) and thus unleashing revolutionary forces. It is the
presence of crisis or the excitement of revolutionary political change that
gives mayors the opportunity for *radical* as opposed to *incremental* institutional reform. The entrance into political power of indigenous peoples
after 500 years of domination, exploitation, and exclusion constitutes
an extraordinary time. The collapse of political-party systems, increased

[5] This conclusion resulted from an interesting conversation I had with José Antonio Lucero.
[6] The attribution of "situational charisma" to mayors as leaders of parties should not
be construed as indicating that such parties constitute "charismatic parties," which are
formed by leaders as their personal vehicles and exist only to advance their personal
agendas (Panebianco 1988: 143–7). Whereas Felipe Quispe's MIP might represent such
a party, the other three parties studied do not. In both countries charismatic, personalist parties are common. Pachakutik, the MAS, and Amauta Jatari/Yuyay stand out as
unusually rooted in organizational life and programmatic agendas.

public conceptions of political corruption and decreased confidence in parties, the dramatic consequences of structural adjustment and its deleterious effects on rural Andean economies, and the overthrow of a succession of presidents in both countries, constitute a time of severe social stress.

Charismatic authority is the least stable of Weber's three types because the leader must continually demonstrate its existence and continually produce the outstanding goods that followers expect from extraordinary people. Leaders, then, must possess other skills that produce substantive results (Bernhard 1998: 2–3; Eisenstadt 1968: 50–1; Weber 1947: 248–9; Weber 1968: 50–1). But no matter how skilled, charismatic leaders eventually lose or leave power. Their charismatic authority is "routinized" and succeeded by traditional or rational–legal authority, or a mixture of both, as the "extraordinary states of devotion and fervor" they engender cool off (Kitschelt 2000: 855; Weber 1978: 1121, cited in Bernhard 1998: 2). The result is the emergence of "incipient institutions," and here is where Weber offers us a useful way to assess the role of leaders in institutional innovation.

In operationalizing charisma I stress the skills and behaviors that leaders use to gain cooperation and support. I concur with Kitschelt that charisma "pertains to an individual's unique personal skills and powers of persuasion that instill followers with faith in the leader's ability to end suffering and create a better future" (2000: 849). I use the term to denote a set of personal qualities that includes an attractive appearance and public personality; an ability to communicate ideas in a way that inculcates support, loyalty, and trust in the face of negative facts concerning the leader's performance or the larger political and economic contexts; the ability to listen to diverse constituencies and *seem to understand* their distinct perspectives and needs; and an intensity or energy that conveys readiness for action and the ability to overcome opposition. I do not share Kitschelt's view that politicians who rely on charismatic authority do so solely in order to "maintain maximum personal discretion over the strategy of their party vehicle" or to sabotage the construction of organizational infrastructure (ibid.). Panebianco similarly argues that charismatic authority is "incompatible with the simultaneous presence of the sponsoring organization" (1988: 66). Both authors interpret charismatic leadership as a tool that leaders use to dominate a political organization and prevent the institutionalization of rival decision-making authority. Like external organizations that sponsor electoral vehicles to achieve instrumental ends, charismatic leaders, Kitschelt and Panebianco argue, have no interest in the institutionalization of the parties they control.

However, in Bolivia and Ecuador, mayors used charisma to construct democratic institutions that *reduced* their personal prerogatives because their goal was not to seize power but to use power to radically change political institutions. Furthermore, the construction of alternative, authoritative deliberative spaces enables mayors to outmaneuver reactionary political parties controlling existing institutions. Innovating mayors therefore have an incentive to rapidly institutionalize alternative spaces as a counterweight to municipal legislatures. Indigenous mayors' aspirations to construct a personalist power base are especially constrained in the settings studied, where they rely on the continuous support of an indigenous-movement–party organization. Indigenous mayors do not enter office with large fortunes or networks of well-placed benefactors. Their electoral base expects swift action on programmatic agendas and watches closely for signs of cooptation or corruption. Mayors perceived as corrupt are swiftly punished – as the mass lynching of the mayor of Ayo Ayo vividly attests.

Personal charisma enables a mayor to continually negotiate ambiguities and complexities with respect to the lines of authority and the institutional prerogatives of weak, new democratic institutions. It facilitates negotiations among competing individuals and political factions within and outside the mayor's political organization. Such factionalism is endemic in indigenous movements in the Andes. The popularity that charisma engenders among constituents also increases the confidence of mayors, who may be more likely to demand greater resources and responsibilities from the central government. In fact, in their study of Ecuadorian municipalities, Faust and Harbers discovered a positive and highly significant relationship between the percentage of votes won by a mayor and the probability that he/she will solicit administrative responsibilities from the national government (2007: 16–17).

Although modern conceptions of leadership typically denigrate charismatic authority, in many indigenous cultures it is an accepted aspect of authoritative leadership, albeit one that others gradually are replacing (Lauer 2006: 58). And in societies where rational–legal authority is under construction and contested, state actors must generate alternative sources. Leaders may use charismatic authority to foster democracy through its routinization in new democratic institutions. In Weberian terms, the consent to be dominated is transferred from the leader to the institution (Bernhard 1998: 1–3). The personal authority that leaders construct, and their ability to use that to outshine other local officials, is crucial to the transfer of state power to new participatory spaces. As Wampler observes, before they transfer power to citizens, mayors must capture and command that power (2008).

My informants, as well as scholarly and journalistic accounts, attribute high levels of charismatic authority to four mayors in the cases studied: Auki Tituaña, three-time mayor of Cotacachi; Mario Conejo, two-time mayor of Otavalo; Arturo Yumbay of Guaranda; and Mariano Curicama, two-time mayor of Guamote and subsequently provincial prefect of Chimborazo (interviews, Ecuador). For example, Pachakutik Vice–Mayor Washington Bazante describes the late Arturo Yumbay, emphasizing both his personal charisma and constant presence in the community:

> Mayor Yumbay was more active, more *aglutinador* [linking together] of the masses, more enterprising, he had another *mística* [mystical quality] in the work.... And he worked with the indigenous and mestizo sectors through *mingas*. And he was always present in these works, he was with the government apparatus, he was a very charismatic man. He was a man who had innate qualities of knowing how to approach the community, the collective. (My translation; interview, July 4, 2005.)

Visible and Continuous Physical Presence

Present leaders are those who engage in repeated, face-to-face interactions with individual citizens and organized groups in structured state-sponsored assemblies and meetings and more informal settings outside government offices. This intimate, repeated, personal contact with citizens enables a mayor to construct trust between citizens and the government based on their personal loyalty and faith in the mayor's commitment and talents. Present mayors visit projects-in-progress to ensure compliance and to motivate participants. They spend a high proportion of their time in their municipality in contact with constituents. In contrast, mayors who are rarely seen outside their office, who travel frequently outside of the municipality, or who avoid contact with the press and mobilized constituents, foster distrust and resentment, particularly in times of significant change or crisis.[7]

---

[7] A case in point is the leadership style exhibited by Mayor Ray Nagin of New Orleans after Hurricane Katrina. His frequent travel outside the city and absence from public view in the two years following the storm led one influential newspaper columnist (Chris Rose of the *Times-Picayune*) to frequently inquire on behalf of citizens: "Where's my mayor?"

Visiting far-flung areas of the municipality is particularly important in rural towns where transportation is costly and time consuming. Mariano Curicama, the Pachakutik mayor of Guamote, a 95% indigenous town in Chimborazo, Ecuador, observed at a 1997 seminar in Bolivia, it is his responsibility to visit his constituents because he has a salary and transportation (Centro de Desarrollo Integral de la Mujer Aymara 2000: 37). Mayors in my cases also established their presence by participating in the collective, unpaid labor that is a part of community life in the Andes and that many indigenous mayors use to stretch scarce financial resources. Others held open office hours so that individuals and group representatives could directly present grievances. For example, Curicama established a practice of being available every Thursday morning from 7:00 A.M. on a first-come–first-serve basis. Citizens often visit Guamote's center for the Thursday market, so this is a convenient time. Prior to indigenous peoples' capturing local government in 1992, municipal employees refused to meet with indigenous citizens (Cameron 2003b: 225–6). Curicama's Pachakutik successor continued the popular practice. Finally, present mayors participate in – and sometimes support with municipal resources – the political mobilizations that indigenous social movements organize at higher geographic levels. Thus they establish a physical presence on the front lines of struggles between constituents and their political opponents.

In Pachakutik-governed municipalities there is a great deal of this face-to-face interaction. In smaller, more rural cantons, municipal officials and staff visit distant communities, communicate with their representatives, and hold public meetings (Barona 2003). In larger cantons, distant communities are less able to participate but receive regular communications in their own language from municipal authorities. And in provincial capitols, such as Guaranda (Bolívar) and Riobamba (Chimborazo), publicly funded Indigenous Houses serve as spaces for regular interaction between Pachakutik government officials and indigenous leaders. An example of a present Pachakutik mayor is Arturo Yumbay, who was praised in the previous section. After Yumbay assumed office in August 2000, he began working with urban neighborhoods, the provincial campesino federation, and other civil society organizations to generate ideas for the canton's Participatory Development Plan. As his brother Alberto recalls,

they began first to organize the barrios, because without organization you can't do anything. So they began to make the Participatory Development Plan. All the barrios participated, the clubs, some sindicatos, the youths, the children, and our indigenous communities, which already had an organizational culture. They were not able to achieve massive participation. But, rather, he had to visit all of the barrios in order to encourage them to participate. So they achieved the making of a Strategic Development Plan. (My translation; interview, Alberto Yumbay, July 7, 2005.)

In Bolivia, where population density tends to be lower and geographical distances make regular visits more costly, mayors habitually meet with civil society representatives in regular assemblies of traditional cultural institutions or peasant unions.

Secure Reelection

Mayors who remained in office for two or more terms presided over the most acclaimed and durable institutional innovations. This finding confirms those of scholars of innovative reform elsewhere in Latin America. For example, the popular governor of Ceará, Brazil, Tasso Jereissati, elected in 1987, sustained his PB initiative by choosing and electing his successor after his term expired in 1991 and winning election again four years later (Tendler 1997: 9). In contrast, in the Brazilian state of Recife, three different mayors representing different parties presided over wide fluctuations in the operation and impact of PB between 1994 and 2004 (Wampler 2008). Grindle discovered that Mexico's legal prohibition on reelection was an obstacle to institutional continuity as each election brought new faces and new priorities to office every three years (2007: 17, 165). Reelection has become more of a possibility throughout the region since the decentralizing reforms of the 1980s and 1990s, which changed the political incentives for once-appointed mayors (Campbell and Fuhr 2004: 436).

How does reelection help? First, mayors have more incentive to please constituents and undertake long-term institutional reforms if reelection is legal. Second, mayors who stay in office improve their skills, expand their knowledge of local conditions, and develop a wider set of external contacts (Bebbington and Carroll 2000: 33). Third, because infant institutions are so dependent upon their mayoral midwives, reelection helps to consolidate newly learned values and practices through repeated practice. In the absence of strong institutions, reelection enables mayors to see projects to fruition and to use their personal political capital to institutionalize participatory processes, as people have a longer time to get involved and to feel a sense of ownership. As Andersson and Van Laerhoven observe, the longer elected and appointed personnel remain in office, the more time they have to design and implement participatory–deliberative institutions (2007: 1099). In Weber's framework, reelection provides sufficient time for charismatic authority to be routinized into rational–bureaucratic institutions, making it more difficult for subsequent administrations to dismantle innovations (Ortiz Crespo 2004: 178).

Codification of institutional innovations into law actually is rare. Ackerman explains that legislatures, which have the powers to codify new institutional practices, are difficult for reformers to navigate. Political parties typically dominate such spaces, and they are likely to resist reforms that constrict their prerogatives. Thus executives are left to promote participatory schemes using only their own authority and resources (2004: 16). Even one of the region's most acclaimed and durable institutional innovations – Porto Alegre's participatory budget – was never codified in law and operated at the discretion of the executive (Baiocchi 2005: 9).

Fourth, reelection provides a longer period of time in which mayors can cultivate trust, which is enhanced by a long-term commitment to serve in local government rather than seek higher office (Campbell and Fuhr 2004: 443). Fifth, reelection makes the work of NGOs easier. In the Andes, NGOs are principally responsible for training new local government personnel. When mayors are reelected NGOs do not have to wait 10 months or more for a new government to take office and appoint personnel, which reduces the need for training programs that consume time and money. The problem of training new personnel is particularly acute in rural areas. Finally, reelection extends the time available for new institutions to yield some visible, substantive results, which helps maintain support for and participation in time-consuming deliberative activities and collective work.

It is important to retain good leaders even after the codification of new participatory processes and spaces, and even if the innovative mayor's party stays in office, because all party militants may not share the same commitment to a new institution. For example, Grindle found that leadership, rather than party affiliation, explained the accomplishments of decentralizing reformers in Mexico. As in the Andes, in small Mexican towns the membership of parties is fluid and militants may change affiliation frequently (Grindle 2007: 86–7). This is particularly the case with respect to new parties within a larger context of partisan dealignment, such as we find throughout the Andes. In Ecuador institutional innovations did not survive the replacement of a mayor from the same party in Guaranda and Guamote after the initiating mayor left office. In Guaranda, Mayor Yumbay died in a car accident in 2002. Incoming Pachakutik mayor Alberto Coles let the participatory procedures fall into disuse and ended many of Yumbay's initiatives. This is partly owing to the prior estrangement between Yumbay and Pachakutik leaders (see Chapter 5). According to Guaranda's Pachakutik contingent, Coles reversed spending priorities to favor urban areas in contrast to his predecessor's greater balance between rural and urban needs. According to Coles, he is trying to continue the participatory and transparent initiatives of his predecessor, but has found difficulty working with urban mestizos, who he says lack interest in collective labor. However, under Yumbay, even urban professionals and mestizos participated in mingas with the mayor; for example, collecting garbage during the night with community brigades (interviews, Alberto Coles, July 5, 2005; Wilfredo Macas, July 5, 2005; Alberto Yumbay, July 7, 2005). Thus, Yumbay possessed leadership qualities that his successor lacked.

In Guamote, two-term mayor Mariano Curicama chose not to run for reelection in 2000. His chosen successor, Pachakutik candidate José Delgado, won the mayor's race, narrowly defeating Amauta Jatari's Juan de Dios Roldán (Cameron 2003b: 216). After 2002, Delgado had the advantage of a 5–2 Pachakutik majority on the municipal council (Delgado, interview in Proyecto Formia 2004: 49–50). Perhaps for this reason, Delgado did not reach across religious, ethnic, geographic, and organizational lines in the way that Curicama had. Bebbington reports that his management style was less transparent, which provoked political opponents' suspicions. He hired more cronies and made less of an effort to include opponents. He alienated NGO representatives by resisting their reporting requirements and expelled smaller ones, depriving the canton of funds and technical assistance (Bebbington 2005: 13–14). Most important, Delgado did not foster cooperation between the indigenous faction that he represented and the increasingly powerful evangelical indigenous faction represented by his rival. While Delgado served as mayor, Roldán served as head of the Indigenous and Popular Parliament, but the rivalry ultimately resulted in their refusal to speak to each other and to constant attacks on each other's institution. The feud continued after the 2004 elections, when the two rivals switched places. Neither Delgado nor Roldán – indigenous mayors representing indigenous parties and operating in the same institutional, political, and economic context – had the ability to negotiate outside their organizational base that their predecessor, Curicama, demonstrated (Andrade 2003; Bebbington 2005: 14; confidential interviews, June 2005).

Reelection is a sensitive issue in indigenous societies, in which annual leadership rotation is the norm. Political leadership is not supposed to be a profession. Compulsory community service for all young couples typically begins after marriage, with men performing the more prestigious and formal roles while women perform more complementary roles. Communities choose leaders based on prior service, individual capabilities, and the need to balance representation of geographic sectors. This system encourages political equality because individuals and families rarely can monopolize power by extending terms in office. Because service in top positions absorbs time and economic resources it has a leveling effect on economic inequalities (see Albó 1985; Arnold 2004; Ticona Aleio 2003: 125–46). In Bolivia's highland ayllus, leadership rotation is also believed to reduce corruption (Lucero 2006: 48). Cultural and peasant-union organizational norms carry over into party politics. In Bolivia, the MAS rotates some leadership positions and access to candidacies. The party even has required elected municipal councilors to resign their terms halfway through in order for their alternates to take their place, with a view toward deconcentrating political power and providing political experience to a larger cohort of potential leaders[8] (Córdova Eguivar 2004; Gray Molina 2003: 360; Lizárraga 1998: 56).

In many Aymara communities of La Paz, ayllus and campesino organizations choose municipal government candidates according to local traditions of leadership selection and rotation. To reduce the extreme internal conflict that a decade of municipal electoral competition has generated, some ayllus have decided to take advantage of a 2004 law that allows indigenous candidates to run for office representing "indigenous peoples" without political-party affiliations. For example, the rural municipality of Jesús de Machaca (pop. 13,535) divided its 24 ayllus into five sections so that each could choose its own mayoral candidate. In large assemblies each community within the section presents its proposed candidate and expresses the merits of its choice. After lengthy discussions, participants line up behind their preferred candidate. Under the system agreed to in August 2004, the mayor's home region will be rotated among each of five territorial sections of the municipality. In addition, the titular (elected) mayor and his or her councillors agree to exercise their positions

---

[8] At a July 2003 national party meeting, MAS leaders decided that legislators who had finished their term would not be allowed to run for municipal office; in 2005, those who had already served in Congress were not allowed to run again so that others could gain experience, denying Evo Morales the opportunity to run again. See Chávez (2005: 8); *La Razón* (2005b, 2005c, 2005d); *Soberanía* (2003: 12). However, Rafael Archondo points out that both the MAS and the MIP are notorious for the *caudillo*-style dominance of their top leaders, Morales and Quispe, and the lack of renovation of their cupula of close advisers (Archondo n.d.a: 1).

for two-and-a-half years and then resign in favor of their alternates, rein-forcing the system of power rotation (Arnold 2004: 52–3; *Construyendo* 2004: 4–5).

This practice of leadership rotation fosters democracy by impeding any particular leader's efforts to accumulate power and resources and by promoting political equality among contending individuals and fac-tions. It reduces divisions caused by competition for coveted positions and educates a larger group of potential leaders. However, high turnover causes problems for institutional innovation, particularly in a society with a low educational level (Andersson and Van Laerhoven 2007: 1099; Córdova Eguivar 2004; Herbas Camacho 2000; Lizárraga 1998). Per-sonal longevity in office is crucial for institutional memory and learning because illiteracy prevents the transfer of vital information by means of books, manuals, or computer files. A 2002 Bolivian Ministry of Municipal Development survey of 30 municipalities discovered the scant persistence of institutional memory regarding the norms of the 1994 LPP owing to the fact that few government workers trained between 1994 and 2001 were still working in government (Ministerio de Desarrollo Municipal 2002: 49–52).

The same survey found a significant, inverse relationship between man-agement capacity and the rotation of mayors (Ministerio de Desarrollo Municipal 2002: 113). An estimated 88% of Bolivian municipal authori-ties elected in December 2004 had no knowledge of or experience in public administration or municipal management. Thus the Bolivian government estimated that in the summer of 2005 officials were still in a process of transition, requiring training and assistance to learn their responsi-bilities. Municipalities were late preparing annual operating plans and submitting reports to the central government and even further delayed in executing scheduled public works projects (García 2005: 12). Appointing and electing leaders for longer terms in office, and allowing reelection, would allow them to develop greater knowledge of municipal procedures and to develop more effective negotiation and oversight skills (Albó 2002: 97). Owing to the challenges of development planning under conditions of annual leadership and staff turnover, two social scientists who are keenly sensitive to Aymara indigenous cultural practices (one of whom is Aymara) recommended in 1997 that indigenous communities lengthen the terms in office for their traditional authorities involved in municipal operations, particularly those serving in the most important offices, in order to avoid the absorption of traditional organizations by bureaucratic municipal norms and struggles over resources, as well as their relegation to "a purely ceremonial role" (my translation; Ticona and Albo 1997: 311).

In addition to the replacement of mayors after brief, often-shortened terms, the custom of new mayors' replacing their entire staffs also inhibits institutional development. Bolivia's Municipal Development Ministry found that in smaller, rural municipalities new mayors typically replace 100% of their staff, whereas in larger municipalities changes in leadership typically result in 30%–40% staff turnover. The problem is exacerbated by the extension of this logic to the vigilance committees and their component social organizations, which also typically rotate leadership annually so that more people have an opportunity to serve (Ministerio de Desarrollo Municipal 2002: 104–5, 109). High staff turnover is less of an issue in Ecuador because of stricter laws that prevent firing many municipal employees; there, the inability to fire superfluous or incompetent staff is a bigger problem (interviews, Proyecto Formia 2004).

Mayoral volatility is particularly high in Bolivia for another reason. Recall that, in Bolivia, mayors are directly elected if they finish first among other candidates for municipal council with more than 50% of the vote. Where they receive less than 50% they are subject annually to "constructive censure," or removal by the municipal council. Because of this rule, the Chapare muncipality of Chimoré had three mayors between 1994 and 1996, along with frequent changes in its municipal council (Lizárraga and Villarroel 1998). Seven replacements of mayors occurred in the department of Cochabamba in 2006. In two cases (Arden Punata and Villa Rivero) this resulted in violence among municipal councilors, vigilance committee members, and mayors. Although several involved disputes between MAS militants and opponents, none of these removals occurred in the Chapare, where the coca growers and the MAS had established hegemony by 2000 (Eid 2007; *La Razón* 2006b).

In Ecuador's indigenous movement there also is pressure to rotate top leadership posts, although popular leaders can and do dominate organizations. In fact, Bebbington observes that the lack of leadership rotation in civil society organizations creates "participatory elites" by allowing some community members to monopolize contacts with the state (2005: 5). Ecuador's indigenous mayors have enjoyed greater longevity than Bolivia's because they are not subject to replacement by opposition muncipal councillors.

For the reasons just described, reelection is a necessary condition for the institutionalization of radical democratic innovations. But it is not sufficient because mayors may still fail to secure support for their reforms.

In fact, reelection is not a reliable indicator of successful leadership. It is only an indicator of political skill or support, which may be secured through patronage and corruption, strong partisan loyalties, the absence or elimination of electoral rivals, the manipulation of valued group identities, coercion, electoral fraud, or the short-term ability to conceal or deflect attention from poor performance. Many incompetent leaders are reelected and some achieve policy objectives. Radically democratic institutional innovation requires additional leadership qualities.

Maintain the Support of Sponsoring Civil Society Groups

Although it is common for political-party militants to expect a mayor from the same party to favor them over nonmilitants, this norm is particularly strong within indigenous social movements, whose members feel they have been ignored for centuries and thus deserve priority treatment. Indigenous-movement-based parties maintain a discourse of ethnic claims against mestizo elites and promise during campaigns to give preference to the once-excluded. Therefore mayors may meet resistance from the social-movement organization on which they base their support if they defy movement commands to prioritize their own group's demands and exclude their oppressors or are perceived to be favoring the nonindigenous at their expense (Ortiz Crespo 1999: 77).

My cases confirm the view that democratic institutional innovations are essentially partnerships between visionary leaders and prodemocracy civil society groups. For example, a comparative analysis of examples of PB reforms in Brazil concluded that mayors with close ties to and deep roots in civil society organizations that possess an ideology promoting greater citizen participation and a goal to hold governments accountable were far more likely to initiate and implement participatory reforms. This distinction held even *within* the PT, which was responsible for the most-admired and emulated cases (Baiocchi 2005; Wampler 2004: 79). Only mayors who can count on citizen support for and participation in new participatory spaces have an incentive to establish and maintain them (Wampler 2008). This is unsurprising, considering that civil society activists' demands for greater leverage in public decision making and oversight typically motivate such innovations. In fact, in their statistical analysis of almost 400 municipal governments in four Latin American countries, Andersson and Van Laerhoven found that the existence of civil society demands for participatory governance institutions had a significant and positive relationship (at the 0.001 level) with the existence of such institutions (2007: 1100). Preexisting organizational and cultural ties among a mayor, his or her staff, and civil society organizations considerably reduce the start-up costs of building state–society partnerships. Some measure of trust already exists between them, along with established patterns of communication and mutual familiarity. These ties contribute to something Peter Evans calls "synergy" (1997). Evans argues that state–society linkages – which I believe are stronger when mayors and civil society groups share cultural and organizational ties – maximize the potential for complementarities by increasing the intimate interactions that build trust between state and society (1997: 204).

Similarly, Campbell and Fuhr found that institutional reforms that achieved their goals were founded upon "social building blocks" rooted in grassroots organizations that came to surpass their original purpose (Campbell and Fuhr 2004: 445). A Bolivian government study of 30 municipalities concurred: It discovered that the form and level of organization of civil society in a municipality was a crucial factor in the success of the state's Popular Participation regime. Municipalities with indigenous organizations were taking advantage of the fact that citizens already had the habit of organizing and participating. The report concluded that high levels of organization typically result in greater support for elected leaders, less political fragmentation, and thus greater governability (Ministerio de Desarrollo Municipal 2002: 109). Not only do civil society organizations help promote change, they make change sustainable by participating in innovative new processes, using organizational solidarity and commitment to sustain enthusiasm in the face of slow or meager initial results, and collectively counteracting resistance to change from the state apparatus and traditional elites (Campbell and Fuhr 2004: 446).

My cases show that support for a mayor from a dynamic civil society organization or set of associations is even more important to institutional innovation and sustainability than municipal council support for the mayor. This finding is corroborated by Faust and Harbers, who studied municipal reform initiated by diverse parties in Ecuador. They found that governments with close ties to organized social groups were more likely to actively pursue decentralization (2007: 21). With civil society support, a charismatic, popular mayor can outmaneuver opposition-dominated municipal councils. In fact, this occurred in Porto Alegre. The mayor overcame the city council's opposition to the first participatory budget by using popular pressure against individual council members. As Baiocchi argues, it is difficult for politicians to oppose a budget that has gained legitimacy through the deliberative process and to appear to oppose the "public will" (2001: 62).

Once participatory, deliberative institutions are established and appropriated by organized civil society, such fora can even replace and marginalize recalcitrant municipal councils – an intentional result in some cases, such as Cotacachi. Reactionary sectors of local society, who otherwise would block comprehensive political and economic reform, often dominate municipal councils. For this reason, based on surveys conducted in Central America and Colombia, Campbell calls municipal councils the "weakest link in the local power system" because councillors often are involved in corrupt relations with private businesses and citizens and use their council votes to extract patronage goods from the mayor (2003: 150). Similarly, Grindle found that municipal councillors were less influential compared with mayors and their staffs with the exception of some outstanding individuals (2007: 171–2). In Puerto Villarroel, Cochabamba, over vociferous municipal council objections, support from the powerful coca growers' Federation enabled the MAS mayor to fulfill a long-term goal of the municipality's majority population and shift the municipal seat to the more convenient city of Ivirgarzama (Lizárraga and Villarroel 1998: 46).

But marginalizing councils also entails costs. It reduces their ability to hold mayors accountable and to represent constituents who oppose the mayor (interviews in Ecuador, July 2005; see also Cameron 2003a: 174, 2003b: 307; interview with Auki Tituaña in Proyecto Formia 2004: 24–5; Wampler 2004: 89–91). Marginalizing councils also tends to increase political tensions between mayors and municipal councillors, from both their own and opposition parties. And, notwithstanding the primacy of civil society–mayoral partnerships, the political composition of municipal councils influences the impact of innovative mayors. A 2002 Bolivian government survey of 30 municipalities concluded that the partisan composition of councils and the coalitions within them had a major impact on municipal governance. The report concluded that councils expressed the distribution of political power within municipalities (Ministerio de Desarrollo Municipal 2002: 102). In municipalities where one political organization has a clear majority on the municipal council – and thus, under Bolivian law, the mayor has an absolute majority – and this organization represents a well-organized social base, it is easier to exercise effective social control because the sponsoring social base has close ties to government officials (Ministerio de Desarrollo Municipal 2002: 103). Elsewhere, partisan conflict can impede reform. However, the authors caution, what appear to be partisan conflicts with respect to policy and planning often are fronts for personal or particular interests, and conflicts like these typically are readily resolved by paying off opponents with patronage jobs and resources (ibid.: 102). Based on his study of PB in Brazilian cities, Wampler concurs that the relationship between mayors and civil society is more important than mayors' ability to gain support of local legislatures, owing in part to the significant autonomy that Brazilian mayors enjoy. Nevertheless, the lack of legislative support requires that mayors pay off opponents in order to compensate them for patronage resources lost to participatory spaces (2008).

Mayors whom indigenous social-movement organizations brought to office have particularly rich social and organizational resources from which to draw. Indigenous communities in both Bolivia and Ecuador possess dense social networks that link cohesive units of community identity to a geographically broad structure of citizens who feel common mutual obligations. These cohesive identities and intracommunity and intercommunity ties constitute a wealth of social capital into which politically and economically marginalized indigenous movements can tap. Social capital is constructed through automatic membership in traditional community life and through voluntary affiliation with modern social-movement organizations at the local, regional, and national levels. Social scientists have documented the contribution to social solidarity and civic competence of participation in civic associations (Kymlicka and Norman 2000: 7; Putnam 1993; Valadez 2001: 344).

The social networks that Andean indigenous cultures possess tend to foster participatory–deliberative institutional innovations because they are markedly horizontal, owing to the aforementioned tradition of leadership rotation and wealth redistribution. The emphasis on equality and horizontal relations fosters the production of social trust and reciprocity. The horizontality of indigenous community cultures generates motivation for participation and deliberation within them. Moreover, the involvement of indigenous mayors in social-movement networks provides permanent channels for sharing lessons with and offering solidarity to other mayors within their organizational and cultural network. In my cases social-movement channels were more important for disseminating ideas than were formal political-party channels, which tend to be characterized by more competition and jealousies, even within indigenous parties.

Strong ties to indigenous grassroots organizations hold mayors accountable to constituents and to the organization's consensualized vision of democracy and development, one that is rooted in local culture and values. The mayor's need to maintain the support of this base reduces incentives to engage in personal corruption or to be coopted by national party leaders, especially nonindigenous parties wishing to harness the appeal of indigenous candidates. This is why mayors' alliances with social-movement-based parties are important. A mayor's indigenous identity alone may attract support from indigenous voters, but it will not provide the support of organized grassroots social-movement organizations that is essential to democratic municipal innovation.[9] Although mayors brought to office by dynamic, deeply rooted social-movement networks have a great advantage, mayors confronting a weaker preexisting endowment of social capital may not be condemned to failure. As Peter Evans and his collaborators found, creating public–private linkages can foster the creation of social capital. When such links provide substantive benefits, individuals have a greater incentive to organize as beneficiaries (1997: 182).

The only study I encountered in which civil society did not play an important role in holding local governments accountable is Grindle's study of decentralization and democratization in Mexico. Grindle attributes this failure largely to the absence of reelection in Mexico because this removed one of society's most important means of motivating good government performance. As a result, government leaders played an exaggerated role in setting agendas and designing institutions compared with experiences in the Andes and elsewhere in South America, where reelection is legal (e.g., Brazil, Chile) (2007: 175).

Communication and Negotiation Across Ethnic Divides

Effective indigenous-party mayors inhabit two worlds: that of the indigenous community, movement, and organization, as well as that of the urban-mestizo professional. They tend to be leaders of indigenous heritage who maintain aspects of indigenous dress and appearance and have

---

[9] Lauer offers a fascinating account of an indigenous mayor, Jaime Turón, who has represented the elite party Democratic Action in a 98% indigenous municipality in Venezuela since 1994. Turón has been reelected twice despite his conviction and imprisonment for embezzlement of public funds, rejection of indigenous identity, hostility toward local indigenous organizations and parties, and violation of democratic governance norms. He has done so by providing bountiful state resources to the community, exploiting his knowledge of Venezuelan political culture, and conforming to indigenous expectations with respect to political leadership (that political leaders live in luxury). See Lauer (2006). However, elsewhere in 49% indigenous Amazonas, where indigenous organizations and the progressive Catholic Church are influential, the indigenous party, United Multiethnic People of Amazonas (Pueblo Unido Multiétnico de Amazonas, or PUAMA), has captured local governments and even elected one of its own governor of Amazonas in 2000 (Van Cott 2005: 207–9).

experience working within indigenous social-movement organizations, but who also have professional training and are comfortable in urban settings. This enables them to draw on Weber's other two ideal types of authority: traditional and rational–legal (see Weber 1946a: 78–9). Indigenous mayors' professional qualifications, ties to public and private bureaucracies, and status as legally elected officials confer rational–legal authority. Indigenous mayors also can tap into traditional authority by incorporating into their governance practices elements of Andean traditions – such as collective labor, rotating leadership service to the community, and participatory assemblies. To do so they must sufficiently personify indigenous constituents' expectations of "authentic" indigenous leaders in terms of their appearance, social status, and knowledge of local culture. As Lucero observes, identity-based movements typically require their leaders to meet high standards of authenticity (2006: 34–5). In Weber's conception, traditional authority rests in the symbols and "everyday routines" of indigenous culture, its patriarchal nature, and the prevailing belief that such practices are of long duration, and thus that they carry the sanctification of long-standing use (1946b: 297) and confer on indigenous leaders considerable traditional authority. Contemporary indigenous traditional authority differs somewhat from Weber's conception inasmuch as authority usually rests with the group, rather than with a particular person or lineage. Indigenous leaders borrow this authority for only relatively short periods of service. Moreover, rather than creating and perpetuating inequality, as Weber perceived traditional authority to do, indigenous traditional authority usually promotes equality through constant leadership rotation and customs that redistribute wealth.

As Weber argued, in the real world all three sources of authority may exist simultaneously to varying degrees. For optimal results, leaders draw on all three and they tend to reinforce each other. Indeed, this is precisely the strength of indigenous-party government when it fulfills its potential: It compensates citizens for the weakness of "rational–legal" democratic institutions by providing other valued and legitimate sources of authority. Indigenous leaders develop charismatic authority by cultivating discursive and interpersonal gifts as they rise through the ranks of indigenous political cultures that privilege these talents. They gain traditional authority by incorporating traditional values and forms of governance that in the last decade have obtained positive connotations beyond indigenous populations.

Drawing on multiple sources of authority enables mayors to develop cross-cultural communication skills and to forge relationships with nonindigenous state, international, and private development actors. In

Panebianco's terms, in the absence of strong, institutionalized party structures, mayors perform a central role of party organizations, that of establishing and maintaining productive relations within the party and between the party and actors in its environment. Relationships with outside actors constitute "a crucial resource" that mayors can spend on the party's behalf or that of the municipality. These relationships enable indigenous-party mayors to perform another crucial party function: financing party activities as well as development projects that the party-as-government sponsors in the municipality (Panebianco 1988: 34–5).

Mayors must gain the confidence of donors in order to attract external resources to augment small municipal budgets and, thus, provide early, substantive benefits to supporters and opponents. These "bonus" resources attract and sustain support for fledgling institutional innovations in the context of meager central-government transfers. Grindle identifies the capacity to secure additional resources above required transfers from higher levels of government to be required "almost universally" and as among the most important responsibilities and skills that local leaders exercise in Mexico (2007: 17, 20, 93). Whereas the most important external contacts that Mexican local government officials made in pursuit of extra funds were officials at higher levels of government (Grindle 2007: 96–9), in Bolivia and Ecuador relationships with NGOs and multilateral donors were more important (Bebbington and Carroll 2000: 9, 32).

The most-lauded indigenous mayor in South America, Auki Tituaña, a Quichua Indian and three-times-elected mayor of Cotacachi, exemplifies the leader who can attract external resources and work across ethnic divides. Tituaña was trained as an economist and had a long history of working with development NGOs through his affiliation with the national indigenous organization CONAIE before Pachakutik selected him as its mayoral candidate. In choosing to support him, the most important indigenous organization in Cotacachi, UNORCAC (an affiliate of a rival national indigenous–peasant federation, the National Federation of Peasant, Indigenous, and Black Organizations [Federación Nacional de Organizaciones Campesinas, Indígenas, y Negras, or FENOCIN]), passed over its own experienced leaders because they believed that Tituaña's academic title and experience working with mestizos would enable the party to better attract mestizo voters, who represent a majority in the canton (Cameron 2003b: 295). Tituaña lived in the urban part of the canton prior to entering politics and was educated in Cuba. Thus he has strong ties both to the indigenous movement and to key domestic and international actors, who have provided to the canton substantial technical and economic assistance (Guerrero 1999: 120). This decision is not unusual among indigenous organizations entering party politics in the Andes. Lauer reports that bilingualism, Western education, knowledge of the formal political system, and the ability to operate in a nonindigenous society now rivals knowledge of cultural traditions and wisdom in bestowing political authority within Amazonian communities in Venezuela (2006: 53). Even in traditional, rural areas of Bolivia, indigenous communities are seeking mayors who are equally adept at managing relations with important external actors and understanding the daily problems and values of their own people (Ticona and Albó 1997: 307).

Tituaña demonstrated other cross-cultural skills. In contrast to prior public officials in Cotacachi, he reached out to diverse social groups and facilitated cooperation, while using a discourse that promotes the construction of a new type of citizenship (Baéz et al. 1999: 64; Ortiz Crespo 2004: 170). As Hambleton argues, good leaders empower underrepresented groups by listening to them and creating space for their participation (2004: 10). One month after taking office Tituaña initiated a series of annual Cantonal Assemblies, which now are institutionalized in municipal law. Realizing that more-organized indigenous sectors would be overrepresented in the assemblies, Tituaña organized mestizo-urban neighborhoods as well as the canton's tropical, multiracial Intag zone (Cameron 2003b: 321–2). Tituaña understood that mestizos would still be overrepresented on the municipal council and would oppose any changes in government that reduced the flow of resources and jobs on which they had become dependent. To soothe the sting of their lost political monopoly, Tituaña continued to channel a disproportionately large share of municipal resources to urban areas and refused to fire a single mestizo municipal employee.

Tituaña's ability to cultivate the trust and loyalty of urban mestizos is demonstrated by the fact that he was able to convince them to participate in collective work projects in their own neighborhoods, despite the fact that collective work was not part of their culture and was associated with the indigenous. Moreover, he was reelected in 2000 with 78% of the vote, having won only 24% of the vote in 1996. Urban residents were seduced by rapid, visual improvements in the town center, which offset a proportional decline in urban spending in favor of rural areas (Cameron 2003b: 299–301). The intercultural, participatory nature of Cotacachi's development model attracted a bonanza of international and domestic NGO money, enabling Tituaña to reduce interethnic competition for resources by attending to the demands of all sectors (Ortiz Crespo 2004: 124).

The influx of resources and national and international attention even gained the mayor support from opposition-party municipal councillors (Cameron 2003b: 303).

Similarly, Quichua sociologist Mario Conejo ran for mayor of Otavalo with Pachakutik in 1996. Although he lost, he won the 2000 election with 45.95% of the vote by securing support from both rival indigenous organizations in the canton (the Imbabura affiliates of CONAIE and of the evangelical indigenous party Amauta Jatari). He also attracted votes from mestizos, who considered him to be a more moderate option than his more-confrontational indigenous rival (Carmen Yamberla, also from CONAIE). He was reelected in 2004 with 54% of the vote (Hurtado 2002: 8; Lalander 2005: 154, 170). Conejo recognized the importance of working across ethnic lines to achieving his goals. At an assembly in Riobamba, Chimborazo, he explained,

> It is important to promote consensus and unity among all of the people of Otavalo. We can't act as individuals or emphasize our differences and prejudices. Mestizos and indigenous must work together. Our motto is: "Construction of the unity of Otavaleños to guarantee our mutual development." We can strengthen our identities as Indians, as mestizos, and as Otavaleños. I am proud of being Indian, of my culture, my history, my present. We must promote mutual respect and interculturality. We must have a vision of the future of men and women, indigenous and mestizos. We must make a collective commitment to create an intercultural vision. (Oral presentation, July 1, 2005, transcribed and translated by the author.)

Conejo's improvement of interethnic relations has been widely recognized within Ecuador. In 2002 the conservative newspaper *El Comercio* singled out Otavalo for making improvement of intercultural relations a major thrust of development policy (Lalander 2005:161). Like Tituaña, Conejo has earned urban-mestizo support by increasing the canton's access to financial resources: In a 2004 interview, Conejo reported having quintupled the annual municipal budget in the previous three years, from U.S.$1,800,000 in 2000 to US$8,700,000 in 2004 (Lalander 2005: 177–8). With a larger financial pie, Conejo can afford to distribute a greater proportion of funds to indigenous communities while also satisfying urban residents.

In Guamote, Chimborazo, Mayor Curicama also reached across ethnic lines to encourage urban mestizos to participate in the new participatory institutions. This initiative is laudable, as Guamote is 95.3% indigenous. Curicama did not need to win mestizo votes for reelection in 1996 and, indeed, the government had been in indigenous hands continuously since 1992. Bebbington argues that Curicama's efforts between 1992 and

2000 resulted in improved interethnic relations and reduced abuse of the indigenous; for example, Quichua passengers received better treatment on mestizo-run buses (Bebbington 2005: 11). Like Conejo and Tituaña, he encouraged the organization of urban mestizos and their incorporation into the Local Development Committee as one of its 12 constitutive organizations, and he incorporated their neighborhood leaders into the Indigenous and Popular Parliament (ibid).

Curicama's professional development also fits the pattern just described. His earliest positions were as an advisor to an important local indigenous organization (Union of Campesino and Indigenous Organizations of Guamote [Unión de Organizaciones Campesinas e Indígenas de Guamote, or UCIG/UOCIG]), a leader of the transport union, and a driver for a state agency. These experiences resulted in a wide set of contacts throughout the canton as well as relationships with the most important NGOs and government agencies (Bebbington 2005: 10). These contacts facilitated the support of numerous domestic and foreign NGOs between 1992 and 2000 and resulted in a significant influx of economic investment. One scholar estimates that, in the late 1990s, 25 billion Ecuadorian sucres were invested in Guamote, compared with the 180 million sucres per year available to the municipality prior to 1992 (Bebbington 2005: 13, citing F. Ramirez 2001). Relations with Curicama were crucial to securing external aid because at times NGOs lost faith in other actors and observed design flaws in Guamote's institutions (Bebbington 2005: 13).

Indigenous mayors need not possess university degrees or experience working with mestizos or state agencies prior to taking office to foster cross-cultural communication. Arturo Yumbay, mayor of Guaranda, was a prominent indigenous-movement leader associated with the provincial indigenous organization the Federation of Peasants of Bolívar (Federación de Campesinos de Bolívar, or FECAB-RUNARI), a CONAIE affiliate, when he was elected mayor representing Pachakutik in 2000. However, he made a great effort to reach out to mestizo groups and won their support. With modest financial support from NGOs and foreign governments, Yumbay fostered participation by personally visiting all of the neighborhoods and convincing them to provide volunteer labor in order to make scarce resources stretch further (interviews, Guaranda, June 21–July 4, 2005). Pachakutik communications director Wilfredo Macas observes:

The minga, which was his great strength, the minga was done at all levels: at the level of the barrios, the communities, for public works. The city was clean.

The garbage was collected for the first time during the night with brigades for the communities and the neighborhoods. And mestizos and professionals participated in these mingas. He achieved the unification of the city and the countryside. This was his great accomplishment. (My translation; interview, July 5, 2005.)

Under Yumbay, Guaranda's participatory government earned national and international acclaim.

In Bolivia, several informants offered the case of Felipe Cáceres, the two-term MAS mayor of Villa Tunari, as an example of a mayor who reached across ethnic lines. Cáceres, of Quechua heritage, reportedly reached out to all sectors of the community, realizing that all would benefit from investment in the area's economic potential, which is derived from tourism, fishing, and coca growing. Although originally affiliated with peasant and agricultural interests, after Cáceres became a hotel owner he realized that promoting blockades would hurt his and others' economic interests, so he established a practice of moderation and consensus-building (Colanzi 2006; Kohl 2001; Lizárraga and Villarroel 1998; interviews, August 2005). I found no other cases in Bolivia in which mayors exhibited a talent for cross-ethnic communication and consensus-seeking.

The mayors just identified perform a crucial role that some deliberative democrats recommend: They ensure that deliberations are confined neither to enclaves of citizens with largely similar identities and interests nor to heterogeneous public spaces in which low–status groups may be silenced or intimidated[10] (e.g., Sunstein 2003: 95). The risk to democracy of allowing one particular group to dominate deliberation while excluding other groups is high. Sunstein provides persuasive evidence that deliberative enclaves tend to promote more extreme views than those originally held by participants because the pool of views expressed will be skewed owing to the homogeneity of the group, and because social pressures will be strong for people to associate themselves with the pole toward which the group's preferences skew (2003: 81). This "group polarization" effect is even more pronounced, he argues, in groups in which members feel a strong sense of shared social identity and solidarity and thus are more influenced by social pressure to conform; in groups in which members feel besieged by external threats; and in groups in which deliberations are held repeatedly (2003: 84–6).

---

[10] See Scott (1990) on "sequestered settings" and Mansbridge on "enclaves of resistance" (1995) as crucial for providing identity-based minorities the opportunity to develop a common critique of the status quo in a nonhostile environment where they can develop confidence and a shared position.

These conditions prevail for indigenous groups studied here and, indeed, in much of the region. Thus, in municipalities where an indigenous majority has the political power to monopolize new deliberative spaces, the democratic quality of the outcome depends on mayors creating mechanisms that promote cross-ethnic and other types of cross-identity/interest deliberation. They also must provide space for oppressed groups to discuss issues among themselves and to develop "clear voices" (Warren 2001: 36) prior to entering into more heterogeneous public spaces. It has been easier for mayors to promote cross-ethnic, heterogeneous deliberative spaces in Ecuador than in Bolivia. In the Ecuadorian municipalities studied, indigenous groups are more internally heterogeneous, are less physically and culturally isolated from other groups, and perceive a less-immediate threat from external actors, compared with coca growers in the Chapare of Cochabamba or Aymara campesinos in the rural highlands. In Bolivia, indigenous organizations controlling local government have a longer history of violent confrontation with the state and elites and less experience with successful negotiation with outsiders.

Finally, as Shönwälder argues, diversifying alliances is a way of protecting social movements from cooptation by a single alliance partner, which is a particular danger at the local level (1997: 768). The strategy also maximizes the potential to attract resources from multiple actors and institutions (ibid.). Mayors with multiple allies are better able to fulfill the next challenge, discussed in the next section: avoiding cooptation by their core constituency.

Establish a Degree of Autonomy From Social-Movement Organizations

Although mayors must maintain social-movement support in order to overcome political resistance, they must avoid the perception that they are the captive of a particular social group or political faction. They are better positioned to negotiate convincingly with diverse actors if they have the autonomy to limit the demands of their base. For example, Cotacachi Mayor Tituaña resisted repeated efforts by UNORCAC – the peasant–indigenous organization that initially sponsored his candidacy – to exercise greater influence over his decisions and to insert more of its members into local government. The organization complains that smaller, often newer, organizations are overrepresented in the Cantonal Assembly (Cameron 2003b: 343–4; Ortiz Crespo 2004: 155; Pallares 2002; Anrango Ch. 2004: 77). Although it weakened the ability of an important indigenous organization to directly represent its members, Tituaña's autonomy enabled him to gain the trust of local and national actors beyond the indigenous movement.

In contrast, in many Chapare municipalities the greatest threat to democratic governance is the political hegemony of coca growers' federations. The federations have subordinated municipal government officials to their own authority, which is not constrained by any formal legal norms or horizontal institutions. In Chimoré, for example, Lizárraga and Villarroel describe the "notorious" extent to which coca growers subordinate public officials. Conflicts emerged there when municipal councillors refused to follow federation directives (1998: 15). In Puerto Villarroel, Córdova observed that coca-growing *sindicatos* exercised a high degree of "social control" over the mayor, municipal council, and local government. The federation frequently reminded officials that they gained their offices with the support of the *sindicatos*. This control in the Chapare is exercised notwithstanding the fact that coca growers' federations also dominate the vigilance committees, which are empowered to hold municipal governments accountable (Córdova Eguivar 2004).

During the period Córdova studied (1996–1999) the federation in Puerto Villarroel was so powerful relative to the municipal government that it was able to sanction municipal officials and the vigilance committee for failing to follow its instructions and comply with promises. It also forcibly froze municipal spending on projects that were not proceeding according to federation guidelines and illegally secured funding for projects not envisioned. Under pressure, the mayor responded to federation demands with ad hoc projects, while ignoring objections from urban residents, whose projects had been approved in the annual operating plan, but for which funding no longer was available. This eventually led the national Controlaría to freeze the municipality's coparticipation resources. After the original mayor was replaced in 1999 the federation designated a successor (Córdova Eguivar 2004: 188–9).

The tendency of hegemonic civil society organizations and their electoral vehicles to dominate and weaken municipal governments can be found throughout Bolivia. Although the Municipal Development Ministry found this correlation of political forces to result in more effective social control by citizens of their governments, it also was found to result in greater problems for the institutionalization of effective management practices (Ministerio de Desarrollo Municipal 2002: 103, 107). Similarly, Wampler discovered that in Recife a well-organized and highly mobilized civil society circumvented PB rules by pressuring governments to put their projects ahead of those approved through the process (2008). In

TABLE 3.1. *The Impact of Context on Leadership*

Favorable Contextual Condition	Leadership Quality Promoted
Flexible decentralization regime allows mayors to innovate	Mayors maintain support of civil society base
Mayors unlikely to be removed during term in office. Few cultural or legal barriers to reelection and office retention	Reelection and office retention
Vigorous internal debate permitted	Communication across ethnic lines
Habit of nonviolent dispute resolution	Leaders hold base together and maintain its support and can communicate across ethnic lines
Moderate political pluralism provides multiple power contenders, none are hegemonic	Communication across ethnic lines Autonomy from social-movement base

sum, participatory–deliberative democracy requires a balance between state and civil society because the state must be able to enforce rules that govern civil society's participation in new spaces.

THE IMPORTANCE OF CONTEXT

Bolivia and Ecuador provide distinct institutional, organizational, cultural, and political contexts for aspiring innovative leaders, and these contextual differences had a significant impact on the operation of the six variables previously discussed (see Table 3.1). First, the Ecuadorian context of flexibility with respect to the degree and nature of decentralization and local institutional design offers an opening for entrepreneurial mayors to initiate and codify institutional change with relatively little higher-tier state resistance. In Bolivia, in contrast, mayors must work within a highly regulated and monitored institutional environment and within complex, prescribed institutions, such as the vigilance committees and participatory planning methodology. Innovation occurs at the margins and is usually derived from local civil society practices, such as campesino assemblies and traditional means for choosing authorities. Ecuadorian mayors face relatively fewer legal obstacles to innovation.

Second, Ecuadorian mayors can count on finishing their terms in office, provided they avoid unlawful mistakes. If they are skillful they can amass sufficient support for reelection, even without their civil society or party base, as Mayor Coles did in Guaranda after he lost Pachakutik's support. But in Bolivia, outside the Chapare, mayors with minority electoral support can be replaced after one year and thus may not pursue institutional initiatives that would take years to bring to fruition. Innovations created are likely to be demolished by opposition politicians, who have a short–term interest in the defeat of rivals. Outside the Chapare, electoral volatility is high and few mayors are reelected. Within the Chapare, campesino norms of leadership rotation work against the duration of mayors in office, even through their elected terms. Bolivian mayors have less opportunity to develop leadership skills and little incentive to invest their political capital in promoting change that does not produce the immediate benefits they need to maintain political support.

Third, political culture also varies between the two countries. The political culture within the Ecuadorian indigenous movement and its main partisan representative, Pachakutik, rewards effective, publicly supported leadership with greater possibilities for reelection; allows for vigorous internal debate that rarely results in violence; and is slowly reducing barriers for women in public, formal roles. Pachakutik and its local indigenous social-movement affiliates operate relatively autonomously from each other, and, in fact, there have been a number of serious divisions between the two. In contrast, within Bolivia's indigenous movement and its two political parties the political culture is more authoritarian and sexist and civil society organizations that are dismissive of democratic norms and laws concerning municipal governance often control political parties. Political disputes often result in violence, and the threat of violence hangs over politics in the Chapare and Aymara highlands. Therefore, although factionalism within indigenous populations is endemic in both countries, in Ecuador internal disputes are less likely to result in violence and thus become irreconcilable. This makes it easier for mayors to maintain unity within their social and political bases. The reduced threat of internal conflict gives Ecuadorian mayors greater credibility in negotiating on behalf of their base and absorbs less energy and political capital, providing them relatively more freedom to pursue cross-ethnic alliances.

Fourth, the degree of competitiveness and pluralism in the local party system also affects the context for leadership. In Ecuador local politics is characterized most often by vibrant pluralistic competition for power among three–five real contenders and additional challengers hoping to win a council seat. In the highlands, where the indigenous population is rarely a majority but often a significant minority, there is an incentive for all politicians to try to appeal across ethnic lines. Indigenous mayors and mayoral candidates realize that election and reelection depends upon successful appeals to a portion of the mestizo population, and thus they have an incentive to maintain some autonomy from their sponsoring indigenous movement so as not to appear beholden to one ethnic group. In Bolivia, in contrast, local politics often is characterized by one of two extremes: the hegemony of one dominant vehicle or extreme party-system fragmentation. Neither context is conducive to cross-ethnic appeals.

The Chapare exemplifies the first scenario. MAS municipalities have enjoyed political stability since the party asserted hegemonic control in the late 1990s and several mayors have been reelected. Chapare municipalities lack the interpartisan conflict that has paralyzed Bolivian municipalities elsewhere and has delayed or prevented the institutionalization of municipal structures established by the 1994 LPP, as well as the execution of public works (confidential interviews, August 2005). However, the hegemony of one party provides an inauspicious context for high-quality leadership because leaders do not have an incentive to reach across ethnic lines or to please diverse constituencies. Thus the institutions they build are less likely to tolerate dissent and promote unfettered deliberation.

The second extreme, partisan fragmentation, is common throughout Bolivian municipalities outside the Chapare. A 2002 Bolivian government study of a representative sample of Bolivian municipalities found high levels of partisan atomization in almost 50%. In 5 of the 30 municipalities studied, each council member represented a different party (100% atomization), whereas in another 9 municipalities partisan atomization was reported to be 80%. The authors found that these high levels of atomization result in low levels of governability because governing alliances can be suspended with the change of one vote. In fact, the bivariate inverse correlation between political atomization on the municipal council and municipal management capacity is statistically significant. Atomization tends to be higher in smaller municipal councils, which are likely to be found in rural areas (Ministerio de Desarrollo Municipal 2002: 112). The negative impact of partisan atomization was found to be ameliorated only in municipalities where a strong, collective indigenous identity provides a countervailing basis for unity. The example of the predominantly indigenous municipality of Charagua is given. Here, despite the fact that each councillor represents a different party, council members pursue their common interests as an indigenous community (Ministerio de Desarrollo Municipal 2002: 102). Thus indigenous communities have the potential to overcome extreme partisan fragmentation.

This has not occurred in the highland Aymara communities of La Paz, where a decade of competition has generated extreme political fragmentation and electoral volatility. This is partially attributable to the fact that mestizo parties have for years offered a vehicle for impoverished, individual, indigenous militants to compete for access to extremely scarce state and party financial resources. In conditions of resource scarcity and external manipulation, widely shared cultural identities have been unable to produce political cohesion. In the 2004 race in Achacachi, 11 political parties and approximately half a dozen citizens' groupings and indigenous peoples competed for 11 municipal council seats, whereas in Ayo Ayo, where 5 seats were at stake, 9 political parties competed (*La Prensa* 2004). Extreme fragmentation makes alliance formation difficult and provides to leaders an incentive to eliminate and exclude rivals. In the context of high political atomization, in which mayors frequently win office with less than 20% of the vote, there is greater incentive for a leader to appeal to his or her base constituency in order to ensure a seat on the municipal council than there is to make broader alliances. Power is achieved and maintained through log rolling and pacts among political leaders, rather than through winning broad public support.

CONCLUSION

Analysis of democratic institutional innovations in the Andes reveals that six leadership qualities are associated with innovative mayors: (1) considerable personal charisma; (2) the ability to be reelected; (3) the support of civil society groups that elected them; (4) a continuous, visible presence in the community and frequent interaction with constituents; (5) the capacity and will to communicate and negotiate effectively across ethnic divides and with external actors, especially donors; and (6) a degree of autonomy from their organizational benefactors. Table 3.2 presents the extent to which the six qualities discussed in this chapter were present in my cases. It is impossible to quantify the intensity of those qualities or to compute an aggregate score for each mayor. Moreover, effective leadership depends on the interaction of particular categories of leadership: For example, the ability to maintain both social-movement support and social-movement autonomy represents a high degree of skill with respect to constituent relations. Notwithstanding these measurement difficulties, we can see that the Ecuadorian mayors Tituaña (Cotacachi), Curicama (Guamote), and Conejo (Otavalo) stand out as extraordinarily talented and effective mayors. Yumbay of Guaranda was perhaps an equally talented mayor, but because he died in office he did not have the opportunity for reelection. These mayors are associated with the most-lauded democratic institutional innovations.

TABLE 3.2. *Scoring of Cases on Six Qualities of Leadership*

Municipality	Charisma	Presence	Crosses Ethnic Divide	Reelected	Social-Movement Support	Social-Movement Autonom
Ecuador						
Colta						
Curichumbi	No	Moderate	Moderate	Yes	High	Moderate
Cotacachi						
Tituaña	Yes	High	High	Yes, twice	High	High
Guamote						
Curicama	Yes	High	High	Yes	High	High
Delgado	No	High	Moderate	No	Moderate	Moderate
Guaranda						
Yumbay	Yes	High	High	No	High	Moderate
Coles	No	Low	Moderate	Yes	Low	High
Otavalo						
Conejo	Yes	High	High	Yes	High	High
Bolivia						
Achacachi	No data	No data	Low	No	Fragmented	Moderate, fragmente
Ayo Ayo	No	Low	Low	No	Fragmented	Low
Chimoré						
Cruz	No	High	Low	Yes	High	Low
P. Villarroel						
Tarqui	No	No data	Low	No	Low	Low
Mita	No	No data	Low	No	Moderate	Low
Villa Tunari						
Cáceres	No	Moderate	High	Yes	Moderate	Low

These findings suggest theoretical implications. First, radical democrats tend to understate the impact of leaders on substantive outcomes and their role in decision-making processes. For most participatory democrats, leaders are irrelevant because the subject of participation is the individual citizen or civil association. The objective of participatory visions is to maximize the role of ordinary individuals while reducing the importance of power hierarchies (Budge 2000: 206). An exception is Fung and Wright, who acknowledge the problem of undertheorized leadership (2003b: 33) and emphasize the role of political leaders in mobilizing "collaborative countervailing power." Political leaders and parties, they argue, have an incentive to promote participatory processes because such processes more efficiently provide substantive benefits to constituents, which politicians need in order to maintain political support (Fung and

Wright 2003a: 284). Apart from the mayor, trained facilitators worked within each district in Porto Alegre (Baiocchi 2005: 37). Thus the idea of citizens deliberating and making decisions without any sort of leadership to structure discussions and move them toward outcomes is belied by empirical data.

Similarly, associative democrats emphasize the democratizing potential of civil society groups that mobilize collective identities and resources autonomously – theoretically without the manipulation of leaders. The emphasis again is on "ordinary people" acting in concert, seemingly without leadership or the need for representation (Cohen and Rogers 2003: 240). Many associational democrats fail to address how precisely they would or should operate (Budge 2000: 199). Some deliberative democrats do a better job of accounting for the role of moderators in reasoned argument[11] (e.g. Ackerman and Fishkin 2002; Humphreys et al. 2006). But, on the whole, this literature underestimates the importance of leadership to institutional innovation and its durability.

Second, indigenous intellectuals also underplay the role of leaders. They typically idealize leaders as receptacles of the community's will, who "serve obeying" in constant deference to an autonomous, evolving, group consensus, as if they had no will of their own. The truth is otherwise. Indigenous leaders who moderate deliberative assemblies or smaller decision-making workshops are charged with the important task of facilitating deliberations, identifying a consensus within a group, articulating it clearly, and encouraging participants to converge around it. But indigenous activists and ethnographic accounts say little or nothing about the role of leaders in generating the preferences around which consensus ultimately forms. As Humphreys et al. (2006) demonstrate, even in ideal deliberative settings moderators can devise subtle means to privilege particular topics and approaches while marginalizing others. Mayors can press for a consensus before alternatives have been sufficiently aired. They can establish the rules for "reasoned argument" in ways that exclude speakers of Spanish or less-dominant indigenous languages and that exclude women, who often feel uncomfortable with public speaking.

Indigenous visions of democracy also typically ignore the fact that indigenous representatives in government have vastly greater access to

---

[11] For example, Ackerman and Fishkin observe that political-party leaders have an incentive to volunteer to serve as moderators in deliberative polls in order to set the issue agenda and affect citizens' preferences (2002: 139) and that group leaders will be tempted to abuse their power (142).

information and resources than do leaders of the community organizations from which today's elected officials emerged. Thus, the gap in access to information between elected and appointed government leaders and their indigenous followers is greater than that between social-movement organization leaders and followers. The more stratified, vertical relationship between indigenous mayors and citizens has significant implications for the maintenance of Andean indigenous political culture, which is rooted in the rotation of prestigious positions among equals. It is unlikely that in the near term conditions in indigenous municipalities will reach levels of socioeconomic and political equality sufficient to significantly reduce power and knowledge disparities between leaders and common citizens.

In sum, mayoral leadership matters. Indeed, it is hard to imagine the Cotacachi experiment without Auki Tituaña or the Guaranda experience without Arturo Yumbay. The relationship between mayors and their political parties matters too. Mayors are often the local leaders of parties and must constantly keep relations with the party, its militants, and constituents in mind in order to lead effectively. This issue is taken up in the next chapter. Although I do not have enough variation in my cases to test this hypothesis, it is worth considering whether the impact of mayors and their political parties is related to the level of party-system institutionalization. Thus, in countries like Ecuador and Bolivia, where party systems are volatile and fragmented and indigenous parties are relatively new, mayors have relatively more influence. But in countries like Brazil, where the party system in the 1990s was relatively more institutionalized and oriented around several important parties, parties may play a greater role than personalities, as suggested by the durability of participatory budgeting between the early 1990s and 2004 in Porto Alegre under a series of PT mayors.

This effort to better operationalize the impact of leadership on democratic quality improves on existing frameworks that emphasize difficult-to-measure individual qualities. It also foregrounds vital aspects of individual agency that scholars of institutional reform often neglect. It is hoped that others will apply the framework elsewhere so that it can be tested and further refined.

4

Political Parties, Civil Society, and Democratic Institutional Innovation

The opportunity to operate as a social movement in the streets, outside the political system, while also holding elected office, maximizes the leverage that indigenous social movements can bring to bear against opponents. When such movements represent excluded groups, their participation in government improves the quality of local democracy by improving representation and strengthening its legitimacy. But expanding fields of contention into formal institutions carries risks. Powerful elites design institutions to control dissent and exclude challengers. Having surmounted these obstacles to inclusion, entering formal institutions subjects social-movement representatives to the same pressures and incentives that their predecessors faced. The result may be a change of faces in government but not necessarily an improvement in democratic quality.

The ambivalence of indigenous movements with respect to formal and informal politics is reflected in a well-known statement that MIP leader Felipe Quispe made after his election to Congress in 2002. He vowed that while he played with one hand the game of democracy, with the other he would hide a stone under his poncho (*La Prensa* 2002: 8). How can social-movement activists entering new democratic institutions be persuaded to put down their stones? How can they do so without betraying the principles of the social movements that launched their political careers and, consequently, losing support?

I examine here the tensions among the competing goals and logics of social movements, the parties they sponsor, and the governments in which their militants participate. As Glenn observes with respect to post-communist politics in Czechoslovakia (2003), parties and governments derived from oppositional social movements are distinct from those that

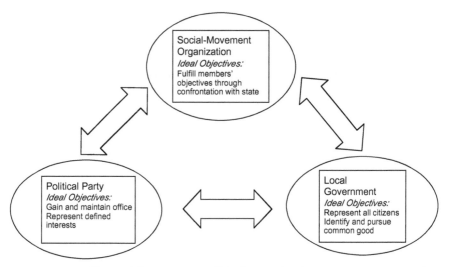

FIGURE 4.1. The social-movement–political-party–local-government nexus and contrasting goals.

arise from more elitist and bureaucratic origins, and they are subject to distinct strains. This is particularly true when they take power at times of great political flux or regime change, when people have such a low view of parties and government that movements seeking or gaining office refuse to self-identify as either. The analogy to contemporary politics in Ecuador and Bolivia is striking. In both countries indigenous parties call themselves movements to distinguish themselves from traditional politicians; the governments they control have incorporated new ceremonies and symbols to signal a break with past governance forms. Yet, despite their disdain for political institutions, social movements must operate within a context in which their inexorable logics determine political outcomes (Glenn 2003: 168). The capacity of social-movement-based governments to manage the tensions among these logics affects their potential to promote democratic institutional reform.

These competing logics are depicted in Figure 4.1. Social movements seek to fulfill their members' particular goals by making demands on the state. They typically disperse or transform themselves once these goals are reached. Political parties are meant to be permanent political actors that gain and maintain a position within the state for the purpose of promoting the interests of party leaders and members. Local governments, in turn, are supposed to represent all citizens, not the members of any particular sector of society or political tendency. They are meant to seek the common good and to moderate conflicts of interest and diverse cultural norms. To create more radically democratic institutions, local government must harness the energy of the social movements and political parties that brought them to power.

For political parties to promote democratic institutional innovation, I argue, first, they must be allied with highly mobilized, cohesive, civil society organizations that can support the party's mayor when fledgling parties falter. These organizations are particularly important to new political parties owing to the high cost of creating organizational infrastructure, recruiting members, and identifying programmatic principles that appeal to voters (Kitschelt 2000: 851). The relationship between leftist-reforming parties and dynamic civil society organizations is symbiotic: As much as parties need movements to sustain them, movements seeking decentralizing, participatory reforms need parties that extend their influence into government in durable and effective ways. As Shönwälder argues, alliances with political parties enhance the influence of local movements (1997: 762). Thus a leftist-party–social-movement alliance provides the best defense against elites capturing and neutralizing participatory reforms while serving as a constructive link between local state institutions and civil society (ibid.).

It is perhaps no coincidence that deliberative–participatory institutions have flourished in Latin American countries with low levels of party-system institutionalization. Mainwaring and Scully's landmark study of party-system institutionalization ranks Ecuador and Bolivia along with Brazil as having the region's most "inchoate" party systems (1995). Where parties are weakly institutionalized they are unable to block efforts by civil society actors to create new forms of state–society linkage that bypass parties and reduce their patronage resources. In a study of deliberative–participatory experiments in Porto Alegre, Brazil, Montevideo, Uruguay, and Caracas, Venezuela, Goldfrank found that the weak institutionalization of local opposition parties was among two main conditions that explain the success of such experiments (2007b). Whereas Goldfrank applies this condition only to local opposition parties, the Ecuadorian and Bolivian cases demonstrate that weakly institutionalized governing parties having organic roots in civil society are more easily permeated by civil society actors demanding greater participation. Moreover, weakly institutionalized parties are more easily managed by innovating mayors, since they present fewer constraints to executive authority.

My second argument with respect to the effectiveness of parties as engines of radically democratic reform is that parties can best promote democratic institutional innovation when they operate in a competitive political environment where they are held accountable for their performance. Conversely, hegemonic parties have no incentive to collaborate with opponents or competitors, and parties unlikely to win more than one or two seats on the municipal council owing to extreme party-system fragmentation must expend most of their energy to outmaneuver opponents and maintain access to patronage resources.

I build upon an extensive literature examining the tensions between social movements and their sister parties, and within social movements that sponsor electoral vehicles.[1] Such parties have an external sponsoring institution upon which the party is dependent for legitimation and through which the party receives "indirect loyalty" (Panebianco 1988: 51, 63). Panebianco cautions that such parties exist as political arms of other organizations that have no interest in allowing them to achieve autonomy. As a result, they never are fully institutionalized (ibid.: 53). Party leaders and candidates enter the organization horizontally from the positions they hold in real life, rather than by rising vertically through the party ranks (ibid., 62).

Within this category, scholars of Latin American parties have focused on relations between leftist parties and social movements, most of which comprise alliances among labor unions, intellectuals, and grassroots organizations.[2] These parties follow what Roberts calls the "organic model," in which a party engages in continuous social mobilization in pursuit of defined programmatic goals, while also competing for political office. In addition, the membership and leadership of the associated electoral vehicle and social movement overlap (Roberts 1998: 75; see also Maguire 1995: 201–5). All organic parties encounter similar challenges: tensions between those seeking to prioritize either the movement or electoral role; the internal diversity of their constituent members, owing to organic parties' roots in diverse popular movements and civil associations that represent different cultures, identities, and interests; and the danger of losing the "antisystem purity" (Eisenstadt 2004: 203) that a movement enjoys when it serves as a direct expression of the people after the party becomes increasingly associated with elections, formal politics, and the state.

---

[1] For a global survey see Goldstone (2003). On left-libertarian and ecology parties, see Kitschelt (1989); Maguire (1995); Mayer and Ely (1998); and Thomas (2001).

[2] On social-movement-based political parties in Latin America, see Eckstein (2001); Foweraker (1995); and K. Roberts (1998, 2002). On Brazil's PT, see Avritzer (2002); Baiocchi (2003, 2005); Keck (1992); and Wampler (2008); on the Mexican Party of the Democratic Revolution, see Bruhn (1997) and T. Eisenstadt (2004).

Neither social scientists nor political philosophers have fully investigated the issues that arise when social movements take on governing roles.[3] Political scientists tend to focus narrowly on formal institutions, whereas sociologists tend to focus on social-movement activity, while failing to place it in an institutional context (Fung and Wright 2003a: 285). Philosophers, in turn, have tended to bracket crucial aspects of the informal–formal, social movement–state problematic, or have offered mainly criticism of existing experiments while dismissing their potential lessons for understanding and improving democratic life (Fung and Wright 2003a: 286). With few exceptions[4] radical democrats have undertheorized political parties' contributions to democratic institutional innovation, emphasizing instead direct participation. Ian Budge attributes this oversight to the "extreme individualistic bias in modern democratic theory," which stems from its origins in Enlightenment and liberal thinking (2000: 199). But parties must be incorporated into any discussion of democratic institutional innovation because it is usually parties that define the issues and preferences that citizens consider, and it is parties in government that implement (or not) those decisions (2000: 196–7).

Indeed, it was parties – specifically left-wing parties – that instituted some of the world's most-admired cases of local government institutional innovation, albeit in close partnership with civil society activists. The principal exceptions to the tendency of the literature on municipal innovation to undertheorize the role of parties are the numerous studies of innovations instituted by the Communist Party in Kerala, India (Desai 2003; Fung and Wright 2003a and 2003b; Heller 2001) and of participatory budgeting that the PT instituted in the early 1990s in the Brazilian city of Porto Alegre (Abers 2000; Avritzer 2002; Baiocchi 2003, 2005; Bruce 2004; Fung and Wright 2003: 36; Goldfrank 2004; Santos 1998; Wampler 2004, 2007, 2008). This fascinating case shares two similarities with those studied here: (1) the leftist, anti-neoliberal orientation of the governing party, and (2) the rootedness of that party in civil society networks. In the Andes, new local institutions directly resulted from a partnership between a visionary mayor and highly mobilized popular movements demanding greater participation in decision making and access

---

[3] Notable efforts include chapters in Goldstone (2003), especially those by Manali Desai and John K. Glenn.
[4] For example, Cohen and Rogers (1995b) view parties as channels through which citizens can check the excesses of undemocratic associations. See also Immergut (1995) and Budge (2000).

to state resources. Similarly, in Brazil popular civil society organizations were at least as important as the PT itself in pushing for PB, designing its principal features, and supporting mayors implementing the model (Ackerman 2004; Avritzer 2002; Baiocchi 2005: 33, 149–51; Wampler and Avritzer 2004: 309).

Domestic and international NGOs helping indigenous parties in the Andes to design and implement participatory governance models promoted the Porto Alegre model, and its chief features may be discerned in many "indigenous" institutional designs. But there are significant differences that limit the relevance of comparisons between the Brazilian and Andean cases. These include: (1) the absence of a focus on *intercultural* participation in Porto Alegre; (2) the size and scale of the municipalities studied (Porto Alegre has a metropolitan area of almost 3 million people, whereas the Andean municipalities studied contain less than 100,000 persons); (3) variations with respect to the political and institutional environments (highly decentralized, federal Brazil versus unitary Bolivia and Ecuador); and (4) the far-higher level of economic and social development and the greater availability of economic resources in Porto Alegre (Baiocchi 2001: 47, 65). Moreover, whereas the PT had been competing in elections for 10 years before adopting PB, indigenous parties began to experiment with institutional design less than a year after their formation.[5]

The parties studied here are classic examples of organic parties. Three (Pachakutik, the MAS, and the Ecuadorian evangelical indigenous party Amauta Jatari) were formed by leaders of well-established indigenous social-movement organizations with a broad geographic base and a dense network of affiliates. The youngest indigenous-movement organization forming a party was 10 years old at the time and the oldest had existed for 18 years (Van Cott 2005: 44). The fourth indigenous party studied (Bolivia's Pachakuti Indigenous Movement, MIP) was formed by Felipe Quispe as a personal vehicle, but he built upon close ties to the national campesino organization and traditional community organizations. Whereas the first three established national party organizations distinct from their highest-tier social-movement affiliate, at the local level the boundary between party and social movement is blurred. This is

---

[5] The PT had experimented with participatory processes since initial victories in 1982 and 1985. Personal communication, Brian Wampler, October 19, 2007. None of these attracted the local or international enthusiasm that PB would 10 years later.

particularly so for the MIP, which lacks a party apparatus beyond Quispe. Given their lack of electoral experience, many electoral candidates come directly from sponsoring civil society organizations.

Indigenous parties in the Andes are distinct from other organic parties because they are grounded in deeply rooted, long-established, authoritative, traditional and contemporary social-movement institutions that provide more than a vehicle for collective political action and decision making. They are imbued with cultural and spiritual meanings and norms of solidarity, reciprocity, and obligatory service.[6] Thus we might expect them to be even more effective in harnessing the energy of civil society actors and transferring political cultures governing informal politics to local governance.

Organic parties must serve as crucial actors in the advancement and defense of democratic institutional innovation. But the obstacles they face are numerous and difficult. I begin this chapter by illustrating the challenges that organic parties encounter when they campaign for office. The second section elaborates a particularly vexing problem for organic parties: internal factionalism generated by the diverse social movements and the civil society organizations that they comprise. In the third section I identify the challenges that indigenous political parties encounter in the Andes when they enter government office, some of which they share with other organic parties. In the fourth section I examine how the political context affects the potential of indigenous parties to promote democratic institutional innovation. I show how high levels of party-system fragmentation, poor choices with respect to political alliances, and the interference of NGOs exacerbated divisions within indigenous parties and inhibited their ability to promote institutional reform. In contrast, where parties operate under conditions of moderate pluralism, they are more likely to make better alliance choices and to be motivated to collaborate with political opponents.

THE CHALLENGES OF POLITICAL CAMPAIGNS

Indigenous social-movement organizations that launch electoral vehicles find it difficult to extend the logic of social movements to these competitive, individualistic, and formal political spaces. Whereas indigenous social movements are governed by norms of leadership selection and

---

[6] For example, two of the parties studied invoke the mythic ruler Pachakuti, who governed the pre-Colombian civilization of Tawantinsuyo (based around Lake Titicaca) during its golden age (De la Cadena 2000: 165).

decision making rooted in traditional cultural practices or developed through years of struggle as contentious movements, elections are regulated by legal norms as well as political exigencies. Moreover, indigenous political parties have a hard time with the logic of democratic representation because of the intensity of communitarian norms within the indigenous social movements that sponsor them. When the two logics collide, conflict and confusion often result. Three challenges are particularly difficult: confusion regarding steering generated by the coexistence of political-party and social-movement structures; the dispersion of human and financial resources from movement activity to political campaigns; and the need to shift from a logic of movement discipline to the logic of pluralism and negotiation.

Confusion With Respect to Steering

Shönwälder identifies the steering conflicts that emerge when social movements make pragmatic alliances with political parties (1997: 763). The mere coexistence of party and movement generates confusion with regard to decision-making hierarchies and steering. Steering conflicts are more intense and distressing when the alliance is between a party and movement with organic links and overlapping membership. At the national level one leader may retain responsibility for leading both party and movement, as Evo Morales and Felipe Quispe have done. But at the local level, long-standing leadership hierarchies typically become bifurcated as a segment of the movement takes on the role of competing in elections. Relations of authority and accountability change. The experience in Ecuador and Bolivia departs from Shönwälder's expectation that the party ultimately remains the dominant partner in such alliances and that social movements almost inevitably are absorbed by political vehicles (1997: 763–5). In the Andes, movements are more likely to embody the authenticity and dynamism that are necessary for political success and party leaders typically defer to expressions of movement power.

The confusion that occurs as indigenous movements attempt to retain control over their electoral vehicle and its representatives in office, and party leaders struggle for independence, is most commonly encountered with respect to the larger, more heterogeneous parties – Ecuador's Pachakutik and Bolivia's MAS – both of which control local governments that span a wide geographic area through a diverse assortment of alliances. Struggles over steering and ambiguity with regard to lines of

authority seem to be less of a problem for the two minor parties, MIP and
Amauta Jatari, because both of these control municipal government only
in ethnically and socially homogeneous rural areas that constitute their
bastion of support: a few Aymara provinces in the Department of La Paz
and the province of Chimborazo, respectively. In these regions there was
little difference between the local indigenous–campesino organization and
party structures and leaders, as of 2005.

Steering Problems in Bolivia. In Bolivia tensions emerged between local
social-movement organizations and national MAS leaders after 2002,
when the MAS began to construct a more formal party-style apparatus.
When it originally formed, there was little difference between the coca
growers'/campesino movement and the party – the latter was merely the
political instrument of the former. This continues to be the case at the
municipal level in the Chapare (*Atlas del Trópico de Cochabamba* 2004:
44). Similarly, in rural areas of Oruro and Potosí, where a peasant *sindicato* is the main community organization, there is little differentiation
between the social organization and the MAS – the union leaders simply
perform additional political functions.

   After two rounds of municipal elections, the MAS began to acquire
a more formal and separate structure and national leaders increasingly
interfered in local politics. Whereas in 1999 it was the norm for coca
growers' centrals to choose candidates, in 2004 higher-tier MAS leaders tried to impose their choices. Sometimes they succeeded, sometimes
not. Where the MAS was expanding outside of its base to urban and
more heterogeneous areas, it faced more competition and thus had to
form alliances with diverse popular and middle-class movements. In such
cases it has been common for national MAS leaders to intervene to settle
disputes over candidacies, often at the expense of local peasant organizations. The shift to more partisan behavior has caused some movement
militants to feel that the MAS has betrayed the original goals of the
coca growers' movement – to defend its territory and right to grow coca
leaf. Even in the Chapare, conflicts have occurred, particularly between
provincial campesino centrals and the partisan apparatus of the MAS
(interviews, Rafael Archondo, August 1, 2005; Abraham Borda, July 26,
2005; Fernando Mayorga, August 8, 2005; Eduardo Córdova, August
3, 2005; Pablo Regalsky, August 8, 2005). As Bolivian social scientist
Pablo Regalsky explains, "[t]he apparatus of the MAS is configuring
itself increasingly according to a partisan logic, a logic of reproduction

of the party. It has established its own interests, such as deputies that want to continue to have their posts and receive money as deputies" (my translation; interview, August 8, 2005). At the local level this struggle to define movement goals and lines of authority and to maintain account-ability has resulted in open conflict as MAS leaders try to make the social movement organization an instrument of the party (*Atlas del Trópico de Cochabamba* 2004: 44).

Prior to 2005, when Evo Morales assumed the presidency, the MAS had not had to deal with open confrontation between movement and party, although there had been numerous confrontations between indi-vidual MAS elected officials and Evo Morales – particularly at the national level. For the MAS, the more vexing problem has been establishing dis-tinct decision-making hierarchies and clear boundaries between party and movement. This is illustrated by the fact that Evo Morales served simul-taneously as head of the Six Federations of Cochabamba coca growers, MAS party chair, and national deputy of the MAS between 1997–2002, and continues to serve as president of Bolivia, MAS leader, and coca growers leader. Political scientist Fernando Mayorga describes the prob-lem generated by blurred party–social-movement boundaries:

There is no central committee or directive of the party. Spaces such as the par-liamentary delegation, regional leaders that meet with national leaders to make decisions, which is the classic form of decision-making, don't exist. There is no link or dialogue between regional and national leaders.... So, who decides? The leaders of the MAS, the parliamentarians of the MAS, the militants of the MAS, or the *cocalero sindicatos*? All of them. So there is a very diffuse frontier between the MAS as party and its followers and allies, and those who actually make deci-sions. Decisions are made at particular moments when the head of the party needs to make important decisions, for example when to begin a march to La Paz. (My translation; interview, Cochabamba, August 8, 2005.)

Ad hoc, multilayered, ambiguous lines of authority create misun-derstandings within the movement–party and provoke struggles over decision-making power in the absence of clear procedures, particularly in municipalities where MAS affiliates are relatively weak and internally fragmented (e.g., El Alto, Sucre). In these urban areas, campesinos com-prise a minority struggling for power against other popular and middle-class sectors (interview, Rafael Archondo, August 1, 2005).

Relations between parties and affiliated communities changed in 2004 when the Bolivian Congress enacted a constitutional change that allowed citizens groupings and indigenous peoples to participate in elections with-out registering as a political party. Numerous indigenous organizations took advantage of this opportunity and ended alliances with parties.[7] There is a clear tendency since the 2004 elections for indigenous and campesino organizations to prefer to run on their own and not as affiliates of the increasingly bureaucratized and hierarchical MAS or the increasingly marginalized and authoritarian MIP (confidential interviews, La Paz, July 2005).

Steering Problems in Ecuador. The issue of who steers the indigenous movement has been contentious in Ecuador because soon after its creation CONAIE rejected Pachakutik as its representative. A major problem was the refusal of the sierra indigenous organization, Awakening of the Ecuadorian Indian (Ecuador Runacunapac Riccharimui, or ECUARUNARI) to submit to any other organization or party (confidential interview, Quito, June 2005). In fact, ECUARUNARI only grudgingly agreed to create Pachakutik after the lowland organization CONFENIAE already had announced its intention to compete in the 1996 national election with its own vehicle (Lucero 2008). CONAIE leader Nina Pacari set off a major rift between party and movement in 1999 when she entered Congress with Pachakutik and accepted the second vice presidency of the legislature in a deal with the conservative Social Christian Party. Many movement leaders assumed this implied an alliance with the neoliberal governing coalition. That year CONAIE led major protests in the capital of Quito, from which it excluded the Pachakutik delegation. As a result, Pachakutik's public image declined. Then again in January 2000, when CONAIE led a movement to overthrow the Ecuadorian government, it called on all political parties to resign – including the Pachakutik delegation. Pachakutik leaders rejected CONAIE's demand for a plebiscite to revoke the legislature's mandate (*Boletín ICCI–Rimay* 2002; Collins 2000; Van Cott 2005: 130–1). A Pachakutik militant from Guaranda described to me the resulting confusion and conflict:

Look, we have not been able to conjugate the realities. . . . We have prioritized the relationship with the government and not the relationship with our communities. There should be some specialized people who have a relationship with the

---

[7] Many new indigenous mayors and councillors represent affiliates of the highland-based Council of Ayllus and Markas of Qullasuyu (Consejo de Ayllus y Markas del Qullasuyu, or CONAMAQ). In Paz groups that had belonged to CONAMAQ before a 2003 internal split ran on their own (confidential interview, July 2005, La Paz).

government and the rest of the leaders work with the bases. But there isn't. Yes, we have created many spaces, but we haven't been capable of regulating what is the function of each one of the spaces. The Pachakutik leaders do what CONAIE should be doing; the leaders of CONAIE are doing everything except what they should be doing.... So this is chaos really. If we don't regulate the specific activities for which each type of leader at each level is responsible, we are not going to be able to move forward. Because there is competition with respect to who does what. (My translation; confidential interview, July 2005.)

Competing and blurred lines of authority dispersed the leadership that democratic institutions need to take root and thrive. Internal disagreements within the movement–party reduce the attention and energy that can be invested in nurturing new, fragile institutions and may even result in attacks on institutions associated with a particular faction. This challenge was minimized in Porto Alegre because Brazilian mayors enjoy exaggerated powers that better enable them to consolidate authority and control steering (Brian Wampler, personal communication, Oct. 19, 2007).

The Dispersion of Scarce Human and Financial Resources

When social movements form electoral vehicles, they must shift energy and resources away from efforts to pressure the government for policy changes. Both movement and party leaders have less time to meet with local affiliates and to build the movement. Movements lose some of their best leaders and advisors to electoral campaigns and public office (Yashar 2005: 302–3). Often, leaders' motivation is financial because government offices provide salaries, whereas social-movement offices are unpaid, with the exception of modest expense reimbursements, and leadership often entails significant financial sacrifice.

When indigenous candidates win office, the national government and international institutions may prefer to negotiate indigenous policy issues with elected indigenous officials rather than representatives of the movement, whom they may perceive as less pragmatic. Social-movement leaders accustomed to serving as movement interlocutors resent their marginalization. Conversely, social-movement leaders may attempt to marginalize elected officials, as CONAIE has on several occasions. As a result, social movements may lose political impact even as they elect their militants because elected officials may feel more professional pressures to negotiate with opponents and compromise movement positions and ideals in exchange for professional rewards or modest policy gains. This problem is not unique to indigenous parties and movements. In Porto

Alegre, as citizens participated more in PB activities, their involvement in "contentious activity" declined (Baiocchi 2005: 44). Social movements that lose political power to elected militants may be forced to moderate their demands. As a result, radically democratic innovations may have less empowering results.

Shifting From the Logic of "Movement Discipline" to a Logic of Democracy and Pluralism

Social movements with a long history of confronting the state develop an operating logic that maintains cohesion through discipline and enforced conformity. When they enter formal politics they must shift away from authoritarian norms that guaranteed survival. The shift has been difficult for indigenous movements in the Andes, who entered electoral politics after centuries of violent confrontation with the state. Years of repression and persecution have inculcated a practice of "campesino discipline." State–indigenous violence historically has been more intense in the Bolivian highlands, with state massacres of indigenous protesters extending to 2003. Thus violence is a more common part of politics in Bolivia compared with Ecuador, and as indigenous parties entered politics violent altercations have occurred between militants of opposing parties. Coercion and physical abuse have carried over into local governance. This may entail monetary fines, physical punishment, or expulsion from the group. Chapare coca growers even have their own police that enforce leaders' decisions. In the absence of state authority in rural areas, even disputes within or between indigenous communities may be settled through force.

For example, as confrontation escalated in Puerto Villarroel between factions of the coca growers' movement in 1999, the coca growers' federation FSUTCC imposed customary sanctions to punish contempt for its authority: physical aggression and humiliation, such as dressing disobedient municipal councillors in a skirt, and ritual whipping with a stick tipped with nettles (the Law of the Ithapallu) (Herbas and Lizárraga 2001: 46). Córdova argues that the same logic and the same processes of leadership selection and rotation that govern the coca growers' movement were imposed on the municipal sphere in place of legal norms. The federation's treatment of elected municipal officials was identical to treatment of leaders in the movement (Córdova Eguivar 2004: 203).

Indigenous parties that maintain practices that outsiders consider authoritarian have trouble expanding beyond a narrow base. For example, during the 2002 national and 2004 municipal elections campaigns, both MAS and MIP drew criticism because their militants prevented other parties from campaigning in their strongholds in the Chapare (Cochabamba) and Achacachi (La Paz), respectively. Ecuadorian indigenous leaders acknowledged a similar problem when they drafted the 1999 Guamote Development Plan, which recognized that authoritarian leadership styles are a problem. As in Bolivia, an ethic of "sindicato/campesino discipline" pervades the political culture among populations where agrarian reform struggles were particularly violent and protracted, since leaders learned to impose discipline on peasants who did not contribute to the collective struggle (Cameron 2003b: 235). The isolation of Bolivia's indigenous peoples and their long history of exclusion partly explains their high propensity for violence. As Sunstein argues, when "like-minded people" deliberate regularly within "isolated enclaves" – particularly when they share a strong social identity and maintain strong bonds of solidarity as the coca growers do – they are prone to increasing extremism and even violence, a tendency that is intensified for "insulated 'out groups'" (2003: 82–8).

Organic parties that enter local office must shift from a logic of internal discipline and enforced conformity to one of negotiation, pluralism, tolerance, and fairness if they are to promote democratic improvements. If they do not, the result is either stalemate and inaction or the oppression of a minority or dissenting group, neither of which fosters democratization (Mansbridge 1983: 32–3). Tolerance of pluralism can be enormously difficult because it requires leaders of a persecuted group to trust their erstwhile persecutors and to risk eroding the unity that enabled the group to gain power. As parties become more institutionalized and autonomous from their parent movements, adjustments are made. Lizárraga and Villarroel observe that, as the MAS consolidated its organizational structure in the Chapare, the coca growers' federations were required to incorporate norms that respond to the time pressures and legal exigencies of electoral authority, even though they conflict with those of social organizations that prioritize direct, lengthy, continuous consultation with members (1998: 7). But the pressure of strong norms fostering internal discipline and group solidarity enables indigenous parties to maintain legitimacy and public support in the face of difficult electoral challenges.

THE CHALLENGE OF INTERNAL DIVISIONS

The challenge of fostering and maintaining cohesion among diverse social movements bedevils most organic parties. First, the opportunity to shift from usually nonpaid roles to paid government positions with access to state resources intensifies interpersonal and factional competition (Albó 2002; Foweraker 1995: 84; Wade 1997: 17; Yashar 2005: 305). Second, "new-left" parties are particularly susceptible to internal factions because they unite a variety of tendencies and social classes (Goldfrank 2007b: 152). Indigenous parties, notwithstanding cultural norms promoting in-group solidarity and cohesion, are not immune from these problems. Indigenous social movements have sustained their greatest achievements in moments of unity that, typically, are catalyzed by conjunctural moments of crisis or opportunity. Conversely, it has been impossible for any indigenous-movement organization or political party to sustain this cohesion at the national level for years at a time, although some have demonstrated enduring local-level cohesion. In this section I explore the sources and consequences of internal divisions.

Sources of Internal Division

The experience of indigenous parties in Bolivia and Ecuador demonstrates four principal sources of disunity within indigenous parties: (1) increasing economic and social differentiation; (2) competition for candidacies and paid positions, and the access to resources that they provide; (3) leadership and factional disputes stemming from competition; and (4) disputes concerning policy, strategy, or tactics.

Increasing Economic and Social Differentiation. Some peasants within a sindicato, ayllu, or peasant cooperative get involved in economic activities, such as transportation or tourism, which bring economic rewards unavailable to others. As economic differentiation deepens, the interests of increasingly stratified communities diverge. Economic and social differentiation often results in a greater urban–rural divide within an indigenous population, which may lead some groups to split off and create their own organizations and political conflicts to emerge (*Atlas del Trópico de Cochabamba* 2004: 44). These urban–rural tensions can cause severe political conflicts. In Chimoré (Cochabamba) a councillor representing the urban center for the coca growers' party, ASP, was ousted in 1997 after rural leaders charged that he had proposed too many projects to be built in urban areas (Lizárraga and Villarroel 1998: 13, 34). Conflict occurs within social-movement organizations and their electoral partners when rules, decisions, and leaderships are contested.

Competition for Candidacies Causes Internal Divisions. Electoral politics disproportionately distributes the rewards of victory to a fortunate few. Movement militants accustomed to sharing in movement triumphs have a hard time seeing how they benefit from electoral victories, particularly when they see a small set of insiders improve their standard of living through access to government jobs. Voters may be suspicious of the new wealth and influence of indigenous government officials. Compared with most indigenous incomes, that of a government job is an extraordinary windfall. This may lead to charges of unlawful enrichment. A Pachakutik elected official explains:

Some are privileged – they win positions in office, they get fellowships to study in Cuba, they get trips abroad. Pachakutik has this cupula on top and they concentrate power. And this is why the movement has weakened. Little by little they did not fulfill the philosophy of the movement. They began acting in a different way, not to help the social sectors, but only to enrich a few privileged ones. Day-by-day a feeling of disappointment is growing because within the indigenous movement itself they say, "I serve as a step, I serve so that somebody else rises up, another arrives, and we don't receive anything." (My translation; confidential interview, July 2005.)

The story of Pachakutik exemplifies this challenge. At the time that CONAIE created Pachakutik the indigenous movement enjoyed considerable strength and unity. Subsequently, individuals and groups that were shut out of access to power when Pachakutik entered government joined rival political parties as these attempted to weaken and divide Pachakutik. In response, Pachakutik began to exhibit many of the problems of the traditional parties it sought to replace, such as corruption and competition for power and influence.

Fragmentation among leaders seeking access to office intensified in 2003 after the Gutiérrez government expelled Pachakutik. Many militants had rejected the alliance. A senior leader of the Izquierda Democrática (ID, or Democratic Left), Pachakutik's main leftist rival, interprets what happened next:

There always was this relationship that ECUARUNARI was an extraordinary political force, they have the best leaders. Recognizing that things are this way, each time there are weaknesses ECUARUNARI always separates. Whenever there are problems affecting CONAIE or an agrarian conflict, they separate, go their own way, and confuse all the rest. So, clearly, in the political struggle, when CONAIE was struggling, because they were saying that "Lucio Gutiérrez abandoned us," there was a fundamental problem of having won an electoral process with promises and then later they were in another phase.... So the indigenous movement remained outside; that is, Pachakutik remained outside. But CONAIE, through other organizations, began to occupy the political spaces that Pachakutik had left. So you have in the Ministry of Social Welfare an indigenous group, and what was more grave, you had an ex-president of CONAIE, Antonio Vargas, in the government. So this was very confusing. Naturally this produced division. (Confidential interview, Quito, June 23, 2005.)

Once Pachakutik left the Gutiérrez government, its mayors lost favor and thus access to resources they needed to maintain support. When municipal elections approached, Pachakutik leaders and social-movement allies joined or allied with other political parties, particularly the ID, dismembering both Pachakutik and the indigenous movement.

Jorge Leon views the desertion of Pachakutik by many important indigenous leaders as the natural result of CONAIE's and Pachakutik's success in forming a large pool of experienced, aspiring indigenous politicians. The fact that there were more aspiring candidates than places on Pachakutik's lists inevitably led frustrated leaders to seek other opportunities. Although this has weakened Pachakutik, and the indigenous movement more generally, it has revitalized political parties, particularly in the highlands. Ironically, Pachakutik may have succeeded in constructing the conditions for its eventual obsolescence as indigenous people gain access to choice candidate slots with the major parties. In response, Pachakutik now has to redefine itself in relation to a party system that is becoming increasingly multiethnic (interview, Quito, June 16, 2005).

Competition for candidacies increases as higher-tier party leaders attempt to consolidate the party's organizational structure. It is in the interest of national leaders to maximize their control over local and regional affiliates so as to enjoy greater license to make political alliances. Whereas local affiliates may be relatively homogeneous, culturally and socially, at higher geographic levels and in electoral districts with small indigenous populations, alliances with other ethnic groups, political parties, and social movements may be necessary for electoral victory. National leaders typically try to impose candidates who are *not* prominent leaders from the local indigenous-movement affiliate in order to broaden alliances and satisfy national goals – such as increasing the number of female mayors to conform to national norms of gender equity.[8]

---

[8] In Chimoré national MAS leaders imposed Juana Quispe as candidate for mayor in 2004 over the objection of the local coca growers' federation. Once she was elected they refused to accept her and drove her from office (see Chapter 6). Similarly, national CONAIE leaders attempted to impose Carmen Yamberla as mayoral candidate in Otavalo (see Chapter 5). The local affiliate prevailed, but in both cases intense conflict ensued.

They also may choose candidates who reflect the ideological tendencies of national leaders, which may be more radical or more pragmatic than those of local leaders. These practices foster conflicts between local and national party leaders, and between local party leaders and local indigenous social movements. As Immergut observes, when parties interfere with interest group activities, "the party system may reinforce rather than provide a counterweight to the problems of faction" (1995: 203).

Competition continues to generate internal divisions as indigenous parties enter office. Many indigenous militants are seduced by opportunities for salaried employment and access to government resources – opportunities that were scarce in both countries before 1995. In a few short years, indigenous leaders shifted from the habit of rotating through unpaid or modestly remunerated authority positions within their social-movement organization, more or less on equal terms, to a situation in which some exercise considerable power over others. Customary norms of leadership rotation are altered: Some leaders are able to serve repeated terms in municipal government and to rise out of the community to sub-national and national positions. Resentment builds as some are passed over.

Capturing local government power has had the perverse impact of intensifying competition among individuals and groups within indigenous communities for access to and control over state resources. In some municipalities individual neighborhoods resist efforts to let deliberation involving the entire municipality determine the use of resources. Neighborhood representatives demand that the budget be distributed to each district so that each controls its own. For example, in Chimoré, in response to Mayor Epifanio Cruz's suggestion that, to maximize the utility of available resources, projects be undertaken that benefit a larger number of communities grouped together under a *central*, independent sindicato, leaders demanded their own projects and the right to manage them. This generated conflict among the sindicatos for control of resources and access to municipal influence – notwithstanding the fact that the municipal government consisted of former sindicato and *central* leaders. As Cruz explains, sindicatos belonging to the same federation fought among themselves to have public works constructed in their own territories and even interfered with projects already approved in municipality-wide participatory fora (Cruz 1998: 29). The arrival of government resources and competition for control over this windfall generated considerable conflict even when collective identity and group solidarity were strong (1998: 28).

Leadership Disputes Generate Factions. Competition among individuals for leadership positions generates factional conflicts as militants choose sides. A particularly consequential dispute occurred in the Chapare. By 1997 campesino leaders Alejo Véliz and Evo Morales were at odds. A national coca growers' assembly chose Véliz to lead the IU–ASP 1997 national ticket, whereas Morales and others were chosen to compete for single-member-district seats in the Chamber of Deputies. Véliz's supporters claim that Morales instructed his followers to vote for a rival party in order to deny Véliz a seat in Congress, an allegation supported by electoral results: Whereas the majority of campesinos in the Chapare supported Morales and his ally Roman Loayza – who easily won – they rejected the Véliz contingent (Herbas and Lizárraga 2001: 44; interview, Córdova Eguivar).

Resulting resentments exacerbated the split within the campesino movement and within the MAS. In 1998 Véliz seized control of the ASP and Morales formed the IPSP in 1999 (Córdova Eguivar 2004: 92; Herbas and Lizárraga 2001: 44; *La Razón* 1998; *Los Tiempos* 1999a). A power struggle subsequently ensued over leadership of the coca federation FSUTCC. The national split had a significant impact on municipal politics. In Puerto Villarroel some leaders stayed with Véliz whereas others sided with Morales, tearing apart sindicatos within the FSUTCC (Córdova Eguivar 2004: 91). The conflict was reproduced within the new Puerto Villarroel municipal government after the ASP president of the municipal council left in 1997 to serve as Morales' alternate in Congress. His replacement, Guido Tarqui, remained with the ASP, whereas the FSUTCC supported Morales. Three of the sitting municipal councillors sided with Véliz; their alternates all supported Morales. Although those elected in 1995 had promised to resign in the middle of their term in order to give alternates a chance to govern, the ASP councillors refused. The leadership dispute deteriorated into open conflict in March 1999. The federation forced out the elected councillors by using Morales' allies on the council to convene meetings in remote locations that were impossible for the Véliz-allied councillors to attend. The latter thus were removed on April 5 for absenteeism and replaced. In addition, the FSUTCC produced the letters of resignation that all ASP councillors had signed when the federation nominated them to run for office (Córdova Eguivar 2004; Herbas and Lizárraga 2001).

Meanwhile, the FSUTCC-controlled vigilance committee accused Mayor Tarqui of stealing from the municipality, failing to complete public works, and favoring his political allies. The committee seized control of the planning process. When the elected mayor and municipal council refused to approve their plan, the coca growers' sindicatos forced the resignation of the municipal council and mayor and swore in their alternates, who approved the coca growers' annual operating plan with minor technical changes (Córdova Eguivar 2004: 185–7).

Mayor Tarqui recouped his seat on the council after a March 17, 1999, Constitutional Court ruling, as did two of the other council members in a separate April 27 ruling. But the federation ignored these legal rulings. During 1999, two parallel councils with two different mayors convened meetings: the titular councillors in the traditional urban center of Puerto Villarroel and the rival MAS-linked council in the coca growers' headquarters of Ivirgarzama (Córdova Eguivar 2004; Herbas and Lizárraga 2001). The federation was unable to resolve the dispute, and the functioning of the municipality – and its ability to provide for the welfare of the people – suffered until new elections were held.

Ecuador also has witnessed severe leadership conflicts that threaten institutional innovation. In many Pachakutik districts indigenous parties must compete against well-funded opponents. A significant struggle over leadership occurred in Guaranda after Pachakutik Mayor Arturo Yumbay died in a 2002 car accident. Conflict erupted when the local Pachakutik organization and its primary sponsor, the CONAIE affiliate FECAB, tried to prevent Pachakutik indigenous vice mayor Alberto Coles from exercising his legal right to assume office.[9] Yumbay's refusal to step aside angered Pachakutik and FECAB leaders, who expelled Coles from the party for "lack of discipline." Coles prevailed and was reelected in 2004 with the ID, the dominant mestizo center–left party in the highlands (interviews in Guaranda, June 2005). The popular assembly ended and Pachakutik subsequently lost power.

Disputes Concerning Policy, Strategy, or Tactics. All organic parties represent diverse views with respect to goals and the means to achieve them. Indigenous parties must grapple with additional sources of division, such as linguistic and regional divisions. The most severe ideological fissure lies between factions oriented toward emphasizing the racial and

---

[9] In municipal elections, each party presents a list of candidates in the order they want them elected, with their most-favored candidates at the top. Voters, however, may give their votes to lower-ranked candidates. More voters chose Coles over Pachakutik's choice.

cultural roots of contemporary exploitation and exclusion, and class-oriented organizations and leaders, who identify more strongly with socialist goals. Whereas class-oriented sectors actively pursue cross-ethnic alliances, ethnonationalist organizations reject such alliances, which they believe coopt leaders and undermine collective indigenous identity. Indianist leader Felipe Quispe exemplifies this attitude. He told a reporter in 2005, "MAS is a hybrid, a mixture. They are not the expression of the indigenous nation. They are from the middle class and the sour destitute left. MAS is like a whorehouse where leftist prostitutes work. We are different. We are indigenists" (cited in Albro 2006: 416).

The Consequences of Disunity for Institutional Innovation

Fractiousness is endemic to organic parties owing to their low level of institutionalization and dependence upon external sponsors (Panebianco 1988: 168). Fractiousness presents serious challenges for institutional innovation: When factions refuse to cooperate and do not trust each other, it is difficult to foster the reciprocity necessary for developing new institutions. The larger the number of deliberating and participating groups the more difficult it is to reach agreement (Immergut 1995: 204). Movement energy and resources are diverted to internal struggles rather than confronting reactionary elites. Constant squabbling turns off voters, who may refuse to participate in deliberative and participatory processes and abandon electoral movements absorbed with infighting. Moreover, when the indigenous movement is divided it is easier for political rivals to outmaneuver the movement and thwart its institutional agenda. Discredited party leaders may no longer be able to convoke participation in municipal projects. Leaders losing internal battles may move to rival political parties, bringing voters with them. Both Pachakutik and MAS have expelled numerous local, regional, and national leaders from the party in an effort to stifle dissent, losing many popular militants, against whom the party must now compete in elections.

Disunity within the party–movement makes it harder for mayors to perform the key leadership tasks identified in Chapter 3. Disunity makes it harder for the mayor to harness the energy, dynamism, and resources of sponsoring movements. He or she may not be able to credibly promise compliance with commitments made by groups if their internal factions disavow each other's authority. Mayors may even need to engage in authoritarian practices to keep institutional reform on track: They may pay off rivals and allow clientelist practices to persist in order to restrain opposition. When internal disputes are repeatedly resolved through the intervention of a dominant personality, political actors learn the importance of personal relationships and the futility of working through institutions.

When interests diverge within the municipality and paralyze decision-making processes, municipal leaders may be forced to allow districts, parishes, or neighborhoods to seize control of their "share" of municipal resources. For example, after conflict between the evangelical indigenous movement and Pachakutik ended the Indigenous and Popular Parliament, Mayor Juan de Dios Roldán initiated a process in which each parish is given its corresponding share of development funds to spend as its parish junta decides. Canton-wide deliberations no longer occur (confidential interviews; Naula Yangol 2003). This may ease internal conflicts, but it has many negative repercussions. Resources are not used as efficiently and are not targeted to the most needy, who are likely to be concentrated in particular neighborhoods. In addition, smaller, more-homogeneous units do not foster high-quality deliberation because interests are less divergent and citizens are not required to debate with each other about their common responsibilities and identities. In any political context there is a necessary trade-off between promoting deliberation across interests and perspectives and facilitating the participation of a larger proportion of affected citizens in the deliberations (Cohen and Fung 2004: 28). At smaller scales more people will influence the outcome, but the benefits of broader deliberation are lost.

When a mayor faces a municipal council or party that is unable to make decisions or reach consensus owing to internal conflict, the mayor may have to devise means to achieve democratic goals that marginalize representative institutions. Party or government disunity may thus drive mayors to "delegative" democracy (O'Donnell 1994). Even where indigenous-party council majorities exist, internal conflicts can generate desertions or expulsions from the party, which may cost the party its majority. For example, Pachakutik leaders threw away a majority on the Guaranda municipal council (five of nine seats) in 2004 over personal jealousies and ethnic indigenous chauvinism. The local party had placed mestizo university professor Bazante in the fifth spot on its list, underestimating his popularity with voters. After Bazante finished second in the preferential vote he refused to relinquish his right to serve as vice-mayor in favor of a FECAB-endorsed, indigenous candidate; local

Pachakutik leaders expelled him, leaving themselves with a minority and an opposition-party mayor (interview, Washington Bazante, July 4, 2005). As Archondo warns, when social-movement leaders are divided and competing against each other it opens an additional front for struggle; in addition to the struggle against state authorities, movement leaders compete against each other by attempting to please an increasingly radicalized and impatient base. A "spiral of radicalism" may be generated, with negative consequences for democratic institutions. As some sectors of the movement become more radicalized than others, individuals and subgroups seek to maximize their own gains, leadership loyalties fragment the movement, and collective action is paralyzed (Archondo 2004: 9–10).

Finally, internal disputes distract from the municipal government's mission of improving the quality of life for constituents. Sometimes, such as the case of Puerto Villarroel, while conflicts persist for months or years, governments cease to function. In other cases, promising institutional experiments ended, as occurred in Guamote after 2003 when competition between Pachakutik and Amauta Jatari over control of the municipality ended the Indigenous and Popular Parliament (confidential interviews, June 2005). Substantive early benefits are crucial for maintaining citizen support for new institutions.

It may be useful to think about the consequences of internal conflicts within organic parties in terms of ideal types derived from two dimensions: sociopolitical disunity and political-party fragmentation. Each dimension can be divided into three ideal types. With respect to sociopolitical disunity, the politicized social sector is so unified as to constitute a hegemonic social force. There is little room for dissent within the movement, and it is difficult for alternative movements to contend for political power. An example of this "hegemonic social force" ideal type is the coca growers' federations in the Chapare, which have crowded out all other political and social forces in municipal politics. At the opposite extreme lies a fragmented civil society in which no social-movement organization or party can gain majority representation in government or forge consensus on a course of action. Leaders within the movement are more absorbed with defeating rival contenders for movement–party leadership than they are with uniting to defeat common adversaries. An example of this type may be found in many rural municipalities of the Bolivian highlands. Here, a cadre of male leaders competes for control of departmental and national organizations representing traditional ethnic organizational structures.[10] The severity of these internal struggles for local power is exemplified by the assassination of Ayo Ayo mayor Benjamín Altamirano by political rivals affiliated with the Movement of the Landless (Movimiento Sin Tierra, or MST) in June 2004 (*La Razón* 2004a). Internal struggles typically intensify prior to elections because social-movement politics is intimately intertwined with partisan competition.

Between these extremes is our most desirable ideal type: pluralism with overarching cohesion, or what many indigenous political activists call "unity in diversity." Here one social movement or political party may represent a politicized social sector but there is sufficient space for dissent and debate over selecting candidates for office, setting movement priorities, and choosing strategies such that the outcome of internal political contests is both uncertain and unlikely to paralyze the movement. Several organizations or parties may compete against each other to represent the social sector but they are sufficiently committed to common goals, values, and identities to cooperate on movement campaigns or municipal councils. This type is exemplified by Cotacachi, Ecuador. In Cotacachi, both rival indigenous organizations have supported the same mayoral candidate and party since 1996 (Pallares 2002: 104–6). Similarly, in Otavalo, after a bitter fight within Pachakutik over its choice of mayoral candidate, the indigenous population united behind the candidacy of Mario Conejo – including the evangelical indigenous party Amauta Jatari.

The second dimension consists of ideal types with respect to the fragmentation and competitiveness of political-party systems. This dimension emphasizes the political context in which organic parties operate. At one extreme we have hegemonic traditional parties, denoting a system dominated by one or several parties representing traditional rural economic elites, who maintain sufficient support among the electorate that contesting social forces are unable to win sufficient representation in government to affect policy decisions. Although there is intraelite competition, elites

---

[10] Between 2000 and 2004 struggles for leadership of these organizational structures intensified. As the Bolivian government lost control of rural areas, their local and provincial affiliates fought to fill the vacuum of authority (*La Razón* 2004a). The most important split occurred within the CSUTCB, when Felipe Quispe refused to step down in 2004. He now leads one sector while rival Roman Loayza leads another. Prior to the 2004 elections, two men struggled for control of the CSUTCB's departmental affiliate, the Federation of Peasants of La Paz, exchanging corruption charges. Similarly, two leaders competing for control of MST during a 2002 Congress hurled bitter accusations, including (credible) charges that the two contestants represented political parties. In Aroma province the younger generation became frustrated with the options provided by senior leaders "and even the sons of the mallkus rebelled against their parents" (*La Razón* 2004a).

unite to exclude new system entrants. None of my cases exemplifies the first ideal type because I chose not to study cases in which indigenous parties did not reach office. However, this condition of hegemonic, exclusionary traditional elite parties existed in most rural municipalities in the Andes prior to the emergence of indigenous parties in the mid-1990s and it persists in many places where they have not taken hold. At the other end of the spectrum we find fragmented and volatile party systems in which more than four parties typically each win double-digit vote support. Consequently it is difficult for municipal councils to reach a consensus on policy issues and unlikely that an elected mayor will enjoy a council majority. Fragmented and volatile party systems are common in rural municipalities in both countries; in fact, this is the defining feature of Andean political systems. The slim margin that separates each party ensures that elections are hotly contested and control of the mayor's office changes after virtually every election; in Bolivia, this may even occur between elections.

Between these two extremes lies our preferred ideal type: a competitive party system of two-to-three parties, each of which attempts to win a majority by appealing across ethnic lines and building political coalitions. In the long term, municipal power rotates among the parties but reelection is possible for popular mayors who maintain absolute majority or plurality support. The Ecuadorian towns of Cotacachi, Otavalo, and Guaranda exemplify this type.

Table 4.1 presents the likely outcomes of combinations along these two dimensions. Our preferred outcome – durable, democratic institutional innovations – results when social-movement pluralism exists in a competitive, pluralistic party system. This outcome corresponds to the conditions that Armony identifies for optimal civic engagement (2004: 206). Armony argues that this optimal level of civic engagement results from improving the "mobilization capacities" and diversity of civil society groups (ibid.). Political incentives encourage political actors to reach consensus on the choice of candidates and policies and to cooperate in order to maintain access to decision-making power and resources. Disincentives discourage actors from seeking to appeal to one ethnic group only or to monopolize political power.

GOVERNING CHALLENGES

The tension between the disparate logics of social movement and partisan politics grows when organic parties enter office. As Warren (2001) and

TABLE 4.1. *The Impact of Political Pluralism and Social-Movement Cohesion on the Democratizing Potential of Institutional Innovation*

	Fragmented and Volatile Party System	Competitive and Plural Party System	Hegemonic Party System
Hegemonic social force	Social force gains political hegemony, captures existing participatory mechanisms, imposes its own decision-making rules (e.g. Chapare [MAS], rural ayllus of La Paz, Oruro)	Persistent electoral and informal conflict for absolute control of power prevents innovation	Political instability, violence, confrontation
Sociopolitical pluralism with overarching cohesion	Social-movement-dominated innovation with exclusion of former elite (Guamote under Pachakutik)	Intercultural institutional innovation (Cotacachi, Otavalo under Pachakutik)	Struggle for power, instability, insufficient majority to innovate or to sustain innovation
Fragmented civil society	Lack of consensus for innovation, individualism, inability to take advantage of existing spaces (Achacachi, Ayo Ayo)	Parties coopt social movements, no incentive for innovation, struggle for access to existing participatory spheres	Traditional elites prevent institutional innovation or capture state-imposed participation mechanisms

Szasz (1995) warn, advocacy organizations – particularly those representing identity groups – have trouble shifting from the logic of struggle against adversaries to the logic of democracy, in which participants must respect the rights and interests of others. This shift also implies a change in the relationship between organic party leaders in government and other popular movement supporters. Governments may be dismayed to find affiliated civil society groups protesting against them (Bebbington et al. 2005: 9). Some problems result simply from inexperience. For example, the Bolivian Aymara party MIP first entered mayoral offices in 2004. According to a source working with the muncipalities in the Department of La Paz,

[I]nitially they were having problems because they tried to run the municipality as if it were a *sindicato*. They continued to be in a demand-making mode, but no, they were in power and they have to make decisions. So this is something they are still trying to understand, but I think they will be able to overcome this.... If you are the government, you have to consult with everyone, not just your own force.... If they don't, the municipality loses and it's not a good management. (Confidential interview, July 2005.)

The shift from movement to government is particularly difficult for indigenous movements, which typically make decisions by consensus. As Mansbridge observes, such groups find it difficult to resolve internal conflicts "by allowing bargains, distributing benefits proportionately, taking turns, or making decisions by majority rule" (1983: 33). They may find it difficult even to acknowledge that conflicts of interest exist within the group (ibid.).

When indigenous parties enter office they encounter the following four challenges, which are less daunting for other organic parties.

Strengthen the Rule of Law While Respecting Indigenous Norms and Values

Merging state municipal government norms with those of indigenous cultures involves trade-offs. Municipal norms may require that decisions be made on schedule to meet firm deadlines. It may be impossible to convene public assemblies to make important decisions quickly. Once taken, decisions must be definitive to allow for long-term planning and to accommodate municipal reporting requirements, as well as those of NGOs and international donors. This may preclude the customary practice of periodically reconsidering decisions. Moreover, municipal spending intended to respond to constituents' demands may result in the incarceration of municipal leaders if it is invested in the wrong sector, at the wrong time, or otherwise violates legal norms, even if no diversion of funds was intended. In the Chapare, after coca growers' union leaders first gained municipal office in 1995 legal problems emerged because they governed according to sindicato rather than legal norms. Under pressure from coca growers, mayors and municipal councils disregarded laws governing accounting and spending of public resources. They dispensed funds for projects that the coca growers' federation considered urgent and failed to spend money according to legally required annual operating plans. In Puerto Villarroel, after the municipality failed to carry out projects designated in annual operating plans, the Controlaría in 1999 withheld its funds. Over time, MAS leaders learned to fuse sindicato and municipal norms in order to avoid national government audits (interview, Eduardo Córdova, August 3, 2005).

Indigenous–campesino leaders often bring antistate attitudes into the government that reflect a culture with low esteem for laws and regulations created by mestizo elites, which mainly have been used to oppress rather than protect them. Indigenous leaders also tend to have a low opinion of government and public administration. The main model they have to follow is the corrupt, clientelist model of traditional parties, and many fall into the same practices: They reward their supporters with jobs and resources and ignore their opponents, including indigenous opponents. If they are to foster meaningful change and establish legitimacy, indigenous officials must foster respect for government and for laws, even practices and rules with which they may disagree. They must be scrupulously honest and transparent in order to send a signal that something different is happening (confidential interviews).

Officials Lack Political Experience, Basic Education, and Management Skills

Educational quality in rural areas is dismal throughout the Andes. Many indigenous mayors and councillors lack basic education and literacy in Spanish. Once in office they must rapidly acquire an understanding of complex municipal rules and procedures that are available only in writing and in Spanish. Mestizo politicians with more experience, knowledge of the law, and political ties to higher levels of government that monitor municipal behavior may outmaneuver inexperienced mayors and council members – particularly women. As a result, most indigenous mayors rely on professional advisers, some of whom NGOs provide. It is in the financial interest of these advisers to maintain their positions by avoiding the transfer of their knowledge to municipal staff. This problem perpetuates the dependence of indigenous governments on outsiders. High turnover in municipal government owing to indigenous norms of leadership rotation as well as political volatility exacerbates this problem. These norms are not specific to the Andes but rather are common in indigenous societies elsewhere in the Americas and thus present a problem for indigenous cultures entering formal governance. NGOs must constantly train new personnel who are either incapable or unwilling to transfer institutional memory and technical capacity to their replacements. While learning takes place, little can be done in terms of institutional innovations or development projects (interviews, Ecuadorian government representatives, NGO personnel, Quito, June 2005; international agency representatives, NGO personnel, La Paz, July–August 2005).

Attract NGO and Donor Money Without Being Coopted

As indigenous parties entered office they attracted attention and resources from domestic and international development professionals, particularly those associated with the political left. Julio Yuquilema, who directs the Ecuadorian government's project to provide technical support to indigenous governments, explains:

Once Pachakutik emerged, different institutions, universities, NGOs became interested. It also was the fashion in the world to promote local development. So there was an important initiative to shift from leaders to authorities, from leaders to functionaries/bureaucrats/administrators. The institutions, universities, and NGOs played an extremely important role in facilitating this transition with respect to the technical aspects, by providing norms, procedures, and regulations. The indigenous organizations have been working hard to learn the new processes and regulations so that they can develop themselves, without assistance from NGOs acting on their behalf. So that indigenous organizations themselves can take over the leadership and management. (My translation; interview, Quito, June 16, 2005.)

The shift from movement to government entails a loss of control over rule making and decision making because officials are constrained by existing laws enforced by higher tiers of government. Indigenous leaders also are dependent upon external actors to prevent them from making costly mistakes, such as misappropriating funds or failing to fulfill reporting requirements, which could result in their expulsion or prosecution. Social movements involved in local governance face what Shönwälder calls "the dilemma of autonomy and co-optation": they must choose whether to seek greater influence in government by forming alliances with ideologically sympathetic actors within state institutions at the risk of losing movement autonomy and diluting their political and cultural identity, or to prioritize movement autonomy by maintaining a righteous distance from state institutions and other political actors, but at the risk of having little political impact (1997: 755).

Although their intentions may be benevolent, and their assistance of great benefit to indigenous governments, NGOs have their own political and ideological agendas. Most receive financing from foreign governments and international institutions that have missions, reporting requirements, and restrictions that they impose on NGO partners and their clients. The problem is exacerbated in Bolivia where political parties sponsor NGOs and use development programs to gain political support. In some cases NGOs may sponsor competing candidates for office in an effort to influence local government, thereby deepening internal political conflicts (confidential interviews in Bolivia and Ecuador).

Surviving the Inevitable Disappointment of Indigenous Followers

All organic parties face the problem of high expectations. Their close ties to civil society generate expectations that – once they are elected – measurable improvements in the relationship between state and society, and the benefits that society receives from the state, are likely to occur. When politics seems to follow past patterns and social and economic benefits are not provided, the disappointment and cynicism generated delegitimize civil society leaders and reduce political participation and interest (see Hiskey and Seligson 2003; Wampler 2008: 31). When indigenous parties first enter office at local, regional, and national levels, they face the problem of not being able to have an impact on policy outcomes owing to their small number relative to opponents. As Yashar observes, this presents the dilemma of either resigning themselves to ideologically unassailable ineffectiveness or risking their representational reputations by engaging in political horse trading with sworn enemies (2005: 303). Indigenous representatives who enter politics with a pure heart may find themselves unable to extract themselves from the patronage vortex (Wade 1997: 17).

When indigenous representatives control a majority in local government it is even harder to explain to constituents that their expectations are too high. And these expectations of immediate change are particularly high for indigenous political parties because voters expect that seizing power after centuries of exclusion will result in radical and rapid changes in their lives. However, the scarcity of municipal resources, the enormous social deficit and high poverty in indigenous communities, as well as external political and economic policy constraints, prevent this from happening. Expectations are highest among indigenous populations themselves, who expect immediate and dramatic flows of resources to the poor and indigenous, but nonindigenous citizens also sought change when they voted for indigenous parties. A Pachakutik provincial counselor explained to Arévelo and Chela Amangandi that the election of Guaranda's first indigenous mayor created high expectations and excited the "popular imagination" by presenting the possibility of replacing the government of "notables and illustrious citizens" with a new "alternative culture" (2001: 40). After 2003 disappointment was palpable within the indigenous movement because in most cases Pachakutik had failed to achieve its primary goals: a fundamental change in the structure and norms of government and a greater consolidation of the indigenous movement and its affiliated organizations. To many, Pachakutik became like any other party, with too many self-serving leaders (confidential interviews, Pachakutik leaders, Riobamba, June 29, 2005; Guaranda, July 4, 2005).

As Jorge Leon explains, after 10 years in municipal government, Pachakutik reached the stage of executing projects, from which results can be observed and measured. As these results prove to be meager, the party's organizational sponsors are pulling back from their association with failing local regimes in order to preserve their reputations and maintain unity. Similarly, political scandals – accusations of corruption and favoritism – have led to widespread disillusionment with the party and, as a result, inspired affiliated indigenous organizations to disown the party and retire from electoral politics in order to reduce the politicization that most have suffered through their connection to electoral politics (interview, Quito, June 16, 2005). An indigenous leader in Guaranda expressed to me the disillusionment that many indigenous people now feel:

They don't have any confidence in Pachakutik. Neither do I because our leaders seem to be acting in their own interests.... They don't work with the bases but, rather, they act above them. Traditionally, before Pachakutik existed, when any national problem existed, our leaders always came down to talk with the bases to inform and socialize them in order to jointly act. Once Pachakutik had been created, this no longer existed. They make a resolution above and they want us to obey them. So this has changed and it is more vertical. In contrast, at the beginning, when there was no Pachakutik, it was from the bottom up to the top. This has changed lately. Above all in the view of [my organization]. I believe this has happened as well in other sectors, because I see that they have been separating themselves from the organization. So surely we all feel this way. At times we feel that our *compañeros* have passed from being our leaders to being with the traditional political parties, for their own personal interests, they begin to manage the bases in order to enter into some job. And later, when they have entered, they forget them. (My translation; confidential interview, Guaranda, July 2005.)

With respect to the situation in Guamote, Naula Yangol observes that civil society leaders feel that no change has occurred because social conditions have not improved, and because municipal institutions have "absorbed activities that secondary base organizations had been realizing," leading to a decline in independent civil society action (my translation; 2003: 74).

In Bolivia, notwithstanding the astounding political success of the MAS in elections between 1995 and 2004, by mid-2005 many within the MAS coalition already had become disillusioned with the blatant careerism

126Radical Democracy in the Andes

that many elected and appointed officials exhibited. Even Morales publicly denounced MAS local officials who had been shirking their duties and maximizing the privileges that accrue from holding office (interview, Rafael Archondo, La Paz, August 1, 2005). Bolivian political analyst Rafael Archondo describes the potential for further disillusionment: "This is going to be a problem in the future. Because what I see is that the MAS, the MIP, the entire MAS is used by some as a staircase or a vehicle for social advancement, for social mobility, for many of its members" (my translation; interview, La Paz, August 1, 2005). Whereas in the past Bolivian political leaders had "arrived from above" by virtue of their exceptional wealth, power, or relationship to an existing leader, the emergence of a leader from the base of a social-movement organization has inspired more militants of such organizations to follow this new path to power (ibid.). Indeed, the problem of careerism exploded after the MAS won the 2005 national elections. In February 2007 disillusionment with the MAS – from within and outside the coalition – increased owing to the revelation of extensive corruption within the Morales government, specifically in reference to nepotism and job selling (*Los Tiempos* 2007).

Disillusionment is a natural part of the organizational development of parties. It follows initial periods of enthusiasm as politics becomes more difficult than expected and leaders pursue personal goals at the expense of collective incentives. Disillusionment develops as parties become institutionalized and shift from activities that actively stimulate their base to greater bureaucratization and professionalization of party offices (Panebianco 1988: 17–18). The problem is exacerbated when the party is unable to "distribute identity incentives to its followers" owing to failed strategies (ibid.: 41). Throughout the Andes the immediate impact on indigenous movements appears to have been a weakening and fragmentation of movement energy. This has caused great disillusionment and a pulling back from close ties between indigenous social movements and affiliated political parties and, in some cases, from electoral participation altogether. This is because indigenous movements do not perceive electoral participation or electoral victories as a way of integrating into the state and dominant society but, rather, as one of several tools to strengthen the movement itself for a broader struggle for self-determination (Arévalo and Chela Amangandi 2001: 74; confidential interviews, Pachakutik militants, July 4–7, 2005).

In some cases the adverse political consequences of internal disunity for the indigenous parties are long term. The loss of its municipal governments in Chimborazo left Pachakutik and its CONAIE affiliate in disarray and its base-level support greatly weakened (*El Comercio* 2004b). Internal squabbles reduce the patience of voters with the slow pace of reform and the long wait for substantive improvements in well-being. When they lose faith in their leaders, citizens will not participate in the activities required of innovative institutional models. Discredited leaders cannot convene mingas or require attendance at assemblies.

THE POLITICAL CONTEXT IN WHICH PARTIES OPERATE

Parties operate within a political environment that exerts pressures that may generate fissures within even the most cohesive movements. The most important external sources of disunity that indigenous parties faced in the Andes were the extent of historic and contemporary party-system fragmentation; disputes arising over the question of forming political alliances with nonindigenous actors; and the interference of NGOs.

Historic Party-System Fragmentation After the Opening to Democracy

Party politics in both Ecuador and Bolivia traditionally has been extremely fragmented. Only in the last 10 years have electorally viable, autonomous, indigenous parties been available as options. Until that time both countries demonstrated high levels of electoral volatility as indigenous voters sampled a buffet of leftist and clientelist parties offering material rewards in a context of economic scarcity (Birnir and Van Cott 2007; Madrid 2005). Political fragmentation is worse in Bolivia, particularly in the department of La Paz. This fragmentation, the presence of entrenched rival political parties, and the open hostility that traditional ethnic authorities express toward MAS militants present a distinct political challenge for the MAS there. Conflicts are partisan and personal and generate divisions within the highland campesino movement. Fragmentation and associated volatility reduce incentives for trust and cooperation and make it difficult for any mayor to sustain institutional innovation.

Using Panebianco's analytical framework, we can see that in areas of Bolivia and Ecuador where indigenous parties must compete against each other for the same voters – i.e., the department of La Paz, the province of Chimborazo – party-system fragmentation and volatility are particularly pernicious because they destabilize indigenous parties' claim to represent indigenous voters. It is more difficult for party leaders to control environmental uncertainty and to reduce internal party divisions in the presence of "electoral fluidity" and changes in the partisan balance of power (Panebianco 1988: 208). The greater hostility and aggression exercised by parties against close competitors cause differences of opinion with respect to strategy within the dominant coalition and raise the stakes for all (ibid.). Panebianco concludes that a high number of competitors for the same vote generate "environmental complexity," which increases uncertainty and the propensity for internal conflicts (1988: 210).

Alliances With External Actors

Alliances with actors outside the indigenous movement also raise questions of strategy and identity on which militants may disagree intensely. Such alliances exacerbate competition for candidacies because available positions must be shared with alliance partners. For example, in the 2005 national elections the MAS significantly extended its geographic coverage by making alliances with diverse civil society organizations and leftist parties. The strategy extended the party's base into urban areas and the middle class and enabled it to construct a broad leftist front. But it was costly: Electoral support was exchanged for access to government jobs. Three months before the elections the daily *La Razón* reported that the MAS had made alliances with 50 sectors, including the country's most important social movements and leftist parties. As a MAS congressional deputy warned, there are not enough positions in the government to satisfy so many allies (*La Razón* 2005b). Moreover, the expansion of its base beyond the peasant and union movements exacerbated tensions with older allies (ibid.).

Alliances can lead to disaster when an ally perceived as an equal or junior partner becomes the dominant partner. Then movement militants must decide whether or not to reject the alliance and accept the repercussions. For example, in 2003 Pachakutik entered national government in a coalition with Lucio Gutiérrez's PSP. But there were misgivings within Pachakutik about the alliance, which a majority of the party's executive committee approved without input from the movement's bases. The decision represented the interests of a sector of the leadership that sought government jobs, rather than a consensualized decision of the movement and its major organizations (Santana 2004: 255–6). Bitter divisions quickly emerged between Pachakutik and Gutiérrez as the president promoted conservative economic policies. The alliance ended in August 2003, after which the president set out to cripple the indigenous movement. An official electoral alliance was formed for the 2004 local elections between Gutiérrez's PSP and Pachakutik's main rival, Amauta

Yuyay. These national alliance issues significantly affected local politics (*El Comercio* 2003a, 2003b; *Hoy* 2003; Ronquillo 2003).

Alliances With NGOs

Development organizations prefer to create new, subservient client organizations as counterparts for their projects rather than to work with existing indigenous-community-based groups that have their own agendas, leaders, and self-governance norms. Indigenous leaders compete with each other for access to external aid by forming rival development NGOs (Bretón 2001). Thus, for example, rather than a sign of a thriving civil society, Guamote's 13 OSGs represent the perverse consequences of access to development resources when civil society leaders compete for resources and authority (Cameron 2003b: 204). In fact, many OSGs do not represent any organic level of social cohesion or have any common identity and purpose (Cameron 2003b: 205). In Bolivia, when rival parties sponsored NGOs in the same canton, the stakes of electoral competition rise and conflicts intensified.

CONCLUSION

Political parties rooted in civil society networks are the ideal partners for innovating mayors, but severe challenges constrain their capacity to foster institutional innovation. As they enter the electoral arena they must manage the confusion regarding decision-making hierarchies and steering generated by the coexistence of a political party and a sponsoring social-movement organization; they must minimize the disunity generated by competition over access to candidacies and appointed positions; they must withstand a reduction in social-movement impact as human and financial resources are diverted from activism to political campaigns; and they must shift from a logic of movement discipline to a logic of pluralism and collaboration. Once they enter office, organic parties face another set of challenges. For indigenous peoples' political parties these problems are particularly acute. They must accommodate new governance norms to traditional cultural norms while strengthening the rule of law. They must do so with less political experience and basic education and weaker management skills than other party-system entrants generally possess. The extreme poverty of most indigenous populations requires them to attract economic assistance from external actors in order to have sufficient funds to make an impact on constituents' lives, but they must do so without being coopted or perceived by constituents as having been bought by external actors. They must survive the inevitable disappointment that their limitations generate among followers who expect immediate and substantive changes after their representatives seize power following centuries of exploitation. Above all, organic parties must maintain cooperative relations with their civil society bases and their mayors. This allows them to maximize their advantages as organic parties while minimizing the challenges such parties encounter. Based on data collected in each case with respect to relations among parties, movements, and governments, I score my 10 cases in Table 4.2.

Radical democrats are aware of the most compelling issue discussed here: the conflicting logics of social-movement activism and interest group advocacy, on the one hand, and democratic governance, on the other. My findings largely confirm their low expectations. Skeptics of associative democracy warn us of the authoritarian nature of many civil society groups (particularly those based on shared identity), their tendency to squash internal dissent in the interest of movement cohesion, and the difficulty of incorporating them into schemes of radical democracy that require respect for the opinions of others and internal norms of democracy (Armony 2004: 8; Szasz 1995; Warren 2001: 27, 36, 211–12).

Deliberative democrats also warn that the logics of activism and deliberation are fundamentally opposed. As Iris Marion Young argues, *activism* is located mainly in the informal sphere, uses tactics of confrontation, coercion, and emotional appeals, and is governed by the norms of righteous disregard for the interests of opponents and a commitment toward furthering movement goals. *Democratic deliberation*, in contrast, is located mainly in formal political institutions, uses reasoned argument, and is governed by norms of respect for the views of others and a commitment toward the common good. Thus it can be extremely difficult for activists to make the transition to democratic deliberation because (1) they do not trust opponents; (2) they view participation in deliberative schemes as constituting cooptation, particularly when it involves longstanding enemies; and (3) they cannot let go of the anger, frustration, and outrage they are accustomed to expressing (Young 2003: 102–4). Rage trumps reason.

Similarly, Fung and Wright argue that adversarial social movements will resist the "risky, costly, and demobilizing" shift "from adversarial to collaborative forms of governance" (2003a: 263). Three additional barriers typically prevent the conversion of "adversarial countervailing

TABLE 4.2. *Scoring of Cases on Management of the Political-Party–Social-Movement–Local-Government Nexus*

Municipality	Relations Between Party and Movement	Relations Between Party and Government	Relations Between Movement and Government	Overall Assessment
Ecuador				
Colta				
Curichumbi	Close/organic	Close/organic	Close/organic	Close/organic
Cotacachi				
Tituaña	Strained/competitive	Close/competitive	Distanced/cooperative	Cooperation occurs despite strains and competition between movement and other actors
Guamote				
Curicama	Close	Close	Warm/cooperative	Close/cooperative
Delgado	Distanced	Close	Distanced	Distance between party in government and movement base
Guaranda				
Yambay	Close/organic	Warm/close	Warm/cooperative	Warm/cooperative
Coles	Strained	Cold/distanced	Cold/hostile	Cold/hostile
Otavalo				
Conejo	Competitive	Strained/competitive	Warm/cooperative	Warm, cooperative relations between movement and government, strains between these and party
Bolivia				
Achacachi				
Ayo Ayo	Competitive/Volatile	Competitive	Volatile	Conflictual and fragmented
Chimoré	Competitive/Volatile	Competitive	Volatile	Conflictual and fragmented
Cruz	Close/organic	Warm/cooperative	Government subordinated to movement	Government subordinated to fused movement–party
P. Villarroel				
Tarqui	Strained/competitive	Hostile	Hostile	Government subordinated to fused movement–party
Mita	Organic/fused	Cooperative/fused	Cooperative/fused	
Villa Tunari				
Cáceres	Close/organic	Warm/cooperative	Warm/cooperative	Fused, cooperative

power" into collaborative forms of governance. First, adversarial groups tend to operate at the national level so that they can maximize their impact on centrally made policies and are ill-suited to resolving local conflicts. National organizations may even pressure local affiliates to adopt more intransigent positions, as I observed with respect to the MAS in the Chapare and Pachakutik leaders in the Ecuadorian highlands. Second, they argue that adversarial communication styles and action repertoires are narrowly suited to pressuring the powerful and demonizing opponents rather than resolving problems and implementing policies. Third, adversarial groups possess mindsets that resist wholesale change. It may be impossible for adversarial movements to dismantle their own "injustice frames," which divide political actors into innocent, noble victims and evil oppressors, and to work in a sustained and cooperative fashion with former adversaries. Such a transformation may destroy the movement's major organizations and even "call into question the deep purposes of leaders and the very reasons that those organizations exist" (Fung and Wright 2003a: 280–2).

My observations confirm the concerns that radical democrats have about deliberative enclaves while demonstrating that Andean indigenous peoples are particularly prone to some of the worst problems that philosophers have identified, problems that intensify the more geographically and socially isolated the group is, the more cohesive and socially salient the group's identity, the more long-standing the relevance of the main political issues around which the group mobilizes, and the more iterative the nature of group deliberations. Indeed, Sunstein argues that deliberative enclaves themselves are not merely evidence of social fragmentation; they also are a great source of social fragmentation because they tend to promote more extreme, polarizing views (2003: 90). In the best of cases, proponents of a moderate alternative may persuade the group to abandon extremist options or a norm of pragmatism may convince group leaders that moderation would best secure collective goals (2003: 85). Such circumstances only arise under ideal conditions of sociopolitical pluralism, which provide the strongest incentives for the accommodation of opponents' preferences.

However, I am not as pessimistic as most radical democrats. My findings demonstrate that it is possible for movement-based parties to make the shift from activism to democratic governance, provided that they can overcome the challenges previously described. Identity-based political movements, particularly when identity groups are impoverished, must surmount a higher set of barriers. But indigenous peoples have a unique set of tools for promoting movement–party coherence and cohesion because they are rooted in cultures and forms of organization governed by strong norms of solidarity and reciprocity. In most cases indigenous peoples' local organizations preceded the inauguration of institutional innovations studied here. They stand in contrast to the instrumental, conjunctural civil society organizations that Grindle and Fox encountered in rural Mexico. These were predominantly clientelistic and formed solely to obtain access to government funds, rather than to sustain a group identity or to maintain valued customs (Fox 1996: 1091; Grindle 2007: 126–39).

Grindle found in her comparison of Mexican cases that an active, claims-making civil society is not sufficient to promote democratic institutional innovations: Civil society's energy must be harnessed by parties (2007: 142). In partnership with civil society activists, political parties play a central role in setting the agenda for institutional reform and convincing citizens to adopt particular options. They provide the structure and access to formal political institutions that even the most effective and cohesive social movements lack. When they are rooted in popular, grassroots civil society organizations, they can mobilize citizens to participate in the design and functioning of institutional innovations and thus increase access to decision-making spheres for excluded groups (Armony 2004: 206; Posner 2003: 43). Political-party leaders can champion collaborative governance institutions, forge partnerships with political allies beyond their insular social-movement base, and link movement goals to larger policy issues. They can gently transform existing cognitive frameworks in ways that are more acceptable to movement militants because they offer quicker substantive results and because they trade more narrow, particularist frames for more attractive, expansive, and encompassing ones (Fung and Wright 2003a).

5

Institutional Innovation in Ecuador

Within the same legal and macropolitical framework, Ecuadorian municipalities responded differently to the opportunity presented by decentralization and the political ascent of indigenous social movements and their electoral vehicles. In this chapter I describe the evolution of local government institutions in five cantons in which Pachakutik won office in 1996 or 2000. In two, Pachakutik remains in power and presides over what outsiders consider to be "model" radical democratic institutions. In three others, Pachakutik lost power to rival indigenous sectors and leadership cupulas: to the evangelical party Amauta Jatari/Amauta Yuyay in Chimborazo province and to the mestizo party ID in Guaranda. The five case studies presented represent two distinct geographic biopsies of Ecuadorian democracy. The two model cases, Cotacachi and Otavalo, are located contiguously in the northern sierra province of Imbabura. The three more-problematic cases lie contiguously across the two southern sierra provinces of Chimborazo and Guaranda. Comparable socioeconomic statistics for each municipality are presented in Table 5.1.

Despite the lack of top-down diffusion of specific participatory-deliberative or traditional–cultural institutions, some common features may be observed in all five Pachakutik-led municipalities. First, mayors made a great effort to meet with constituents as individuals or in groups. In small, rural, majority-indigenous cantons Pachakutik mayors and councillors engage in considerable face-to-face interaction with indigenous communities. In larger cantons, distant communities are less able to participate directly but receive regular communications in their own language from municipal authorities. In provincial capitols – such as Guaranda (Bolívar) and Riobamba (Chimborazo) – publicly funded

TABLE 5.1. *Ecuadorian Cases: Socioeconomic Characteristics*

	2001 Population	% Population Indigenous 2001	% In Poverty 2001	%Illiteracy/ Female Illiteracy	%Urban/ Rural
Ecuador	12,156,608	6.6–25[a]	61.3	9/10.3	61/38.9
Imbabura	344,044	39.6	84.5	11.9/14.9	50/50
Cotacachi	37,215	40.0	84.2	19.2/22.3	18/82
Otavalo	90,188	69.6	87.8	19.5/24.4	48.7/52.3
Chimborazo	403,632	49.3	84.8	16.5/20.7	39/61
Colta	44,701	79.5	88.7	31.2/37.8	5/95
Guamote	35,210	95.3	90.5	27.4/34.3	14.4/85.6
Bolívar	169,370	28.4	81.7	15.2/18.6	26/74
Guaranda	81,643	55.9	86.7	20.1/24.8	25/75

[a] This is a controversial measure. The SIISE estimates 6.6%, The Inter-American Indigenous Institute and the Ecuadorian government's website (www.ecuador.edu) list 25%, and Ecuadorian indigenous organizations claim 45%.
Sources: Instituto Nacional de Estadística y Censos, 2001, www.inec.gov.ec; Sistema Integrado de Indicadores Sociales del Ecuador-SIISE Versión 3.5 (2003). Both sources based on 2001 Censo Nacional de Población y Vivienda (Quito: República de Ecuador).

Casas Indígenas (Indigenous Houses) serve as spaces for regular inter-action between Pachakutik governments and indigenous leaders. Second, Pachakutik municipalities, notwithstanding significant internal variations, are typically led by mayors with a history of social-movement activism and/or professional training and relationships with external donors that facilitate access to technical assistance and supplementary financing. Third, Pachakutik mayors infused governing institutions with symbols and practices derived from indigenous culture. Although not all Pachakutik administrations instituted participatory–deliberative spaces in which civil society actors can debate and influence public policy decisions, most of Ecuador's noteworthy experiences are associated with Pachakutik mayors.

I subsequently describe the political developments in each canton that led to the maintenance or loss of political power and the resulting impact on fledgling institutional innovations. I emphasize how the performance of mayors and political parties, and the relationship of both to civil society, influenced the development of institutional innovations. Each of the five Ecuadorian cases is presented within the context of the province in which the canton is located. I begin with Imbabura, home to the country's most durable institutional innovations, moving next to Chimborazo, Ecuador's most-indigenous province, and finishing with the province of

Bolívar, where Pachakutik rapidly established itself as a leading party in the late 1990s. Although an effort was made to present parallel case studies of a similar length with emphasis on similar features, the number of cases studied and the scarcity of data with respect to some of the features of interest necessarily resulted in some lopsidedness. Cantons on which more data were available and for which interview subjects were more accessible receive more attention. Case studies also are more detailed where indigenous parties remained in office longer and where participatory–deliberative institutions were established.

IMBABURA

Imbabura is home to two of Ecuador's most-acclaimed experiments in participatory–deliberative local government. The two distinct models developed in Cotacachi and Otavalo inspired experiments in indigenous and mestizo municipalities throughout the Andes. Imbabura is Ecuador's third-most-indigenous province, at an estimated 39.6% of the population (SIISE 2003). The Ecuadorian government classifies Imbabura as having a "medium economic tendency," owing to the fact that agricultural and manufacturing production provides a modest degree of economic growth (Hurtado 2002: 3). Nevertheless, 84.5% of families live in poverty (Bretón 2001: 145). Imbabura attracts a significant amount of development assistance from NGOs owing to its large indigenous population and that population's high level of organization. In 1999 the province was home to 16 secondary base organizations (11.3% of those in the country) and 26 development NGOs undertook operations there (15.3% of those in the country) (ibid.: 131).

Cotacachi

Cotacachi merits extensive examination because it is one of the earliest and by far the most-celebrated example of indigenous-party-led institutional innovation in Ecuador – perhaps in the Andes. In 2000 Cotacachi received the Dubai International Prize for the use of democratic management techniques that promote equality and sustainable development in local government (UN–Habitat and Municipality of Dubai 2000, cited in Cameron 2003a: 173), and in 2002 it received UNESCO's Cities for Peace Prize for achievements in "democratization and citizen participation" (Cameron 2003b: 267–8). In 2001 the Ecuadorian government awarded Cotacachi the "Little Dreamer" prize for promoting civic consciousness and leadership skills among children and youths. Its mayor is a frequent nominee for president and perhaps the most well-known and admired Ecuadorian mayor.

Cotacachi is a canton of 37,215 people that lies 60 km from the equator, between Quito and the Colombian border. Three urban and eight rural parishes surround the Cotacachi volcano, encompassing high, dry mountain settlements, high and low forests, and the subtropical zone of Intag (Cameron 2003a: 169). Approximately 40% of the inhabitants are indigenous, 6% are Afro-Ecuadorian, and the remainder are mestizo (Ortiz Crespo 2004: 59).

A primarily agricultural region, Cotacachi is marked by unequal distribution of land, leaving most indigenous families without sufficient land for subsistence and prompting approximately 60% of indigenous residents to migrate for seasonal or permanent paid labor. These are disproportionately men (Báez et al. 1999: 18; Guerrero 1999: 114–5; Ortiz Crespo 2004: 99). Extreme land inequality limits economic options and, as a result, 84.15% of the population live in poverty (Cameron 2003a:169).

Leftist organizers began working in Cotacachi in the 1960s through leftist political parties and the Ecuadorian Federation of Indians (Federación Ecuatoriana de Indios, or FEI). The most important contemporary indigenous organization in Cotacachi, the UNORCAC, an affiliate of the national campesino organization FENOCIN, formed in 1977. It represented 43 campesino, indigenous, and Afro-Ecuadorian communities in 2004. UNORCAC's member communities meet monthly, and organization-wide meetings are held annually (Ortiz Crespo 2004: 92, 104).

UNORCAC was by far the most important popular organization until the Pachakutik government that took office in 1996 encouraged unorganized sectors – the tropical, multiracial Intag zone and urban neighborhoods – to organize themselves. Owing to the incipient nature of these efforts, Bretón's 1999 data list only one OSG in the canton (UNORCAC), as well as eight development organizations. The canton has the lowest ranking of NGO density relative to indigenous population in our case sample (21). The paucity of OSGs and NGOs is particularly striking in comparison with the canton of Guamote, whose population size is comparable; there were 12 OSGs and 15 development NGOs there in 1999 (Bretón 2001: 139). Rather than a sign of weak civil society, the small number of popular OSGs demonstrates the unity and coherence of a multiethnic peasant movement in Cotacachi.

In alliance with the Broad Leftist Front (Frente Amplio de la Izquierda, or FADI), in 1979 UNORCAC elected its leader to the municipal council. Since then, UNORCAC has held between one and three of seven council seats. Despite its minority status, before capturing the mayor's office in 1996, UNORCAC municipal councillors used their presence to channel to rural areas' public works spending that previously had been nil (Anrango Ch. 2004; Cameron 2003b: 293, 296; Guerrero 1999: 17; Pallares 2002: 90–1).

In 1996 UNORCAC allied with the new indigenous party Pachakutik, despite the fact that it was not affiliated with the party's social-movement parent CONAIE, but, rather, with its rival FENOCIN. Pachakutik and UNORCAC chose as their first mayoral candidate Auki Tituaña, a Quichua Indian and economist affiliated with CONAIE, who had extensive experience working with development NGOs. The choice followed a lengthy and contentious debate within UNORCAC; many militants worried about Tituaña's close affiliation with rival CONAIE and his lack of membership in UNORCAC. Others argued that Tituaña's social prestige, owing to his academic title, would attract urban-mestizo votes. Eventually a consensus was reached and UNORCAC-affiliated communities voted for Tituaña, who was elected in May 1996 with 24.11% of the vote. He received 73 more votes than his closest rival, providing a thin mandate for change. That year Pachakutik elected only one municipal councillor (Cameron 2003b: 295–7).

After taking office in August, Tituaña convoked a canton-wide meeting to determine budget priorities. He presided over the First Assembly of Cantonal Unity September 11–13, 1996 (Guerrero 1999: 119–20; Proyecto Formia 2004: 22). According to Guerrero, during this first assembly, participants reached consensus on the goals and broad outlines of participatory planning in ways that gave legitimacy to the new processes in the eyes of both indigenous communities and urban residents (Guerrero 1999: 120). The assembly subsequently has met each year for three days in September. The first four annual assemblies were devoted to the collective formulation of a canton-wide development plan (Ortiz Crespo 2004: 123). Prior to the second assembly, civil society groups undertook workshops in which participants diagnosed the needs of the canton's various social and territorial groups (broken down into urban, rural, and Intag zones) and identified their priorities. Thus the objective of the second assembly, held September 18–19, 1997, was to form working groups on specific issues – e.g., education, economic development, and protecting the environment – that sorted through the results of the self-diagnostics. In addition, participants debated options for the institutionalization of the participatory planning process, the nature of citizen participation, and the role of the municipal government. Also in

1997 Cotacachi completed its first development plan, which is intended to guide development through 2011 (Cameron 2003b: 273, 328). Although adult males dominated the first two assemblies, the participation of women, whose role had been increasing in their own social organizations and in municipal government, increased during the third assembly. Children also were included. Development NGOs joined a working group with assembly participants in order to identify ways that they could support the fulfillment of the 1997 Cantonal Development Plan (Bretón 2001: 134; Guerrero 1999: 120–1). By 1999 the municipality had become less dependent upon NGOs to organize and run the assemblies and municipal staff were able to take on most of this responsibility (Cameron 2003b: 173–4). The assembly was institutionalized more formally in 2000 by virtue of a municipal ordinance, which specifically characterized it as a space for the exercise of "social control," the "expression of citizenship," and for participatory planning, in which "decisions are based on the principles of respect, solidarity, and tolerance of the existing pluricultural and multiethnic diversity" (my translation; Anrango Ch. 2004: 62). The legal codification of the assembly is a unique accomplishment in a region where most institutional innovations remain informal and lack legal protection – including the paradigmatic case of Porto Alegre, Brazil.

The Cotacachi model developed in 1996–1997 consisted of a Council for Development and Management that oversees five working groups that focus on particular issues, such as education or environmental protection. It meets approximately every two months and represents municipal authorities and civil society organizations. Below each working group are parish juntas (legally recognized neighborhood councils) and urban neighborhood organizations, as well as youth and women's groups. In annual assemblies, on average 23% of the municipal budget is decided collectively and earmarked for projects that benefit the canton as a whole, while the remainder is divided among individual neighborhoods to manage themselves (interview, Segundo Andrango, Quito, July 8, 2005).

Civil society and territorial organizations meet directly with members of the Council throughout the year (Ortiz Crespo 2004: 126). The Council meets biannually with all NGOs undertaking local development projects in order to oversee their plans and progress in an effort to better control NGO activities (Cameron 2003b: 312). The Council acts as the "executive authority of the Assembly" (Ortiz Crespo 2004: 125). The two social organizations (UNORCAC and the Intag Zonal Committee) are the most crucial to the economic development process, revealing a bias within the committee toward rural and popular groups and against the participation of often-less-organized urban neighborhoods and elite economic and political interests (Guerrero 1999; Báez et al 1999: 9).

Mayor Tituaña was concerned that mestizo-urban residents would reject the assembly if they perceived it to be a rural-indigenous domain. Thus he fostered the formation of a Federation of Neighborhoods in 1998. All of the new neighborhood associations' presidents supported his reelection in 2000 (Cameron 2003b: 321–2). Leaders of these urban neighborhood federations typically meet every two weeks, but individual families and members participate only sporadically (Ortiz Crespo 2004: 92). Thus, urban citizens are less in the habit of direct political participation through social organizations, voluntary collective labor, or mutual assistance, and are less likely to feel a strong cultural or ethnic identification with an organization, compared with rural and indigenous citizens. By 2002 the membership of the Council for Development and Management had grown to 16 members representing government and civil society groups, with three seats reserved for women (Cameron 2003b). By 2004, the council had expanded further, adding greater territorial representation (Ortiz Crespo 2004: 157). Its work is divided into sectoral working groups responsible for implementing the goals and objectives of the Cantonal Development Plan in their sector (Anrango Ch. 2004: 82).

During the first four years citizens in all three ecological zones organized themselves into groups and affiliated with the planning process. In addition, substantive improvements were made with respect to the provision of basic services and electricity, investment in physical infrastructure, and investment in the expansion of tourism. The Pachakutik administration doubled its budget by attracting financial and technical assistance from 16 NGOs that committed themselves to working through the assembly process to implement the development plan (Ortiz Crespo 2004: 123–4). Tituaña attracted on average one-half-million U.S. dollars of NGO money each year between 1996 and 1999. This enabled him to satisfy his main constituencies and to gain early support for institutional innovation. Urban residents were seduced by rapid, visual improvements in the town center, which offset a proportional decline in urban spending in favor of rural areas (Cameron 2003b: 299–301).

Participation increased in Cotacachi's annual assemblies between 1996 and 2001: from 177 mostly indigenous participants from the highlands in 1996; to more than 500 participants, including significantly more urban-mestizos in 1999; to over 600 participants in 2001 (Cameron 2003b: 308–11). A qualitative improvement also occurred as a wider variety of groups and people internalized the new norms. Participants shifted from presenting lists of public works projects for their own communities to discussing broader development themes with greater geographic and temporal scope (Cameron 2003b: 309). In particular, urban groups increased their involvement. The composition of the Fifth Assembly demonstrates the increased organizational activity in urban areas: 50% of delegates represented the urban zone, whereas the Andean and subtropical zones were allotted 26% and 24% of delegates, respectively. This indicates an urban bias, as 80% of the population live in rural areas, but regional representation tends to vary from year to year; in 2004 the subtropical Intag zone was overrepresented (Ortiz Crespo 2004: 156–7).

Mayor Tituaña proved to be a master at attracting external donations and fostering cross-ethnic support. In 2002 he reported that since 1996 the canton's annual budget had averaged US$2.5 million (Ortiz Crespo 2004: 125). In 2002 the budget for social and economic investment doubled from $1,457,000 the previous year, owing to international loans and donations; in 2005 the municipality had $1,510,000 of its own money plus $1,386,000 in international donations (Ospina 2005: 14). In addition to its dependency on external financial support, Cotacachi, like many poor rural cantons, is heavily dependent on national government transfers. Only 5% of the municipal budget comes from Cotacachi's own resources, compared with 95% channeled through the Law of 15% and other national resources. Its ability to increase its own resources is restricted by the poverty of its population, as well as strong resistance from UNORCAC and other poor groups, who argue that their members should not have to pay taxes, owing to the current level of severe inequality and the past exploitation they have suffered. Tituaña has persuaded Cotacacheños to pay higher taxes but the assembly has rejected his suggestions to increase them further[1] (Ortiz Crespo 2004: 144–5).

Like most Pachakutik mayors, Tituaña has convened mandatory mingas in order to stretch scarce resources by harnessing free community labor. This initially was a controversial request. In the 1980s peasant communities organized resistance to mestizo municipal authorities' imposition of forced labor, which they perceived as an effort to pervert indigenous customs. Indigenous peasants had been forced to clean the urban center and build local infrastructure without compensation. However,

---

[1] For example, Mayor Tituaña asked the municipal council to analyze three options for increasing taxes on municipal water services. The council was afraid to make the increase, so the request was referred to the Cantonal Assembly, which "approved by consensus a 100% tax increase" (Tituaña 1998: 14).

Tituaña, using his indigenous identity and the support generated by provision of substantive goods to rural communities, gained the *authority*
to convoke the minga. He even succeeded in convincing urban neighborhoods to participate in collective work days on projects in their own
neighborhoods (Cameron 2003b: 283, 302).

In 2001, after Tituaña was reelected with 78.03% of the vote, the
methodology for PB was further specified (Anrango Ch. 2004: 64, 329–
33; Tituaña in Proyecto Formia 2004: 19–20). By this time Cotacachi
had received considerable international attention. Tituaña himself con-
fessed that Cotacachi's innovations were based on the Porto Alegre
experience, among others, which technical advisers had offered as a
model. He believed that the Porto Alegre model could be even more
successful in Cotacachi, owing to the smaller scale of the canton and
the fact that its population already was better organized, particularly
the indigenous sector (Cameron 2003b: 329–31; Tituaña in Proyecto
Formia 2004: 20–1). Nevertheless, in interviews Mayor Tituaña emphasizes the basis of the Cotacachi model in long-standing cultural practices,
which have been operationalized for the modern world through the adoption of Western administrative techniques (Proyecto Formia 2004: 28).
Another important source of Cotacachi's emphasis on collective political participation is the strong socialist influence in the canton, reflected
in the cross-ethnic, class-centered orientation of the strongest indigenous organization, UNORCAC (Ortiz Crespo 2004: 70). Moreover, both
Tituaña and his wife, a medical doctor, studied in Cuba (Cameron 2003b:
294–6).

Implementing the Development Plan, creating a PB, and forging closer
ties with a wider range of social organizations were the main emphases
of the mayor's second term (2000–2004). Communities worked directly
with a technical team hired by the municipal government on four aspects
of PB: exchanging information, setting priorities, achieving consensus,
and evaluating results. The objective was to make municipal spending
completely transparent and to maximize citizen participation in the fulfillment of the Development Plan. Municipal information with respect
to spending, awarding contracts, and executing projects was made more
accessible (Ortiz Crespo 2004: 128). During this term in a typical year,
one-quarter of the budget was invested in projects affecting the entire
canton while the remainder was distributed to each zone according to the
following formula: urban zone 32%, Andean/rural 32%, Intag 30%,
assembly expenses 5% (Anrango Ch. 2004: 86; Ortiz Crespo 2004:
124–5). This formula was intended to reduce interzonal conflicts. The

drawback is that it failed to channel resources based on important criteria, such as population or unmet basic needs. The relatively more prosperous urban zone is home to approximately 20% of the population yet it receives one third of the budget (Cameron 2003b: 331). Of the annual budget, approximately 70.93% is invested in public works projects and programs, all of which is spent according to the participatory methodologies adopted. According to Ortiz Crespo this is one of the highest percentages in Latin America[2] (2004: 135). However, Cameron argues that the budgeting process is "more consultative than participatory" because the mayor, municipal council, and technical staff maintain final decision-making authority (2003b: 331). Cotacachi established a leadership school in 2001 to cultivate new leaders and to develop ways to shorten and streamline the numerous meetings associated with the assembly process, an effort to address the problem of "participatory burnout" (Cameron 2003b: 310, 313).

In the policy realm, Cotacachi was Ecuador's first canton to decentralize the provision of health services (Ortiz Crespo 2004). A significant portion of the results in the area of health care is attributable directly to UNORCAC, which undertook an NGO-sponsored project called Jambi Mascari. Indigenous women were principally in charge of that project (Ortiz Crespo 2004: 126). By 2002 the assembly had acquired its own budget and permanent staff of seven technical advisers (e.g., engineers, planners, accountants) as well as its own building on the central plaza (Cameron 2003b: 312). This is considerably more institutional structure and support than other innovative institutions studied here possess. In 2003 the assembly created mechanisms to improve the monitoring and evaluation of projects (ibid.: 65). By 2004 approximately half the adults in the canton had participated in some organization represented in the assembly. Although originally anyone could participate, as its size grew, accredited organizations were allowed to send a leader, as well as a representative of the women and children in the organization. This guideline reveals the underrepresentation of women as leaders of civil society organizations, as well as a disturbingly common categorization of adult women alongside children. For example, at the Fifth Assembly in 2000, of 606 participants, 46% were women, 53% were men, and 25% were children.

---

[2] In 2002, a typical year, 6.81% of the budget was spent on capital expenses ($139,930), 22.07% was spent on current expenses such as salaries ($453,438), and 70.93% was spent on investment in public works and projects ($1,457,238) (Ortiz Crespo 2004: 135).

Individuals may attend the assembly and have the right to speak, but they do not have a vote. The requirement to send representatives of organized groups is less of a problem than it appears, as decisions in the assemblies typically are made by consensus, rather than by vote (Ortiz Crespo 2004: 158–60). Individuals also may participate in meetings of their territorial and social organizations, at which they decide which proposals their representatives should support. Nevertheless, Tituaña notes that after 2000 as organized sectors gained more prominent spaces in the participation regime it became more difficult for unaffiliated individual citizens to participate (Proyecto Formia 2004: 22). Ospina (2005: 9) reports that only 33% of respondents participating in a September 2005 survey in Cotacachi belong to any organization at all; only 10% reported having participated in any participatory political activity and only half had even heard of the Assembly of Cantonal Unity. Representation by groups also tends to overrepresent members of smaller groups, while underrepresenting members of larger organizations, such as UNORCAC (Ortiz Crespo 2004: 155).

At each assembly the mayor reports on the status of the Development Plan. At the Seventh Assembly Tituaña reported that "55% of the decisions have been fulfilled, 33% were *in progress*, and 12% remained to be completed" (my translation; italics in original; Ortiz Crespo 2004: 125). This substantive success is particularly impressive in light of the fact that at the time Pachakutik entered office the canton was running a deficit of 200 million sucres, lacked any type of development plan, and was oriented toward the distribution of patronage to political clients. The municipal staff consisted of relatives and political allies of the prior administration and lacked appropriate technical qualifications (Báez et al. 1999: 10; Proyecto Formia 2004: 23). In addition, on taking office, Pachakutik had only one seat on the seven-member council.[3] Thus the convocation of the assembly was part of a strategy to neutralize municipal council opposition to Pachakutik–Tituaña's reform agenda. As Tituaña explains,

Given the experience and the testimonies of other municipalities, we knew that control of the majority was important in order to make our themes viable, but we confronted this contrast with the convocation of the citizens, of civil society,

---

[3] Other council members represented the Ecuadorian Roldosista Party (Partido Roldosista Ecuatoriano, or PRE) (three seats), the Popular Democratic Movement (Movimiento Popular Democrático, or MPD) (two seats) and Popular Democracy (Democracia Popular, or DP) (one seat) (Proyecto Formia 2004: 24).

so that they gave support, guidelines, and in some cases mandates, that I would assume directly as obligatory, so the Councilors also began to feel the weight of the decisions of the people....

I think that there was a quite mature attitude among the Councilors, because they really accepted the invitation that we offered to work together, so that there would be a majority; in fact, we clearly delineated the rules of the game, so that there wasn't going to be pressure.... Basically, we sent a signal that there was not going to be pressure for the division of [public] works, and that everything would be done in compliance with the Law. That clarified the role corresponding to the Municipal Executive and Legislature, so the Councilors joined us. (My translation; interview published in Proyecto Formia 2004: 24–5.)

Some opposition councillors became strong supporters of the mayor owing to the national and international recognition that he brought to the canton, not to mention millions of dollars in external aid. Initially, all non-Pachakutik councillors had opposed Tituaña and his democratization agenda (Cameron 2003b: 303).

The severity of the 1997–1998 national political crisis, which led to the expulsion of President Abdalá Bucaram and the convocation of a National Constituent Assembly (Asamblea Nacional Constituyente, or ANC) – both events largely instigated by the indigenous movement – facilitated political cohesion within the politically fragmented municipal council. Pachakutik subsequently amassed a governing majority. Despite this political advantage, the mayor continued to attribute the success of the participatory process to the support of social organizations (Tituaña interviewed in Proyecto Formia 2004: 24). Opposition municipal councillors representing urban elites enjoyed a majority between 2000 and 2004, but their influence was minimized by unfavorable public opinion of opposition municipal councillors (Ortiz Crespo 2004: 153–4). But the assembly's marginalization of the municipal council and expansion of the importance of the mayor's office is a problem. Municipal council members continue to oppose the loss of their control over the public works budget and the clientelist platform it once provided. On the other hand, the existence of the assembly process enables municipal councillors to evade responsibility for politically difficult issues, such as raising taxes (Cameron 2003b: 307). Mayor Tituaña negotiates ambiguities with respect to lines of authority among the council, assembly, and mayor's office using his personal charisma, political skills, and public support (interview, Segundo Andrango, Quito, July 8, 2005; Ortiz Crespo 2004: 145). Another mayor may not be able to keep opposition from municipal council members from undermining assembly decisions.

Otavalo

Otavalo is a municipality of approximately 90,188 people located next to Cotacachi. It is an important stop on the well-traveled Pan-American highway. Many social scientists and development professionals consider Otavalo to be a model of democratic institutional innovation, primarily owing to the talents of its mayor, Mario Conejo. Notwithstanding his short time in office, by 2005 he was considered among the most successful mayors in the country. Lalander effusively concludes that Conejo had quickly accomplished "institutional, political, economic, social and cultural changes" while uniting adversarial ethnic groups (my translation; Lalander 2005: 154). His administration is notable for effective collaboration across ethnic lines, for efficiency in the management of resources, and for an innovative system to promote transparency in government.

Otavalo is world famous for its dynamic artisan sector, which dates back to the colonial period and began a contemporary boom in the 1970s. On average, 145,000 tourists annually flock to the Otavalo market to buy indigenous handicrafts. Otavalo handicraft merchants may be seen on streets throughout the Americas, Europe, and beyond (Hurtado 2002; Lalander 2005: 161; Meisch 2002: 1–3). Thus, compared with other migrants, Otavalo's migrants are more likely to leave the country for extended periods of time, particularly since the 1980s, and Otavalo is more integrated into the international economy and relatively more prosperous than other Ecuadorian cantons (Meisch 2002).

Otavalo's population is approximately 50% indigenous, and the dominant indigenous group is the Otavalo[4] (interview, Santiago Medina, June 24, 2005). The textile, handicraft, and tourism industries are dynamic and attract approximately 49% of the population to urban centers. Thus, compared with Cotacachi, Otavalo is far less rural (Hurtado 2002: 2). Nevertheless, not all Otavaleños benefit from economic growth, and in 1999, an estimated 87.8% of households lived in poverty (Bretón 2001: 146). In 1999 Otavalo received development assistance from 17 development NGOs and was home to 44% of Imbabura's OSGs. These figures place Otavalo in fourth place in the highlands in terms of the density of development NGOs relative to indigenous population and poverty (Bretón 2001: 134).

Successful trade in Otavalan handicrafts and tourism economically and socially transformed the canton. Wealthy Indians came to purchase

[4] "Otavalos" are members of this ethnic group; Otavaleños are residents of Otavalo.

more and more property in the city center and diversified their busi-ness interests, eclipsing once-dominant mestizo-white elites. According to sociologist and Mayor (2000–present) Mario Conejo, by the 1980s the indigenous had achieved a "massive presence" in urban areas of the canton, owning perhaps 80% of the major buildings in the city center. This created conflicts between upwardly mobile indigenous business elites and mestizo-white urban elites, who continue to hold racist views of their indigenous neighbors and were not prepared for the "invasion" of spaces that they had held for years[5] (interviewed in Lalander 2005: 164). The sig-nificant wealth of many indigenous business owners also has generated tensions between them and poorer, more rural, traditional, indigenous campesinos (Conejo interviewed in Lalander 2005: 167; Lalander 2005: 164; Meisch 2002: 77–8). Unlike the populations of many other cantons, which are shrinking owing to a lack of economic opportunities, the popu-lation of Otavalo has grown steadily: The 2001 census reported 59.11% growth over the previous decade (Hurtado 2002: 3).

In 1996 Mario Conejo ran for mayor on the Pachakutik ticket. He lost, but Pachakutik elected a representative to the municipal council. The 2000 local elections demonstrated Conejo's capacity to reach across conflicting indigenous groups. A militant in the evangelical indigenous party Amauta Jatari, and a fierce rival of Conejo's, had planned to run against Conejo/Pachakutik. To promote unity, leaders of both local par-ties and of CONAIE decided to meet together to select a single can-didate. Pachakutik and Amauta Jatari leaders chose Conejo and urged competing indigenous candidates to support him. However, the second-most-supported candidate, Carmen Yamberla, president of the Imbabura CONAIE affiliate (Indigenous and Campesino Federation of Imbabura [Federación Indígena y Campesina de Imbabura, or FICI]), immediately launched a complaint. She involved national leaders, who failed to per-suade Conejo to step aside. In the end, Conejo represented the joint Pachakutik–Amauta Jatari ticket, while Yamberla – as well as another indigenous and two mestizo candidates – ran against him. Conejo was elected mayor with 45.95% of the vote, leaving the other candidates far behind. He attracted votes from those allied with the local indigenous

---

[5] A similar phenomenon emerged in Guamote after the land reform, particularly after the indigenous majority captured the government in 1992. As Torres argues, the occupation by indigenous citizens of the central, urban public space has enormous economic, social, political, and cultural implications: It represents the assertion of "Andean forms of local power" (my translation; Torres 1999, cited in Hurtado 2002: 3).

party leaderships and from mestizos who perceived Conejo to be a moderate alternative to Yamberla (Hurtado 2002: 8).

Conejo also benefited from the increase in power and prestige Pachakutik enjoyed in 2000, the favorable example that Pachakutik presented in neighboring Cotacachi, as well as the personal esteem in which the community held Conejo (Lalander 2005: 170). His popularity and stature increased during his term. He was reelected in 2004 with 54.4% of the vote, notwithstanding the decision of all nonindigenous parties to unite against him behind one candidate. Conejo took the initiative to reformulate the Otavalo Strategic Plan, which the Ecuadorian Association of Municipalities had produced for the canton in 1998–1999. He decided to broaden popular participation in this plan while incorporating the technical expertise and financing that a UNDP project provided (Lalander 2005: 161).

As in Cotacachi, in Otavalo there are two main spaces for canton-wide deliberation and decision making: the Cantonal Citizen Forum and the Cantonal Development Council. At annual fora the mayor reports on government activities during the previous year in relation to guidelines in the plan. Representatives of parish juntas, indigenous *comunas*, and urban neighborhoods discuss issues affecting the entire canton. The Development Council receives demands from territorial and sectoral interests. It is staffed with technical advisers responsible for designing strategies for achieving the plan's goals (interview, Segundo Andrango, Quito, July 8, 2005). At all points in the process, Otavaleños are assisted by technical experts, many of whom are paid by NGOs or are working through the World Bank project, the National Program for the Development of the Indigenous and Black Peoples (Programa Nacional para el Desarrollo de los Pueblos Indígenas y Negros, or PRODEPINE) or the UNDP (Hurtado 2002: 11).

Decision-making power also is located within the parish juntas, indigenous comunas, and urban neighborhoods, which have equivalent administrative status and often are referred to as "neighbors' workshops." The neighbors' workshops hold annual assemblies to prioritize spending of their share of the municipality's financial resources. Rather than establish several canton-wide working groups for different topics or needs, as in Cotacachi, these are discussed within the parish juntas and urban neighborhoods, with participation of civil society organizations and in consultation with the mayor. Some parishes decide to divide the money equally among the various comunas and let each spend it as they wish. Because the amounts given are relatively small – perhaps $2000 – many parishes' participants will pool resources and prioritize collective projects or annually rotate the entire sum among the comunas (interview, Segundo Andrango).

Despite Otavalo's being a much larger municipality, with approximately three times the population, Conejo has constructed a more horizontal, quasi-formal governing institution to link civil society and government officials, omitting the middle layer of intermediation in the Cotacachi model and allowing a larger role for both the elected municipal council and for citizens organized into parochial juntas and urban neighborhood associations (Ortiz Crespo 2004: 145–6; interview, Segundo Andrango, July 8, 2005). Thus, indigenous development expert Segundo Andrango argues, the Otavalo model better facilitates direct communication and coordination, with less administrative effort (interview, Quito, July 8, 2005).

Moreover, compared with Cotacachi, the Otavalo municipal council has a larger role as the legitimate representative and legislative power of the municipal government. Conejo intended to include the council because citizens had elected it and because including it reduces the political tensions that occur when it is marginalized, as in Cotacachi. Nevertheless, Hurtado observes that there were significant tensions during the first two years of Conejo's administration as council members struggled to maintain authority and relevance (2002: 13). In 2004, Conejo assured an interviewer that he was working in harmony with the council and that 95% of municipal decisions involving the council and the mayor's office are taken by consensus (Proyecto Formia 2004: 32). This view is shared by NGO informants interviewed during fieldwork in 2005 (interviews, June 2005).

Mayor Conejo has built a reputation within and outside the canton as a transparent and efficient administrative leader. On taking office in 2000, his highest priority was constructing trust between citizens and their government by making government processes more transparent and by eliminating opportunities for corruption. He believed that his government would not be effective if he could not create conditions of trust and credibility toward municipal officials (oral presentation, Mario Conejo, Riobamba, July 1, 2005). To foster greater popular participation in the government, the mayor established an Office of Citizen Participation and Intercultural Dialogue (Conejo, interviewed in Proyecto Formia 2004: 31–3). Like Tituaña, he has bridged the gap between the rural and urban indigenous populations. For example, in 2003, just before the 2004 elections, Conejo decided that the price of municipal water must increase significantly to become self-sustaining. The people approved the increased cost for the service and he was reelected. This increase, which entailed the removal of an 85% subsidy, was palatable because civil society groups worked with the municipal government to choose, execute, and oversee the new municipal water project. The cost of water was raised to market levels and provided in the most efficient way possible (interview, Santiago Medina, June 24, 2005).

One of the ways that Conejo has developed such a trustworthy and honest image is his initiation of a system of transparent public contracting. In the past, municipal officials had awarded contracts to friends, family members, or political supporters, or in exchange for kickbacks. Projects often were not completed properly, on time, or at all. Conejo oversaw the rewriting of the public contracting law. Now, the politically independent *colegios* (professional schools) of engineers and architects maintain a list of qualified professionals. When the local government needs an engineer, the school sends over the name of the next person on the list. Thus, qualified engineers alternate access to public contracts. Everyone can see that any qualified person has an opportunity to work for the municipality and that the mayor receives nothing in return. After contracts are awarded citizens groups monitor the engineer's performance. This has increased public opinion of the mayor (interview, Segundo Andrango, July 8, 2005; oral communication, Mario Conejo, July 1, 2005; Lalander 2005: 163). Transparency also is facilitated through the Otavalo government's website (http://www.otavalo.gov.ec).

Another Conejo innovation is the "60/40 formula." With respect to the portion of the budget invested by the canton as a whole, a community may be told to wait for another year so that resources can be devoted to a project elsewhere. Communities asked to wait may still have access to resources if they can come up with 60% of the resources themselves in materials or labor. In such cases the municipality will try to come up with the remaining 40% required for the project, often from external sources. Conejo believes this system is a great advance for local development because it requires citizens to invest their own resources in exchange for the services they once received passively. It is more likely that the community truly desires the resulting projects and that these are executed and monitored faithfully. The institution of the 60/40 formula has been accompanied by a more rational tax system in which citizens are taxed according to their wealth and property. As a result, people are more careful with public resources because they know that they are partially their own (interview, Segundo Andrango, July 8, 2005; oral presentation, Mario Conejo, July 1, 2005; Lalander 2005: 162).

As in Cotacachi, Otavalo's Pachakutik mayor has used his personal credibility before both rural–indigenous and urban-mestizo communities to promote greater intercultural cooperation and solidarity. At a 2005 public meeting in Riobamba, Conejo explained his vision:

It is important to promote consensus and unity among all of the people of Otavalo. We cannot act as individuals or emphasize our differences and prejudices. Mestizo and indigenous must work together. [Our motto is] "Construction of the unity of Otavaleños to guarantee our mutual development." We can strengthen our identities as Indians, as mestizos, and as Otavaleños. I am proud of being Indian, of my culture, my history, my present. We must promote mutual respect and interculturality. We must have a vision of the future of men and women, indigenous and mestizos. We must make a collective commitment to create an intercultural vision. (My translation; oral presentation, Mario Conejo, Riobamba, July 1, 2005.)

The result of his efforts is the creation of an efficient administration with considerable support across ethnic groups and urban–rural divides (Lalander 2005: 153). Even the conservative newspaper *El Comercio* in 2002 recognized the Otavalo government for its efforts to improve interethnic relations:

Otavalo is the only city in the country that seeks to improve the intercultural relations of its inhabitants as a development policy. According to the Plan de Vida, the axis of local development, the "convivencia" [harmonious relations] balanced among mestizos and indigenous is the principal goal. (My translation; cited in Lalander 2005: 161.)

One way that this *convivencia* has been accomplished is to make as many decisions as possible by consensus. According to Conejo, at least 95% of decisions are made by consensus rather than simple majority (interview, Proyecto Formia 2004: 32). Making decisions by consensus rather than through imposition or through competitive voting gives beneficiaries a sense of ownership and responsibility. As Conejo explains, "there is no public work if there is no community participation, not just with the *mingas*, but also for us the concept of participation is in the space of dialogue, of discussion and analysis of the problems, of prioritizing the search for alternative solutions" (my translation; interview, Proyecto Formia 2004: 36).

CHIMBORAZO

Located in the central sierra southeast of Quito, Chimborazo is Ecuador's most indigenous province (49.3%) and among its poorest (www.inec.gov.ec; Hurtado 2002: 4). An estimated 84.8% of the population live in poverty (Bretón 2001: 145). Probably owing to the large indigenous population and high poverty, Chimborazo contains both the highest concentration of civil society organizations and the highest concentration of development NGOs in the country. In fact, the province hosts one-quarter of Ecuador's development NGOs (56) and OSGs (36). Development organizations influence politics by generating incentives for the creation of civil society organizations among indigenous communities, providing financial resources to the organizations that they favor and, often as a result, perversely exacerbating existing factionalist tendencies (Bretón 2001).

Chimborazo also is unusual because of its high concentration of evangelical indigenous communities. It is the only province where evangelicals constitute a majority (65%) of the indigenous population (Andrade 2005: 50). Elsewhere in the highlands the evangelical Christian indigenous population averages 12% of the total indigenous population (Andrade 2003: 127–23). North American missionaries helped to form the Association of Indigenous Evangelical Churches of Chimborazo (Asociación de Iglesias Indígenas Evangélicos de Chimborazo, or AIIECH) in 1967. The name eventually was changed to the Confederation of Indigenous Peoples, Organizations, and Evangelical Churches of Chimborazo (Confederación de los Pueblos, Organizaciones, e Iglesias Indígenas Evangélicos de Chimborazo, or CONPOCIIECH), which better evokes recent trends in the Catholic indigenous movement. The attraction of evangelical churches is partly attributable to the support that the local Catholic Church traditionally has given to a system of labor servitude and political oppression (*gamonalismo*) that virtually enslaved the indigenous population until the land reform of the 1970s (Cameron 2003b: 183). In recent decades indigenous leaders increasingly have seized control of their organizations from foreign missionaries because the latter have discouraged them from political participation, particularly activism in opposition to the state (Andrade 2005: 53; Lucero 2006: 36, 39–40).

Only in Chimborazo has an evangelical indigenous party elected a mayor. Having observed the success of rival CONAIE in launching an electoral vehicle and participating in the 1997 ANC, evangelical Indians became more interested in participating in party politics. Dr. Vicente

Chucho, Amauta Jatari provincial councillor in Chimborazo, told me
how this changed:

> This movement began in the year 1997 when the government convoked the ANC.
> They reformed the law of elections. Before, to participate it was only for those
> who belonged to a political party and you had to register with the Supreme
> Electoral Tribunal, and those who are members of these could be candidates
> for mayors, prefects, deputies and whatever. This was reformed. Thereafter, this
> signified that independent movements could participate without being obliged to
> be part of any political party. In this context, in 1997, Colta in particular had
> been a very important center for indigenous organization, especially the Protes-
> tant evangelical movement. The organization united more than 550 indigenous
> churches throughout Chimborazo. So we're talking about 25,000 or more people
> who belonged to this movement. . . .
> Then, I remember that we united some 160 representatives of the 550, in
> which we analyzed the Electoral Reform Law, and we saw the necessity that the
> indigenous groups also take part in the political participation of the state. Because
> before this the indigenous were excluded, there was no space for us to participate
> in the public administration of the state. So we saw this need and we also, with
> the knowledge of evangelism, and the professional formation some indigenous
> had attained – some had entered teaching – particularly at the primary, medium,
> and kindergarten levels. So the people began to think in this manner that the
> problems that we were living with, it was necessary that we, who had suffered in
> our own bodies these problems, that we propose our own point of view. From this
> the Amauta Jatari Independent Political Movement was born. (My translation;
> interview, Riobamba, June 29, 2005.)

Indigenous evangelicals increasingly questioned foreign missionaries'
commands to eschew worldly politics (Andrade 2005: 53).

Evangelicals fought to counter the political hegemony of CONAIE
in the sierra as the latter became the dominant interlocutor for the
indigenous population (Andrade 2005). In Chimborazo, Pachakutik–
Amauta relations are hostile and aggressive – notwithstanding the solidarity engendered by a shared indigenous–peasant identity – owing to the
predominance of two indigenous parties competing in the same "hunting
ground" (Panebianco 1988: 217–8). The evangelical movement only had
an incentive to ally with Pachakutik when leaders did not believe they
could compete in elections on their own. Once Amauta Jatari enjoyed
electoral success, organizational dynamics ensured that alliances would
be avoided, since they threaten the identity and cohesion of both parties
that purport to represent exclusively the indigenous electorate. In fact,
as the two cases from the province of Imbabura demonstrate, interparty
alliances with *opponents* – parties representing distinct social sectors,
in this case mestizos – are easier and more stable than alliances among

competitors (ibid.: 219). Pachakutik frequently forms electoral governing alliances throughout the highlands with mestizo center and center–right and left parties.

Amauta Jatari's success was insufficient to maintain its legal registration. In December 2003 the Supreme Electoral Tribunal (Tribunal Supremo Electoral, or TSE) disqualified the party for not having presented candidates in 10 provincial elections, as is required to maintain registration. It reemerged in 2004 as Amauta Yuyay. This time it benefited from the divorce between President Gutiérrez and Pachakutik, the party that had brought him the presidency. After a fallout in mid-2003, Gutiérrez made the newly constituted Amauta Yuyay its partner in Chimborazo and nearby provinces (Lucero 2006: 49; interviews in Quito, Riobamba, June 2005).

Guamote

Like Cotacachi, Guamote was among the first Pachakutik municipalities to establish innovative democratic institutions. Its two-term mayor also earned national attention; he was elected provincial governor in 2000 and served as minister of Social Welfare (2001–2003). The subsequent collapse of one of the country's most-promising alternative governments exemplifies the critical importance of mayoral leadership to, as well as the disastrous implications of disunity within political movements for radically democratic reform.

Guamote is a rural, 95% indigenous canton of approximately 35,000 people (SIISE 2003). Thus Guamote is approximately the same size as Cotacachi, but much more indigenous. It is Chimborazo's poorest canton and Ecuador's fifth poorest, with the country's highest percentage of indigent families (Andrade 2003: 128; Santana 2004: 240). Guamote ranks last in Ecuador in terms of rural educational attainment, infant mortality, and child nutrition (Cameron 2003a: 169; Flor 2001: 7–8; Korovkin 2003: 134; www.inec.gov.ec). Guamote's economy is more agricultural than Cotacachi's. The 1970s land reform improved land distribution such that most now is in indigenous hands. However, as in Cotacachi, the low productivity of indigenous lands and the low labor demands of livestock and dairy production have caused many to migrate to cities permanently or seasonally (Cameron 2003b: 258–62).

Bretón ranks Guamote sixth in the sierra in terms of the density of development organizations relative to poverty and indigenous population (Bretón 2001: 134, 139). Santana ranks it highest in the country

and attributes much of the formation of indigenous–peasant organizations to the encouragement and financial support of NGOs (2004: 240).
The strongest, most important organizations emerged after the agrarian
reform (Bebbington 2005: 8). The oldest, most important is the Jatun
Ayllu Federation of Indigenous Organizations, founded in 1974. It is the
local CONAIE affiliate, and the majority of elected officials in Guamote
between 1996 and 2004 (when Amauta Jatari unseated Pachakutik) were
Jatun Ayllu militants (Naula Yangol 2003: 59). In 1989 a government
program to promote rural development created a rival organization,
the UOCIG (later UCIG), which became the operating arm for government development aid (Bebbington 2005: 9; Bretón 2001: 175; Cameron
2003b: 203–4).

Guamote was among Ecuador's first cantons to elect an indigenous
head of local government (at the time, smaller municipalities elected
municipal council presidents, rather than mayors). Prior to the creation
of Pachakutik, leftist parties frequently placed indigenous leaders on
their lists as alternates in order to gain indigenous support without risking actual indigenous power (Cameron 2003b: 215–6). In 1992 veteran
indigenous leader Mariano Curicama won election representing the ID.
Curicama had become Guamote's first indigenous municipal councillor
in 1984, representing the Marxist–Leninist MPD (interview, Mariano
Curicama, June 27, 2005; Korovkin 2003: 132). Curicama's election
as mayor – concurrent with the election of two indigenous municipal
councillors – reflected a rapid shift in political power away from the traditional, feudal elite. Like indigenous organizations elsewhere in Ecuador
and Bolivia, comuna councils and OSGs preselected indigenous candidates by consensus in order to maximize their "moral authority" and
electoral support, although this consensus often was difficult to achieve
among rival groups, particularly after 2000 (Cameron 2003b: 216).

Prior to the shift in political power toward the indigenous majority, the
urban, commercial mestizo minority controlled municipal government.
They barred Indians from entering municipal buildings, confining them
to the steps (interview, José Delgado, in Proyecto Formia 2004: 48). In
fact, mestizo elites tried to prevent Curicama from taking office in 1992.
Indigenous organizations responded with a threat to boycott mestizo
businesses. This threat cleared his path, together with the accompaniment
of approximately 5000 indigenous supporters, who literally stood behind
him as he entered the building (Cameron 2003b: 218).

Guamote's early indigenous electoral success helped convince
CONAIE leaders to launch Pachakutik in 1996, and Guamote was among

the first cantons to form a Pachakutik affiliate (Cameron 2003b: 217). This success partially is attributable to the land reform, which broke up large haciendas and thus, together with a demographic shift among urban-mestizos toward larger cities after the construction of the Pan-American Highway, caused many mestizos to leave (Cameron 2003b: 197). In addition, the intensive process of political organization during the land struggle resulted in the creation of cohesive and experienced indigenous organizations, which became the principal collective actors in local politics in the 1990s (Cameron 2003a: 170). Prior to the land reform, in 1964 Guamote had slavelike labor conditions and the most unequal, concentrated pattern of land ownership in Chimborazo. But the Ecuadorian government made Guamote a priority after 1973 (Cameron 2003b: 178–97; Torres 1999: 92). Indigenous organizing also benefited from a gradual improvement in the quality of and access to rural bilingual education (Torres 1999: 97). Thus, although institutional innovation is less likely to thrive under conditions of extreme inequality and underdevelopment, inauspicious underlying social and economic conditions can be improved with targeted local and national government intervention.

Voters reelected Curicama with Pachakutik in 1996. In addition to Curicama, five of seven municipal councillors were indigenous and all seven represented civil society organizations. The increased numerical presence of indigenous representatives in government thwarted mestizo efforts to isolate and marginalize solitary indigenous councillors (Cameron 2003b: 216–7). According to Torres, Curicama's second term (1996–2000) "radically altered" local politics. As in Cotacachi, the focus of municipal government shifted from providing services to the urban minority to a greater balance in favor of rural services and investments (Torres 1999). Curicama instituted an Indigenous and Popular Parliament in 1997, making it the first such institution in Ecuador. The Parliament immediately attracted international interest and acclaim as "one of Ecuador's most participatory and inclusive municipal governments" (Cameron 2003b: 173).

The Guamote model is similar in structure to that used in Cotacachi. The first Congress of the Parliament took place July 25–26, 1997, and it met on average 5 times a year – ranging from a low of 2 to a high of 12 times a year between 1997 and 2002. The mayor, municipal council, and members of the Parliament have the right to convene it. Delegates were the 121 presidents of the canton's legally recognized indigenous cabildos, which elect presidents each December (Cameron 2003a: 171; Naula

Yangol 2003: 1–11). Comuna presidents are integrated into municipal government by working in coordination with the municipal council, the two together constituting the "Full Council." Cameron points out that the Parliament is unique among indigenous-party innovative institutions because parliamentary representatives have a more formal role in municipal government decision making and because this scheme formally recognizes comuna presidents rather than civil society leaders. These presidents enjoy formal legal recognition and substantial legitimacy among indigenous communities (Cameron 2003b: 227–8). In addition to issuing norms with respect to political participation and overseeing municipal spending, the Parliament supervises elected municipal officials and nominates candidates for cantonal appointments controlled by the national government (Cameron 2003a: 171). Mayor Curicama and his successor José Delgado claim that the Parliament had higher moral authority than any other government institution. Other informants told Cameron that the Parliament prevailed about 80% of the time between 1996 and 2002 in interinstitutional conflicts. As in Cotacachi, the Parliament successfully insisted that all external actors – such as NGOs and national government agencies – work through the Parliament so that development initiatives better met local needs (ibid.: 171; Naula Yangol 2003: 20). Many of Cameron's informants found this to be its greatest substantive achievement (2003b: 229).

In 1997, during its first assembly, the Indigenous and Popular Parliament began to develop a long-term development plan. Completed in 1999, the Unitary Plan of Cantonal Development was crafted in a participatory fashion during 28 one- or two-day community workshops held throughout the canton. Approximately 8% of Guamote's population participated in the workshops, representing 112 of 121 communities. Although only 33% of participants were female, this is high for an area with long-standing sexist norms. An even more interesting participatory advance was the use of the Quichua language during the workshops, constituting the first instance in which the municipality operated in Quichua on such a scale (Cameron 2003b: 241–3).

As in Cotacachi, the Parliament's work is undertaken by working groups devoted to the plan's sectoral goals. The result was a shift in the allocation of the budget away from small, highly visible, mainly urban, projects with little impact, toward strategic, long-term goals, such as literacy and preventative health care. The working groups gave greater authority to civil society leaders compared with the scheme in Cotacachi, where the relative weight of civil society representatives and NGO technical staff on sectoral committees is more balanced (Cameron 2003b: 246).

With a $280,000 grant from the U.S. Inter-American Foundation, Guamote also instituted a Local Development Committee in September 1997 as a "technical institution" over which the mayor presides and in which the 12 presidents of the major civil society organizations in the canton participate. These organizations include associations of farm workers, women's groups, agricultural cooperatives, and the canton's seven urban neighborhoods, represented by a Federation of Urban Neighborhoods similar to the one created in Cotacachi. Many of them formed recently to take advantage of the opportunity to work directly with the municipality on funded projects (Naula Yangol 2003: 57–9). The Development Committee worked at the second level of the participatory structure directly with civil society organizations (e.g., NGOs, indigenous federations), providing technical capacity to support the supervision of development projects. Each municipality-sponsored project had a "functional structure committee" that included a designated responsible civil society organization and typically four other organizations or government entities. As in the other models discussed here, projects were undertaken with a great deal of organized collective labor (Naula Yangol 2003: 22–5). A coordinating group consisting of two representatives each from the committee and the Parliament, as well as one municipal councillor, was established to facilitate harmonious relations among the three entities (Andrade 2003: 129). Even according to authors that admire the Guamote model, coordination among the three entities was extremely difficult, owing to personal and institutional rivalries (Naula Yangol 2003: 65; Torres 1999: 100; confidential interviews).

A crucial problem of the Guamote model was Curicama's failure to secure the formal, legal recognition that the Parliament needed to act independently of the municipality or to secure a permanent source of funding independent from municipal decisions. Under Curicama's leadership institutional conflicts were resolved through the application of his personal charisma and the trust that he had acquired among the population across political, ethnic, and religious divides. He embodied institutional innovation by becoming the accessible mayor. Mayor Curicama greatly improved public access to government through regular, extensive consultations with communities and organizations. Curicama established, and his successors continued, a practice of being available to citizens every Thursday morning from 7:00 A.M., when locals often visit the Thursday market, on a first-come–first-serve basis (Cameron 2003b: 225–6). The exaggerated importance of the mayor in the new participation scheme drew criticism from NGOs and external observers. After Curicama decided not to stand for reelection in 2000,[6] neither of his successors was able to bridge institutional or religious divisions or foster cooperation. The municipality refused to share information with a Parliament dominated by a different political force and relations completely broke down (Bebbington 2005; confidential interviews).

Pachakutik's candidate José Delgado won the 2000 mayor's race with 37.17% of the vote, defeating Amauta Jatari's Juan de Dios Roldán, who attracted 23.3%. This time all seven councillors elected were indigenous, and Pachakutik gained a 5–2 majority (Cameron 2003b: 216). The Delgado administration (2000–2004) represented continuity with Curicama's. Delgado focused on implementing the development plan, modernizing the municipal administration, training municipal staff, and making public financial information more accessible and up-to-date. Delgado reports having strengthened the community minga for implementing public works and promoting more participation of rural communities, particularly of women, youths, and children. In 2004 Ecuador's National Union of Journalists named Delgado the best mayor in the country (Delgado, interview in Proyecto Formia 2004: 49–50).

However, a number of institutional frictions subsequently emerged. The Local Development Committee was not an initiative of the Pachakutik government or civil society. Rather, the Inter-American Foundation had imposed it as a condition of a significant financial grant. According to Cameron, the committee's design was inappropriate because civil society organizations preferred to manage their own projects. Local leaders refused to accept its authority because donors had imposed it. Thus, by 2002, the committee had largely ceased to function and technical staff in the municipality took it over and provided technical assistance for a handful of projects while civil society organizations managed their own, smaller projects (Cameron 2003a: 172; 2003b: 239–40).

---

[6] Curicama is among the few indigenous-party mayors to rise to regional and national office. He served as an adviser to Pachakutik's 27 mayors between 2000 and 2001 until he was invited to serve as subsecretary in the ministry of Social Welfare, under indigenous leader Luis Maldonado (September 2001–January 2003). President Gutiérrez appointed him minister of Urban Development and Housing, where he served from January to September 2003. In 2004 Curicama was elected prefect of Chimborazo in alliance with the regional party Fatherland in Solidarity (Patria Solidaria, or PS) (interview, Mariano Curicama, June 27, 2005).

The availability of increasing budgets helped to smooth over ethnic differences accruing from competition over resources. Curicama demonstrated great skill in attracting resources from the central government and external donors. The municipal budget increased from $60,000 in 1991, to $700,000 in 1993, to $1 million in 1999, and $2.5 million in 2002 (Cameron 2003b: 222n44). In contrast, Mayor Delgado between 2000 and 2004 concentrated on rationalizing local property tax assessments and increasing collections (Cameron 2003b: 223). But external government and nongovernmental donors have been a constant source of disunity and intraindigenous community conflict. Donors prefer to create new, subservient client organizations as counterparts for their development projects, rather than work with existing indigenous-community-based groups that have their own agendas, authoritative leadership, and self-governance norms. This creates an incentive for indigenous leaders to compete with each other for access to external aid through control of rival development NGOs. Rather than a sign of a thriving civil society, Guamote's 13 OSGs (in 2002) represent the perverse consequences of access to development resources when OSG leaders have an incentive to compete for resources and power by forming rival organizations and refusing to cooperate with each other. In fact, many OSGs do not represent any common identity or distinct purpose (Cameron 2003b: 204-5).

The Parliament itself suffered from the scarcity of resources for its operation. With a meager budget ($8,000 in 2002) it could not pay staff or reimburse its members' transportation and incidental expenses. The exception is the president and secretary of the Parliament, who received $100 and $80 per month, respectively. NGOs provided technical support but did not provide substantial funding, perhaps because the Parliament sought to seize from NGOs decision-making control over development policy. Despite the rhetorical support that Pachakutik mayors and municipal councils gave to the Parliament, starving it of resources when it fell under evangelical control effectively enabled them to maintain control. Cameron points out the stark contrast with the Cotacachi model, in which the mayor and NGOs have provided substantial funding for the operation of the Cantonal Assembly (2003b: 233).

Despite these problems, Pachakutik's reforms dramatically improved access to municipal government offices for formerly excluded groups. Once a place where indigenous citizens were abused and neglected, in Cameron's opinion, they became the "focal point" of indigenous political mobilization and indigenous social movements penetrated public spaces as never before (2003b: 173). Under Pachakutik the municipal council held its first open meeting in rural communities. This represents real progress since 1992, when mestizo municipal workers refused to speak to or obey orders from the newly elected indigenous mayor. Municipal officials no longer expect or receive "gifts" of agricultural goods from indigenous citizens in exchange for public services, and the indigenous are no longer subject to physical abuse and humiliation (ibid.: 196–218).

Until approximately 2002, widespread support for the new institutions dampened religious conflict and political rivalries between CONAIE/Pachakutik and FEINE/Amauta Jatari. Many evangelical militants participated in Pachakutik-dominated institutions. (Andrade 2003: 129). Writing in 2002, Andrade proclaimed optimistically that common ethnic identities had eliminated interreligious conflict (my translation; 2003: 129–34). CONAIE leaders had for 10 years led a substantial proportion of the canton's indigenous movement – including evangelicals – in major local protests linked to national protests (Cameron 2003b: 248–51). However, political tensions between evangelicals and Catholics eventually overwhelmed the forces promoting interreligious harmony. A weakening President Gutiérrez exacerbated these tensions when he set out in 2003 to destroy his former alliance partner by funneling money and political support to minority, conservative elements of the indigenous movement (*El Comercio* 2003a, 2003b; *Hoy* 2003; Ronquillo 2003). Most analysts attribute Amauta Yuyay's success in 2004 in Chimborazo to numerous last-minute visits by the president, who distributed small gifts and promised to provide public works spending (*El Comercio* 2004b; Febres Cordero 2004).

Open conflict erupted toward the end of Delgado's administration between the mayor and the head of the Indigenous and Popular Parliament, Amauta Yuyay's Juan de Dios Roldán. In August 2003 – as Pachakutik left the government – Dios Roldán arranged a presidential visit on behalf of the Parliament without consulting that body's members or Mayor Delgado. Gutiérrez brought gifts for Amauta constituents (Ronquillo 2003). The municipal government retaliated, refusing to give information to the Parliament and thus preventing it from performing its monitoring function. Enmity grew between the two parties and the two leaders.[7]

---

[7] After the acrimonious rupture between President Gutiérrez and alliance partner Pachakutik in 2003, Gutiérrez funneled massive amounts of patronage to new ally Amauta Yuyay and made several visits to Chimborazo to support its candidates (*Aguirre* 2003; confidential interviews, Riobamba, June 2005). Pachakutik's claims that Gutiérrez effectively purchased the Guamote municipal government for the evangelicals in the days before the

After Amauta Yuyay won the 2004 mayoral election, Delgado and Dios Roldán switched positions – Pachakutik's Delgado served as president of Parliament, Amauta Yuyay's Dios Roldán as mayor – and the political stalemate continued. Because they refused to work with each other, the Parliament ceased to function (confidential interview, June 24, 2005). Dios Roldán now oversees a process in which each parish junta is given its corresponding share of development funds. The canton as a whole no longer decides how spending will be prioritized or participates in canton-wide deliberations (confidential interviews). Development professionals concur that doling out small amounts of money for projects serving tiny geographic areas is inefficient and tends to foster competition over resources and clientelistism, rather than integrated economic development and democratic deliberation (Bebbington et al. 2005: 19). According to a top Pachakutik official in Chimborazo,

> The style of participation in Guamote since the change in government is that all of the communities come to an assembly and they discuss, but those who make the decisions are the mayor and the municipal council, and this isn't really participatory. Thus, they have not sustained the process, because in Guamote now there is no longer the Indigenous and Popular Parliament. People just go to a meeting and they are told which public works are going to be done. Or they say that each *comuna* will receive $5,000, for example. So the Parliament has almost nothing to do. It doesn't have anything to do. Because the mayor and council decide what each *comuna* will receive. So it is not possible to give priority to a particularly needy community or to make macro projects for the entire zone, to establish priorities at a more macro level that are self-sustaining. (My translation; confidential interview, June 29, 2005.)

This is the same method used in the evangelical stronghold of Colta.

Colta

Colta is our only case in which an evangelical indigenous party governed, and one of two in which Pachakutik lost power to another party. Colta is the geographic heart of the evangelical indigenous movement, which has deep roots dating to the early 20th century. Its population is somewhat larger than Guamote's. It lies northwest of Guamote, which had been part of Colta until 1944. Yet it is equally rural and poor: 95% of Coltans live in rural areas and 89% of households live in poverty (www.inec.gov.ec;

election are supported by an independent newspaper poll conducted earlier in the year showing 87.5% public support for Delgado (Delgado, interviewed in Proyecto Formia 2004: 53).

Bretón 2001: 146). In the late 1990s Colta ranked third on Bretón's list in terms of the density of development organizations working with indigenous populations and was home to five OSGs and 18 development organizations (2001: 134–9). The majority of the 450 indigenous communities in Colta are evangelical Christians, a legacy of evangelical churches established between 1918 and 1953. In 1967 the AIIECH took control of the churches, their influential radio station (Radio Colta), and their schools (Andrade 2003: 130).

During the 1980s Colta's evangelical Indians gained public office in alliance with the ID. An indigenous mayor was elected with the ID in 1988 – Ecuador's first. Subsequently an indigenous evangelical was elected a provincial deputy. In 1996 Colta elected as mayor an evangelical indigenous pastor representing Pachakutik. As Pachakutik was taking off and achieving astounding results in its first elections, many evangelical indigenous militants joined. But evangelical and Pachakutik militants' efforts to fashion a common political project failed (Andrade 2003: 130–2; interview, Vicente Chucho, Riobamba, June 29, 2005).

In launching Amauta Jatari in 1998, evangelical indigenous militants had to overcome intense opposition from evangelical pastors, who had for many years urged them to keep politics and religion separate and even had forbidden their political participation. Over time, indigenous leaders persuaded their neighbors that they must get involved in politics in order to improve their lives. In some cases pastors continued to try to influence and control evangelical indigenous politicians. As the Amauta mayor of Colta explained to Susana Andrade, evangelical pastors often drop by the *alcaldía* and expect mayors to drop what they are doing and "attend to them" (my translation; quoted in Andrade 2005: 57). Andrade concludes that evangelical pastors in Colta essentially have captured local political power and reproduced the old top-down political model in religious form (Andrade 2003: 127). Her view contradicts statements that Amauta Jatari representatives made to me but confirms criticisms that Pachakutik leaders in Chimborazo express (confidential interviews).

By 2000 Amauta Jatari had established dominance in a few cantons and the strongest was Colta. Since then the party has controlled the mayor and all seven indigenous municipal councilors (Andrade 2003: 130). Pedro Curichumbi won the 2000 election with 31.03% of the vote and was reelected in 2004. Amauta Yuyay mayors gained office in neighboring Guamote and Alausí in 2004 as well. These electoral achievements are attributable to the growing strength of the evangelical indigenous movement, the decline in Pachakutik support that followed its alliance with Gutiérrez, and numerous last-minute visits and gifts from the president (Andrade 2005: 60; *El Comercio* 2004a).

According to Vicente Chucho, formerly Colta's administrative director, the canton has developed a participatory, transparent governance model, in contrast to prior models in which public policy making was secret and hidden, elected officials monopolized decision-making power and clientelism determined public spending. Today, he argues,

> in Colta the people decide themselves in an assembly with a minimum of 80 people, up to 500–600 people. And they decide openly – look folks, here is how much money we have. And perhaps there is also some external help as well. So here's how much we have. And this is distributed according to the population and the necessities and problems that each parish and community has. And in Colta there are at least 271 communities, and none of these is left without a budget. So each year they meet and each community knows how much money corresponds to them and they decide what to do with this amount they have. So it doesn't happen that a particular person or community, being a friend of the mayor or of a councilor gets favored. (My translation; interview, Riobamba, June 29, 2005.)

Emilio Guzniay, Chimborazo's Pachakutik coordinator, holds a different view. In Colta, he argues, municipal funds are distributed equally to each comuna. This is a waste because it would be more productive for the canton to invest in businesses that would create employment and thus eliminate the necessity for so many rural residents to migrate to other areas. "So, instead of giving a little bit to each comuna, it is better to invest all or most of the money each year in one larger project that would have more of a sustainable impact" (my translation; interview, June 29, 2005). Thus, although Amauta Yuyay governments may claim to be "alternative" in order to attract external financing, they promote little deliberation because the mayor and municipal council continue to make decisions (ibid.). Periodic assemblies are a mechanism for consultation, rather than participation, and they play no authoritative role in the municipal budget (Andrade 2005).

In 2005, Andrade warned that the evangelical party's inexperience and lack of a clear political project had led it to make easy conjunctural alliances that in the long run would lead the party to ruin. The communities are starting to criticize the party's leaders and demand new leaders that share their rural, indigenous identity. They expect more rapid improvement in poverty alleviation, literacy, and health. Andrade charges that the government had coopted FEINE by providing jobs and resources and that this had destroyed the indigenous movement's unity. Rather than offering a new form of politics, evangelicals are reproducing traditional populist and clientelist relations (my translation; Andrade 2005: 60). Amauta Yuyay leader Vicente Chucho offers a more optimistic view: "People now have a lot of interest and make proposals. They don't want to be left to the side, they want to integrate" (my translation; interview, June 29, 2005).

Indigenous peoples have secured self-government in Colta. Citizens participate in discussions of public-spending priorities with respect to their neighborhood. But there are two main obstacles to democratic progress. First, as in the Chapare of Cochabamba, Bolivia, Colta has one-party rule. Overwhelming support for the evangelical indigenous party has eliminated political pluralism. Only Amauta has representation in the executive or legislative branches. That party and its mayor have no incentive to negotiate with opposing parties or interests or to reach across religious or ethnic lines. This partisan hegemony is mirrored in civil society: The dominant political organization is the canton's affiliate of Chimborazo's evangelical indigenous organization. Second, there is no mechanism for citizens to discuss with their elected leaders canton-wide priorities. Instead, each neighborhood focuses on its own needs without reference to other, possibly more-needy, neighborhoods.

BOLÍVAR

Pachakutik became a major force in politics in Bolívar after the 2000 elections. The party already had elected a mayor and municipal councillor in 1996 and sent a provincial deputy to the national legislature in 1998. In 2000 Pachakutik elected the provincial prefect, two provincial counselors, the mayors of Guaranda and Echeandia, nine municipal councillors (two each in Guaranda and Echeandia), and filled 29 seats on parish juntas (Arévalo and Chela Amangandi 2001: 29). This robust support for Pachakutik in Bolívar – notwithstanding the relatively low percentage of indigenous population – provided an auspicious context for the initiation of new governance models. Not only was Pachakutik a major political party in the province in the late 1990s, as in Cotacachi, indigenous mayors won elections by reaching across ethnic lines.

The southern sierra province of Bolívar is less indigenous and less populous than the other two examined here. Largely for these reasons it has fewer OSGs and fewer development organizations channel resources there (Bretón 2001: 131). Like Chimborazo, Bolívar is among Ecuador's seven most economically stagnant provinces (Hurtado 2002: 4). An estimated 81.7% of families live in poverty (Bretón 2001: 145). The province's relatively more urban nature has led to relatively higher rates of literacy (www.inec.gov.ec).

Guaranda

Guaranda, Colta's northwest neighbor, provides another dramatic illustration of the importance of effective mayoral leadership to democratic institutional innovations. The death of the Pachakutik mayor rapidly unraveled one of the country's most notable efforts to incorporate citizen deliberation and participation in local governance across ethnic lines. Moreover, like the case of Guamote, Guaranda exemplifies how promising, progressive social movements can limit their own political potential by investing in factional and personalistic disputes rather than building alliances across organizational, partisan, and ethnic lines. The authoritarian leadership and organizational style of the local Pachakutik affiliate ultimately turned off potential voters and lost the movement some of its most talented militants.

Guaranda is the provincial capitol of Bolívar and thus the most urban municipality studied here. One-quarter of the population lives in urban areas, and in 2001 an estimated 55.9% of the population consisted of rural indigenous people (www.inec.gov.ec). In 1999 approximately 86.7% of the population lived in poverty (Bretón 2001: 146). In contrast to the relatively low level of civil society organizations and development NGOs in Bolívar, Guaranda is a hothouse of NGO activity. Bretón ranks Guaranda second in the country in terms of development NGO activity, the number of people living in indigenous areas, and the degree of poverty as a function of development NGO concentration (2001: 139).

The CONAIE affiliate FECAB-RUNARI is Pachakutik's provincial partner. Formed in 1973, it is one of Ecuador's oldest and strongest indigenous–campesino organizations. In 1991 it represented more than 80 communities. Pachakutik also draws its candidates from other sectors – professionals, students, unions, and artisans. Bolívar's evangelical Indians belong to one of two rival organizations. The first, the Association of Evangelical Churches of Bolívar, works with FECAB on areas of mutual interest and generally supports the Pachakutik candidates because FECAB allows their candidates on the Pachakutik list. The second, the Federation of Indigenous Evangelical Churches of Bolívar, based in the parish of San Simón, broke away from the association and allied with Amauta Jatari, whose candidates had not yet won in Bolívar as of 2005. The internal splits within the evangelical movement may explain the weakness of Amauta Jatari in the canton, notwithstanding its location in the geographic heartland of evangelism. Although tensions between Catholic and evangelical indigenous organizations do exist, relations have improved in recent years and they never have been as contentious as in Chimborazo (confidential interviews, 2005).

FECAB leaders expect to have the final say on Pachakutik candidates and strategies. Before Pachakutik was formed, the organization participated in elections with the ID, which provided new offices for FECAB in 1993. But FECAB leaders were continually disappointed with the political rewards exchanged for their loyalty. Selverston-Scher describes an incident in 1993 in which indigenous leaders invited local and provincial politicians to the unfinished offices and one-by-one hung them from their chairs in the air to extract promises to fulfill electoral commitments and to furnish the offices (2001: 107). Today Pachakutik leaders work out of the FECAB offices.

The hegemonic intentions of FECAB authorities are indicated by statements with respect to the lack of "discipline" exhibited by some Pachakutik officials. For example, one FECAB leader told me:

We as leaders, we always fight to make it so that our compañeros continue to follow the line of the leaders and of the struggle and that they don't become confused with their title. That they continue to follow the mandate of the traditional leaders. (My translation; confidential interview, July 2005.)

Another indicator of FECAB's hegemonic inclinations is that they have avoided making electoral alliances with other parties, whereas alliances between Pachakutik and a host of other parties are common in other provinces (confidential interview, former Pachakutik militant, July 2005).

In 1996 Pachakutik won the mayor's office. Its candidate, Kléver Guevara Erazo, an urban-mestizo, was a disappointment. FECAB leaders had expected he would give them a better chance of winning than a rural, indigenous candidate, but claim that he betrayed the movement once he gained office (interviews, Pachakutik leaders, July 2005). He eventually left for the ID – the dominant party in the canton for the previous 20 years – in what would become a common pattern for Pachakutik officials that FECAB leaders reject. In 2000 indigenous leader Arturo Yumbay, representing Pachakutik, became the canton's first indigenous mayor. Mayor Yumbay came from the ranks of FECAB and was enormously popular among indigenous-rural constituents. Even the Evangelical Federation supported his candidacy.

Yumbay, with help from NGO advisers and the Pachakutik apparatus, convoked a Citizenship Assembly on August 31, 2001, with the goal of collectively writing a Cantonal Strategic Plan. He invited urban neighborhoods, clubs, *sindicatos*, youth groups, and indigenous communities and sponsored events to promote deliberation among civil society groups. The mayor's office established commissions that included representatives from the municipality and civil society to work on particular themes and created consensus-seeking working groups (Arévalo and Chela Amangandi 2001: 36–38; interviews). A union of parish juntas was convened in which, for the first time, each parish was allocated a portion of the municipal budget. A variety of NGOs played an important role in Yumbay's innovative institutions by elaborating specific participatory methodologies along the lines articulated by the mayor and civil society organizations.

In 2001, a typical budget year under Yumbay, Guaranda received US$3,336,833.08 from national government transfers and raised US$319,270.08 of its own resources; that is, the canton provided just under 9% of its own budget. That year Guaranda also received supplementary funds from NGOs and foreign countries. For example the Japanese government signed a contract with Guaranda to donate $2 million for economic development (Arévalo and Chela Amangandi 2001: 41–4). The administration stretched the money as far as possible by invoking numerous mingas, in which the mayor actively participated (interview, Segundo Pilamunga, Guaranda, July 4, 2005). As a FECAB militant recalled,

The *minga*, which was his great strength, the *minga* was done at all levels: at the level of barrios, the communities, for public works. The city was clean. The garbage was collected for the first time during the night with brigades from the communities and the neighborhoods. And mestizos and professionals participated in these *mingas*. He achieved the unification of the city and the countryside. This was his great accomplishment. To return this dignity and respect – not of everyone, because of course it was a very short time, and because the political predators didn't like it. (My translation; interview, Wilfredo Macas, July 5, 2005.)

Use of the minga was controversial because, prior to the emergence of Pachakutik, Bolívar's mestizo local leaders had imposed forced, collective labor on indigenous communities. Rural, indigenous communities requesting public works in their departments were required to provide the labor because mestizo leaders knew that they could exploit the indigenous tradition of the minga. Far more money was spent in urban neighborhoods, where mestizos did not have to donate labor (Selverston–Scher 2001: 106–7).

After Yumbay died in a 2002 car accident, many participatory processes were discontinued. Conflict erupted when the local Pachakutik organization and FECAB tried to usurp Pachakutik indigenous Vice-Mayor Alberto Coles' legal right to replace Yumbay.[8] Under Coles, reelected in 2004 with the ID, the canton-wide participatory process terminated and the municipal government took charge of canton spending decisions and project implementation. The objectives and aspirations articulated in the 2001 plan are no longer followed. Instead, a portion of the canton's resources is distributed directly to eight rural parish juntas that prioritize decisions in participatory assemblies (confidential interviews, Guaranda, July 2005).

Coles continues to attract external donor support for the canton as an indigenous mayor (interview, Alberto Coles, July 5, 2005). But he lacks the authority to convoke mingas for municipal projects. The conflict between Coles and Pachakutik split the indigenous movement: One sector followed Coles to the ID, which had more money to offer aspiring indigenous candidates; the other stayed with Pachakutik. During his short first term Coles gained significant support from mestizos by giving priority to urban projects and reversing the preferential treatment Yumbay had given to indigenous and rural parishes. According to one of his critics, a former electoral rival, 90% of the budget under Coles goes to urban neighborhoods in a canton in which 74% of the population is rural (interview, Alberto Yumbay, Quito, July 7, 2005). Pachakutik militants even question his authenticity as an Indian, claiming that he has lost the indigenous cosmovision or the ability to think like an Indian (confidential interviews). After 2004 Pachakutik leaders threw away their slim municipal council majority over personal jealousies and ethnic chauvinism when

---

[8] A rift between Coles and Pachakutik emerged in 2000 when Coles refused to relinquish his right to the vice-mayoral position. In municipal elections, each party presents a list of candidates in the order they want them elected, with their most-favored candidates at the top. Voters, however, may give their votes to lower-ranked candidates, enabling them to take the place of party leaders' preferences. In 2000 and 2004 voters preferred lower-ranked candidates to those that Pachakutik had chosen. When Coles finished second after Arturo Yumbay, Pachakutik leaders urged him to step aside in favor of their candidate. His refusal angered Pachakutik and FECAB leaders, who eventually expelled Coles from the party for "lack of discipline."

they expelled Pachakutik mestizo Vice-Mayor Washington Bazante from the party.

Guaranda represents a striking example of the impact of mayoral leadership and political party cohesion on the outcome of institutional innovation. Processes that thrived under Yumbay collapsed under Coles. Pachakutik leaders threw away control of the mayor's office and municipal council when elected officials refused to submit to their commands. Their authoritarian behavior and refusal to build bridges across partisan lines lost the party militants and voters. Why would rational political party leaders behave in ways destined to diminish the party's electoral prospects and access to power? Panebianco explains this phenomenon as the result of dominant coalitions that are unable to adapt to "variable environmental conditions" (1988: 15). When a party has few electoral options, the freedom to adjust to the environment becomes restricted and, as a result, the coalition's position on organizational questions hardens, even to the point of maintaining positions that threaten the survival of the organization (ibid.). Pachakutik's followers rejected the leadership cupula's dogmatic line and sought collective and selective incentives outside the party. The fact that the ID was willing to welcome them with prominent positions made this option attractive. Pachakutik was unable to "monopolize a collective identity" as representative of indigenous or popular demands (Panebianco 1988: 31). Pachakutik could not "drastically change its ways without disorienting its followers (and thereby instilling in them an 'identity crisis')" (ibid.: 42). This inability to adjust to diverse and changing identity needs rigidifies the party's internal conflicts, preventing it from resolving "serious organizational crises" that required a comprehensive change in its strategy and collective ideology. This explains why "dominant coalitions are often unable to reelaborate their political strategies" (ibid.)

CONCLUSION

The Ecuadorian cases illustrate the importance of mayoral leadership to the design and implementation of democratic institutional innovations. This is underscored by the fact that in two cases (Guamote and Guaranda) promising institutional innovations collapsed after a change of mayors because successors lacked the talents of predecessors. As a result, they were unable to hold factions within their sponsoring organizations together or to maintain alliances with political allies.

Relations between and within sponsoring indigenous movements and parties as distinct factions struggled for influence in government and access to resources also affected the durability and democratic quality of innovating reforms. Effective mayors prevented these struggles from derailing innovative reforms in Cotacachi and Otavalo, but they erupted into disruptive public battles in Guamote and Guaranda, where they ultimately cost Pachakutik power. In Colta movement–party dynamics affected institutional innovation in a different way: The political hegemony and numerical weight of the evangelical movement reduced the motivation to promote deliberation across political and confessional divides. (This phenomenon of organizational and ideological hegemony will reappear in Bolivia's Chapare in the next chapter.) Since 2003, owing to attacks by President Gutiérrez and the disillusionment of supporters, at the national and subnational levels, Pachakutik has undergone a painful restructuring to replace failed leaders and redefine its mission and identity.

In Ecuador, some Pachakutik mayors gave civil society organizations a greater role in local government and introduced indigenous–campesino cultural norms into institutions that had excluded them for generations. In every case, poor, rural, indigenous communities saw some increase in the investment of municipal resources in their areas after indigenous parties took power. In some, institutional innovations created space for public deliberation over common development priorities, increased the participation of civil society groups in public decision making, and facilitated greater cross-ethnic cooperation. In others at least a portion of the budget was distributed to submunicipal communities, which gained the opportunity to collectively deliberate the allocation of their resources. Although such sums were small and had a negligible impact on living standards, citizens gained an opportunity to participate in public deliberations about community priorities. This represents a modest improvement in democratic quality.

Other democratic improvements were achieved. All cases saw improved representation of indigenous peoples in local government. Indigenous-party-led governments shifted spending priorities toward rural areas and projects of greatest interest to indigenous communities. All increased the number of indigenous municipal-government staff, although this was difficult owing to labor laws protecting municipal employees from termination. Indigenous languages became widely spoken in government offices, dramatically improving the flow of information to indigenous constituents (Mario Conejo interview, in Proyecto Formia 2004: 35;

interview, José Delgado, in Proyecto Formia 2004: 21). In Guamote, municipal law now requires that *new* employees must be bilingual in Spanish and Quichua (Cameron 2003b: 220).

Scholars of the Cotacachi case agree that interethnic relations have improved since 1996 (Ortiz Crespo 2004: 152; Cameron 2003b: 335). Because Indians were in the minority there, Mayor Tituaña cultivated town-based support. He soothed the sting of urban-mestizos' lost political monopoly by continuing to channel a disproportionate share of municipal resources to projects in urban areas and promoting an alternative to the corrupt, clientelist politics-as-usual. Cameron argues that the construction of a peasant–indigenous–urban–middle-class alliance was crucial to developing political support for participatory institutions (Cameron 2003b: 285, 295). In neighboring Otavalo, Meisch reports that interethnic relations had improved, particularly among the younger generation. Pachakutik militants estimate that Conejo received at least 30% of the mestizo vote in 2000. However, the rapid economic and political ascent of Otavalo's indigenous majority has increased tensions with mestizos who feel displaced by the changes (Meisch 2002: 206–9).

In Guamote, perhaps owing to the overwhelming majority of indigenous citizens, and the more traditional, indigenous culture compared with those of Cotacachi, Otavalo, and Guaranda, Curicama and Delgado made only modest efforts to reach out to mestizo groups and ensure their equitable participation (see Cameron 2003b: 221–2). The most important effort to include mestizos was both mayors' decision not to fire racist and/or incompetent mestizo municipal employees, realizing that firing the minority of employees that the mayor legally *could* fire – department heads – would have inflamed already-tense interethnic relations. Moreover, indigenous replacements with sufficient administrative experience and education were scarce (Cameron 2003b: 219–20). When Pachakutik transferred power to Amauta Yuyay in 2004, in contrast, the new mayor fired the entire technical team that had worked on the new participatory processes (Bebbington 2005).

Throughout the country the representation of women in local office improved after a 2000 law required that political parties include women in 30% of the positions on their candidate lists. The record of predominantly indigenous provinces with respect to women's participation exceeds the national average, although women serve in the least-influential positions and there are few female mayors and no prefects (Radcliffe 2001: 11–12). In our cases women remain underrepresented in representative and participatory institutions and those represented suffer frequent abuse by men. Efforts to incorporate women's participation commonly equate them with children as parallel spaces are created for both. The most progress in improving representation can be seen in Cotacachi, where the number of women working in municipal government doubled from 7 to 14. Between 1996 and 2003, Mayor Tituaña estimates that the number of women participating in the assembly increased from 25% to 40% of total participants. By 2004 the presence of women in the dominant local indigenous organization, UNORCAC, had grown: A woman occupied the vice presidency as well as six seats on the executive committee and women had formed their own coordinating organization (Báez et al. 1999: 57; Ortiz Crespo 2004: 107; Proyecto Formia 2004: 29). Women have served as assembly president and municipal councillors and in 2004 comprised half of the Development Committee's then-16 members (Ortiz Crespo 2004: 123). Ironically, given the image of the rural indigenous as more sexist than modern urban-mestizos, women made less progress in urban organizations. In 2002, 14 of 15 association presidents and the entire Neighborhood Federation's executive committee were male (Cameron 2003b: 323).

Female representation also improved dramatically in majority-indigenous Guamote. A recent municipal law requires that women hold at least three of seven municipal council seats; in 2004 four of seven councillors were female (Proyecto Formia 2004: 51). That year Mayor Delgado noted that Pachakutik had exceeded the legal requirement that 35% of candidates on party lists be female. But female councillors are marginalized, intimidated, and excluded and male councilors challenge their authority (Cameron 2003b: 227). Since women are unlikely to be elected president of their communities they rarely served in the Parliament.[9]

The generally more positive outcomes in Ecuador – beyond the impact of leadership and party–movement influences – also reflect a more favorable political context. Although political fragmentation is high, it does not reach the extremes seen in highland Bolivia. Several of the Ecuadorian cases also are marked by greater cultural-ethnic heterogeneity, which is likely to increase the motivation for political actors to engage in cross-cultural accommodation. Indigenous–campesino politics are relatively less marked by violence and coercion in Ecuador owing to historical

---

[9] In 2002 only 3 of 121 cabildo presidents were female (Cameron 2003a: 185n6). Guamote's umbrella women's organization represents 70 smaller women's organizations in the canton. With financing from the European Union, it has been promoting training in leadership and basic accounting and economic production (Naula Yangol 2003: 60).

factors – e.g., a lesser degree of intraindigenous land conflict, less-violent relations with the military – beyond the scope of this study. Although this factor was not explored systematically, because Pachakutik municipalities are more reliant upon NGOs for financial resources to support institutional innovations, they may be relatively more susceptible to pressure to promote democratic norms, such as gender equality. These contextual differences that distinguish the two country environments are revealed in the next chapter.

6

Institutional Innovation in Bolivia

Owing to the standardization of the LPP throughout Bolivia, there is little variation in the experiences of local government with respect to the *design* of institutional innovations. All municipalities were required to formulate POAs and five-year municipal development plans using a prescribed participatory planning methodology. All were required to form vigilance committees comprising representatives from civil society organizations. As in Ecuador, indigenous political parties added features derived from indigenous and campesino-union cultures, such as the minga, the *fila comunitaria* (community line) method for selecting electoral candidates, and accelerated rotation of elected leaders.

Cases diverge with respect to implementation in relation to the political, social, and economic context. This context varied sharply between the departments of La Paz and Cochabamba. As in Ecuador, I chose a small set of geographically clustered cases from two regions where indigenous parties had their greatest electoral success. I show how distinct political conditions in the departments of La Paz and Cochabamba resulted in variations in implementation affecting the democratic quality of local governance. In contrast with Ecuador, where leadership was decisive, what is notable in Bolivia is not the *impact* of leadership but, rather, its conspicuous absence owing to the overweening influence of local and national movement–party logics and rules, cultural and political norms of accelerated office rotation that prevent mayors from establishing authority, and the top-down imposition of local governance designs that diminished the scope of mayoral initiative. Statistical information with respect to available socioeconomic indicators is presented in Table 6.1. These vary

TABLE 6.1. *Bolivian Cases: Socioeconomic Characteristics*

	1992 Population	2001 Population	% Indigenous 2001	% in Poverty Based on Unsatisfied Basic Needs 1992/2001	% Illiteracy/Female Illiteracy % Rural Illiteracy/Female (2001)[a]	Urban/ Rural
Bolivia		8,274,325	62.05	70.9 / 58.6	37.4/46.6 52.9/64.69	
Cochabamba	1,078,890	1,455,711	74.36	71 / 55.0	14.66 (total)	
Chimoré (Carrasco)	8555	15,264	76.08	94.8 / 82.7	17.18 (total)	3874/11,390 18.93%/81.07%
Puerto Villarroel (Carrasco)	24,637	39,518	82.96	94.9 / 81.7		6366/33,152 indigenous: 12.19%/87.81%
Villa Tunari (Chapare)	48,111	53,996	87	96.8 / 87.2	17.37 (total)	4511/49,485 indigenous: 5.7%/94.3%
La Paz	1,545,033	2,350,466	77.46	71.1 / 66.2	33.82/45.5 44.33/58.08	
Achacachi (Omasuyos)	60,050	70,503	93.11 (65,644)	93.3 / 93.3	24.43 (total)	7540/62,963 indigenous: 9.31%/90.69%
Ayo Ayo (Aroma)	6407	6981	90.79 (6338)	98.9 / 99.3	18.48 (total)	100% indigenous: 100%

[a] Municipal-level illiteracy measures are for persons over the age of six. Illiteracy is likely to be underestimated because the category omits persons not responding to the question.

Source: All data are from the 2001 Censo Nacional de Población y Vivienda (La Paz: República de Bolivia) or the 1992 version of the same study. These data are available at www.ine.gov.bo. The data of the last two columns are from the Bolivian government website www.enlared.org.bo/ficha/municipio.

considerably between the two departments but are remarkably consistent within them.

In 1995 the MAS swept elections in tropical Cochabamba, from which three of my cases were chosen. In two subsequent elections the party maintained or strengthened its absolute control over mayors, municipal councils, and vigilance committees throughout the Chapare. In 2005 it seized the presidency and lower house of Congress, solidifying local MAS hegemony while reducing the threat of government oversight that had moderated the extralegal excesses of MAS local governments. But during the period studied, relations between these and national government authorities were tense. In the Aymara highlands of La Paz a distinct political environment was encountered. MIP mayors took office only in 2004 and they did so under conditions of political fragmentation and instability generated by the proliferation of competitors for the same indigenous vote. These extreme political environments – political hegemony and fragmentation with instability – have reduced the democratic nature of institutional innovations in both regions.

As in Chapter 5, the case studies presented are somewhat lopsided owing to the varying availability of data. Nevertheless, taken together and placed within their regional context, they illuminate the divergent outcomes of attempts to infuse political institutions with opportunities for popular participation in decision making and features of indigenous–campesino culture. We can see the difficulties that new electoral vehicles face in adapting to new governance roles while maintaining support from a social-movement base that expects electoral success to bring immediate improvements in well-being and absolute power.

COCHABAMBA

Cochabamba is 74.4% indigenous, which places it third among Bolivia's nine departments on this measure (Censo Nacional de Población y Vivienda 2001). The poverty rate in 2001 was 55.0%, slightly *below* the national average of 58.6%. Both of these figures represent a significant drop since the 1992 census: from 71% in Cochabamba and 70.9% in Bolivia. Cochabamba presents some advantages and disadvantages as a site for local institutional innovation. The department is relatively more prosperous than others, a prosperity that extends to the Chapare, and poverty is decreasing more rapidly than it is elsewhere. Social indicators also are improving.

Our three cases are taken from the Chapare of Cochabamba, the bastion of the MAS. The Chapare denotes the subtropical region of

Cochabamba and spans three provinces and 6 million acres, with major settlements along the highway linking the cities of Cochabamba and Santa Cruz. Only in these settlements do residents have access to electricity, medical attention, and other basic infrastructure and public services (Vargas and Draper 2004: 67). Today the majority of the population consists of Quechua and Aymara migrants from the highlands of Cochabamba (74%) and the rest of Bolivia (26%). These migrants encroach on the territory of lowland Indians, such as the Yuracaré and the Yuquis, who live today in their own territories in tension with colonists (Herbas Camacho 2000: 33).

State-sponsored colonization intensively settled the Chapare between 1960 and 1980. Thereafter, unplanned migration from Bolivia's highlands increased rapidly, as the state closed mines in the highlands. This migration precipitated a dramatic increase in the production of coca leaf for export (Lizárraga 1998: 54). Migrating kinship groups and neighbors formed self-governing organizations called *sindicatos* in response to the need to gain legal title to land and to demand access to basic and agricultural services (Garcia Linera 2004; Healy 1991).

Sindicatos formed in the 1970s and 1980s provided systems of local justice and dispute resolution and established social and cultural ties of reciprocity and solidarity. Sindicato authority extends to family life; many Chapare sindicatos and regional federations were the only source of legitimate authority until campesinos took political power in 1995 (Córdova Eguivar 2004: 52–60; Healy 1991: 88). As coca growers' leader Evo Morales explained in a 2000 interview,

The sindicatos have managed to convert the Tropics of Cochabamba into a "mini state." The sindicato resolves the issue of health, education and survival. This organization has strengthened itself in the absence of the State and has converted itself into the maximum authority of participatory democracy.... There is political power because the municipalities are in the hands of the MAS. Thus, those who decide the management of the municipalities' popular participation money are the sindicatos and neighborhood juntas. (My translation; *Los Tiempos*, November 19, 2000, reproduced in Córdova Eguivar 2004: 94.)

Thus, a decade before they swept local elections in 1995 with the new ASP, sindicatos exercised statelike powers: They established property boundaries, levied taxes on the coca trade, collected monthly $1 dues from each family, set transportation fares, and invested resources in local public works, such as roads and schools (Healy 1991: 89). Sindicatos established rules for behavior and obligations for membership, without which no family could gain access to land and agrarian services. They had the legitimacy and power to sanction dissident or recalcitrant members through fines or the imposition of community labor (García Linera 2004: 394). Only family members or persons known to existing settlers in a community would be able to obtain land, after they had proven their merit through contributions to collective work projects and other rites of passage (*Atlas del Trópico de Cochabamba* 2004: 43).

By 1985, sindicatos controlled almost the entire Chapare. By 1985, approximately 89% of the sindicatos existing today had formed and their networks covered the entire available space. Political divisions occurred as the base-level sindicatos formed into municipal-level *centrales* and provincial-level federations. Only the physical barriers of mountains and nonnavigable rivers, and the political barriers of national parks, lowland indigenous peoples' territories, and previously occupied lands, limited their expansion. It became untenable to live in the region without being a sindicato member, with the exception of residents of small urban centers or remote indigenous tribes. But the importance of sindicato membership transcends the practical necessities of life on the agricultural frontier in a region devoid of public services. The collective struggle for survival imbues each member with a strong collective identity, an ethic of mutual dependence and accountability, and strict norms of discipline and conformity to the community's will[1](*Atlas del Trópico de Cochabamba* 2004: 42–3).

Sindicatos are ambiguous as "indigenous organizations." Indigenous-community organizations are more ethnically and linguistically homogeneous, and their authority systems have been tied to the same geographic territory for generations. The coca growers' sindicatos, in contrast, include migrants from different areas of Bolivia and most date only to the 1950s (Garcia Linera 2004: 391). Self-governing structures more closely resemble Western, particularly Marxist, institutions – for example, electing authorities formally, rather than rotating them by age and prior experience, as would occur in Andean highland communities (Córdova Eguivar 2004: 59,). No standing is accorded to authority positions that migrants may hold in their sending communities, and there is no effort

---

[1] Sindicatos, and the higher-tier centrals and federations to which they belong, use all three types of organizational power that Etzioni identifies to control members' behavior: They use *coercive* power to threaten and punish members who do not comply with organization norms; *utilitarian* power, by emphasizing the rewards and ends of organizational loyalty; and *normative* power, by fostering values of obligation and reciprocity within the group, often underpinning union traditions with indigenous cultural practices. A. Etzioni cited by Vecchio (1997: 77).

to directly transplant community structures from elsewhere (Córdova Eguivar 2004: 62). Instead, the coca growers' movement gains much of its cultural capital and identity by defending a traditional Andean cultural practice from persecution by domestic elites and foreign powers – the ritual chewing of the "sacred" coca leaf (Healy 1991: 93–4). This discourse of cultural and identity claims was developed in the 1990s as a strategy to forge alliances outside the coca growers' movement, particularly with the 90% of indigenous–campesinos who do not grow coca, as well as urban-middle-class sectors that are receptive to the defense of coca as a defense of national sovereignty (García Linera 2004: 439).

As land became scarce in the 1990s sindicatos could afford to require more of their members and to impose a strict ethical code of conduct. Members routinely are asked to perform collective work in the community, such as constructing and maintaining infrastructure (Córdova Eguivar 2004: 43, 94–5). The government assault on coca growing, and on the sindicatos themselves, after 1985 intensified feelings of obligation to the sindicato (*Atlas del Trópico de Cochabamba* 2004: 42). This sense of vulnerability was heightened by a 1988 law regulating Coca and Controlled Substances (Law 1008), which criminalized coca cultivation in the Chapare and sought the eventual eradication of the crop (Colanzi 2006: 12; Córdova Eguivar 2004: 52–8; Healy 1991: 90; Lizárraga 1998: 55). Failure to participate in coca federation-sponsored protest activities could result in sanctions, such as fines, community work, or the loss of land (García Linera 2004: 427).

The 2001 national census reported a Chapare population of 108,778 (Censo Nacional de Población Vivienda 2001; Córdova Eguivar 2004: 9). This figure dramatically underestimates the population, owing to the methodology used, the absence of seasonal migrants during the time the survey was taken, as well as the refusal of some independent sindicatos to cooperate with government census takers (Kohl 2001: 77–8; Lizárraga and Villarroel 1998: 18). Other sources estimate that the population hovered around 200,000 inhabitants between 1988 and 1996; after 1996, a reduction in the influx of migrants and some outmigration from the region was balanced by natural increase within the region, resulting in a leveling off of the population and an end to the population boom (*Atlas del Trópico de Cochabamba* 2004: 42). The rapid colonization of the region increased pressure for scant vital services and infrastructure. In the late 1990s there were virtually no basic public services outside the urban centers (Córdova Eguivar 2004: 9; Lizárraga 1998: 54).

In response to the explosion of the Chapare population, the sindicato structure developed into a dense network of four tiers, ranging from the local sindicato to the national organization. Within the cocalero movement the location or scale of decision making depends on the geographic scope of the question or problem considered. If local sindicato members cannot reach consensus on a problem it will be raised to the higher level for consideration. Problems are then considered in open assemblies in which all must deliberate on the outcome. For extremely important decisions, massive assemblies may be held so that representation and deliberation are more direct (Córdova Eguivar 2004: 63).

The number of sindicatos increased from 183, organized into 23 centrals and 2 federations, in 1980 at the beginning of the coca boom; to 773 in 1994, organized into 62 centrals and 5 federations. By the late 1990s, there were at least 892 sindicatos, organized into 85 centrals, and a sixth federation was formed to represent coca growers in Tiraque (Córdova Eguivar 2004: 46–71; Colanzi 2006; García Linera 2004: 456; Healy 1991). At the top of the coca growers' hierarchy is the Coordinating Committee of the Six Federations, formed in 1992 and affiliated with the national peasant organization CSUTCB and the Syndical Confederation of Bolivian Colonists (Confederación Sindical de Colonos Bolivianos, or CSCB). The most powerful federation – the Special Federation of Peasant Workers of the Tropics of Cochabamba (Federación Especial de Trabajadores Campesinos del Trópico de Cochabamba, or FETCTC) – through its leader, Evo Morales, has controlled the Coordinating Committee since its creation. It is based in Villa Tunari (Córdova Eguivar 2004: 62). Local-level sindicatos typically represent between 50 and 80 families (Lizárraga 1998:55). Between the local sindicatos and the federations is an intermediate layer of "centrals," which correspond geographically to a canton or district. Above them, Bolivia's nine departmental peasant federations and the Six Federations of the Tropics are represented in the national organization CSUTCB (Córdova Eguivar 2004; García Linera 2004; Healy 1991; Lizárraga 1998: 55). Several coca federations also are affiliated directly with the CSCB.

The efficiency of the coca growers' organizational structure made the movement a formidable political force. Its union structure and mission facilitates rapid, efficient communication, while the size and configuration of the units of the movement's network facilitates efficient management (*Atlas del Trópico de Cochabamba* 2004: 44). Repressive coca-eradication policies actually strengthened the coca growers as a political movement (Healy 1991: 87). Long-standing confrontation with the Bolivian state made the seizure through elections of municipal government structures in 1995 even more meaningful, but at the same time ambiguous and contentious (Córdova Eguivar 2004: 47).

Women's Parallel Political Activity

In Ecuador women's political activity is integrated into the dominant indigenous organizations. Although this activity is often confined to less-prestigious spheres and women continue to struggle for equal status, great improvements have been made in the last decade. In Bolivia, in contrast, women are confined to separate, subordinate institutions. Women began to participate in the activities of the Six Federations in 1992. They had not been allowed to participate in demonstrations until women organized on their own to defend their communities from drug-eradication forces when their husbands were away. The success of their mobilizations convinced some male leaders that they could be an important resource for the movement, although others resisted their inclusion and continue to do so. At a 1994 assembly of the Six Federations, men accepted a proposal to create a female counterpart (Garza 2005: 46–7). Between 1994 and 1997 most federations formed female counterparts and an umbrella organization for women was established in 1997 (Federation of Female Campesinos of the Tropics [Federación de Mujeres Campesinas del Trópico, or FECAMTROP]). Women's status rose after they organized a 31-day march (December 18, 1995–January 17, 1996) in support of male coca-growing family members, who had been jailed and subjected to physical abuse. The only substantive result was the release of a number of political prisoners, but the women had increased their profile within the male-dominated movement (Córdova Eguivar 2004: 82–3; Quispe 1998; Vargas and Draper 2004: 67–9).

The parallel, gendered structure of the coca growers' movement is derived from Andean indigenous views of social organization and political leadership, in which the married couple serves together in leadership roles. It is purported to maintain harmony and equilibrium between the sexes, human beings and nature, and the heavens and the earth, but this formal parity elides the subordinate position of women within the family and the movement (Arnold 2004). Male and female federations meet jointly at the same time but confer separately to work on their own issues and actions. Women are particularly active in promoting health and education projects, as well as small-scale family-based economic development. Men and women today both actively participate in protest demonstrations (Córdova Eguivar 2004: 68; Garza 2005: 54).

Women's primary impediment to obtaining more influence within the movement is macho–sexist attitudes among male leaders, as well as their lack of education and literacy. Even with spousal support, women remain responsible for the majority of domestic and child-rearing responsibilities, as well as contributing to family income (Garza 2005: 59, 87–9). Lack of land ownership disqualifies them from some leadership positions. An example of the difficulty campesino women militants experience in gaining candidacies is demonstrated by the fact that, in 2005, all of the national indigenous candidates that MAS postulated were men; all of the women on the electoral list – required by the 1997 gender quota law – represented mestizo civil society organizations allied with the party (*La Razón* 2005b).

Coca Growers' Control of Municipal Governments

The ASP gained control of the municipal government in the Chapare after the 1995 municipal elections. This constituted a dramatic shift in relations of power away from urban, light-skinned, economic elites toward rural, upwardly mobile indigenous campesinos. As coca growers filled municipal council seats representing the ASP, they also filled the vigilance committees. This defeated the purpose of the innovative committees, which were intended to hold elected officials accountable. While adapting as much as necessary to the rigid legal structure that the LPP and the laws governing the administration of public funds imposed, the coca growers superimposed their own ways of making decisions and controlling resources on to municipal institutions, subjugating elected authorities to federation mandates (Córdova Eguivar 2004).

An example of the infusion of traditional institutions into local democracy is the selection of candidates, which follows sindicato norms derived from traditional practices in highland sending communities. Each sindicato offers one or several possible candidates, who stand before the assembly. Participants in the assembly line up behind the candidate they support; the candidate with the longest line wins the most prestigious or responsible position, followed by the candidate with the second-longest line, etc. Thus elections are held according to "*filas*" (lines), eliminating the need for counting or numeracy (interview, Eduardo Córdova, August 3, 2005; Córdova Eguivar 2004; Lizárraga 1998: 58). Once in office, campesino leaders continue to follow the political practices of their social-movement organizations, rather than conform to the norms of the formal political system to which they have gained access. For example, in much of the Chapare coca federations arrange preelection pacts that require elected municipal council candidates to resign halfway through their terms in favor of their alternates. Elected simultaneously by law, alternates serve in the event that "titular" councillors cannot. This arrangement deconcentrates political power and provides political experience to a larger cohort of leaders. It reflects a wider practice in rural areas of annually rotating campesino leaders through traditional community and sindicato leadership positions (Gray Molina 2003: 360). These leadership rotation practices also govern the vigilance committees, which in the Chapare mainly represent coca growers' federations.

Learning the complex methodology of participatory planning, reporting, accounting, and participation required by the LPP was difficult in the Chapare. In 1995 and 1996 the Bolivian government, often working through NGOs, sponsored numerous workshops (Córdova Eguivar 2004: 5). As in the rest of Bolivia, rural municipalities were the last to receive training and education, notwithstanding persistent pleas for technical assistance (Cruz 1998: 27). Thus, as they awaited training, the coca growers' representatives often disregarded the legal requirement to develop a five-year PDM or an annual operating plan. Often municipal governments carried out work and then retroactively wrote their annual plan, ignoring both the legal requirement to plan as well as the requirement to use a particular methodology. This led to problems with the national Controlaría, which intervened on a number of occasions in 1999. As a result, MAS governments learned to follow the rules more carefully and to at least appear to facilitate the participation of unaffiliated groups (interview, Eduardo Córdova, Cochabamba, August 3, 2005).

The three case studies of municipal government that follow demonstrate striking similarities in the Chapare owing to similar social, economic, and political conditions. We see few examples of effective mayoral leadership owing to norms that require constant rotation and to the lack of incentive to reach out to political opponents and those of other ethnic groups. Most significantly, the fusion of state and civil society prevents mayors from exercising autonomy vis-à-vis social-movement bases, a feature of effective mayors in Ecuador. This fusion prevents the development of distinct spaces to represent diverse social interests. The coca federation dominates governments and no political force or institution within the municipality is able to hold it accountable, including mayors and council members.

Chimoré

Chimoré is a canton of 15,264 people, 75% of whom live in rural areas. Just over three quarters of the population are indigenous and 82.7% lived in poverty in 2001 – a marked decline from the 94.8% measured in 1992. The majority of the population identify themselves as Quechua (67.6%); 5.1% self-identify as Aymara, and the remainder belong to smaller lowland groups (Medina 2003b: 131). There also are approximately 1200 Yuracaré and 160 Yuqui Indians inhabiting protected indigenous territories that span 360,000 hectares (Censo Nacional de Población y Vivienda 2001, 1992; Herbas Camacho 2000: 33). The economic dynamism of Chimoré gives it an Index of Human Development of 0.615, the highest in the department of Cochabamba, including the capital (Lizárraga and Villarroel 1998: 8). Nevertheless, its remote location has impeded access to public services: 14.66% of the population are illiterate, only 35.5% of inhabitants have access to potable water, 41.7% have access to sewer systems; 58% have access to electricity in their homes, and only 5.8% benefit from sanitation services (Lizárraga and Villarroel 1998: 10).

The dominant civil society organization in Chimoré is the Special Federation of the Tropics of Chimoré (Federación Especial del Trópico de Chimoré, or FETCH), an affiliate of the coca growers' Six Federations. In 1998 it comprised 127 sindicatos organized into 13 centrals (Córdova Eguivar 2004: 61; Quispe 1998: 119). Notwithstanding its dominance, there are diverse other expressions of civil society. In 2000, 68 territorial base organizations were recognized, including 58 campesino communities, 6 neighborhood juntas, 1 indigenous community, and 3 additional unspecified community associations (Herbas Camacho 2000: 84). Chimoré also contains 26 state-sponsored producers' associations, many of which came to be the economic arm of the sindicatos (*Atlas del Trópico de Cochabamba* 2004: 43). Those that remain associated with the government are marginalized from the activities of the coca growers' federation. There also are a few associations devoted to artisan production. Ten urban neighborhood juntas representing 833 members are represented on the vigilance committee. The Civic Committee of Chimoré was active in representing urban and business interests prior to the inception of direct elections and Popular Participation. Since then, however, it has been marginalized owing to the political hegemony of the coca growers' federation and the committee's lack of legal standing under the LPP. It increasingly has devoted itself to resisting the coca growers' political hegemony (Herbas Camacho 2000: 37–8).

Prior to the LPP, political parties chose local government candidates, who mainly represented urban neighborhoods. According to Epifanio Cruz, the first ASP mayor of Chimoré, "this situation has been transformed totally" and sindicatos and neighborhood committees now

determine who competes (my translation; Cruz 1998: 24). The ASP dominated the 1995 municipal elections in Chimoré with almost 70% of the
valid vote, winning an absolute majority (four of five seats) on the municipal council (Cruz 1998: 31). The populist party, Civic Union of Solidarity
(Unión Cívica de Solidaridad, or UCS) elected one councillor, who represented urban residents (Lizárraga and Villarroel 1998: 13). Prior to the
election the federation chose Epifanio Cruz to be its mayoral candidate,
and campesino voters obediently voted for him on election day (Quispe
1998: 119). Winning an absolute majority meant that fellow councillors
could not challenge his position as mayor, as has frequently occurred in
more politically fragmented areas throughout Bolivia. According to Cruz,
this political hegemony facilitated considerable coordination between him
and the municipal council and enviable political stability and continuity
notwithstanding minor objections and problems (1998:31).

Prior to 1995 Chimoré never had had a municipal development plan
and the canton had no resources of its own. Projects had been initiated and completed with difficulty and only in urban areas. There was
neither planning nor participation of the population in the execution
of public works in urban areas. Between 1985 and 1995, with their
own resources sindicatos planned and financed the construction of public
works and organized the requisite compulsory labor. This process of community organization and collective work was transferred to the municipal government when the sindicato leadership assumed office (Cruz
1998: 25).

After the promulgation of the LPP, there was a period of confusion as
urban residents endeavored to organize themselves into the urban neighborhood juntas that were the subjects of the new regime and campesino
leaders sought information about the law. Between the promulgation of
the law in 1994 and the December 1995 elections, Chimoré went through
three changes of mayor and frequent changes in the municipal council as
local actors struggled for power and power shifted from urban to rural
areas. This changed after the national government sponsored workshops
to inform citizens about their rights under the new law and to train
municipal elected leaders and employees in its complex methodology for
planning and decision making. Rural areas like Chimoré were the last to
receive this type of training. As Mayor Cruz recalls, many public works
were implemented during this period in a haphazard, unplanned manner
owing to the mayor's need to attend to exigent demands from coca growers' sindicatos and the confrontational attitude of the vigilance committee
representing them. As a result of increased training, Cruz believes that

after 1996 management was more responsive to the law and constituents (Cruz 1998: 26–7).

Political instability persisted, however, as the coca growers asserted control. After urban-mestizo vigilance committee members accused the municipality of misusing funds, the National Controlaría froze Chimoré's funds for eight months, effectively halting work on all projects scheduled for late 1996 and early 1997. In 1998 the secretary of Hacienda criticized the municipality for failing to distribute funds equitably, a problem that Mayor Cruz attributed in part to errors in the 1992 census, which grossly underestimated the number of rural inhabitants by a factor of four to one. The secretary also urged the municipality to undertake projects at a larger geographic scale because these are more cost effective than smaller projects for numerous communities (Cruz 1998). In its 1998 audit the Controlaría determined that half of the problems had been addressed and that the rest should be corrected by the end of 1998 (Lizárraga and Villarroel 1998: 17).

Conflicts persisted within the local federation as leaders struggled for access to power and federation leaders exerted power over elected officials (Herbas Camacho 2000: 70–1, 81). An ASP councillor representing the urban center was ousted by rival members in 1997. Rural leaders argued that he had proposed too many projects for urban areas. In this first administration the federation forced two municipal councillors to resign because it disapproved of their performance (Lizárraga and Villarroel 1998: 13, 34). Another ASP councillor was forced out in 1998 after being accused of illicit activities related to the coca-eradication law (ibid.).

Conflicts also convulsed the vigilance committee. When the ASP government took office, the establishment of district borders and the institution of the vigilance committee had not been concluded. Before 1998 only urban representatives of mestizo political parties served and these did not understand the law or their own responsibilities (Cruz 1998: 31; Lizárraga and Villarroel 1998: 16). The problem was exacerbated in 1997 when the new center–right ADN national government took over and the urban-mestizo vigilance committee representatives gained support from ADN officials in the prefecture. However, after redistricting occurred in 1998 rural representatives of sindicatos dominated the committee (ibid.).

Another challenge the first ASP administration faced was the demand of every sindicato in the municipality that some project be undertaken in its community. Many were confused by the participatory planning process and believed that they were requesting projects from the central government. This created a dilemma, in that only approximately U.S.

$270,000 were available and there were around 80 campesino communities. The budget of the first five-year development plan was, as a result, inflated far beyond the funds available (Cruz 1998: 28; Herbas Camacho 2000: 86). In response to Mayor Cruz's suggestion that, in order to maximize the utility of available resources, projects be undertaken that benefit a larger number of communities grouped together under a *central*, the independent sindicato leaders demanded their own projects and the right to manage them. This generated conflict among the sindicatos for control of resources and access to municipal influence – notwithstanding the fact that the municipal government consisted of former sindicato and *central* leaders. It was this problem that drew national government criticism in 1998.

Thus Cruz identifies a serious disadvantage of the new regime: It tended to cause divisions within the campesino movement, which prior to the LPP and the arrival of government resources was characterized by considerable unity of action and purpose and the ability to manage and undertake its own projects (1998: 28). The dramatic undercounting of the rural population by government census takers exacerbated the problem (Herbas Camacho 2000: 39, 87).

To address the budget shortfall, Cruz and his team devised a program whereby the municipality would provide most of the funding, but each community wanting to have a project must contribute 5%–10% of the cost – a solution similar to but not as demanding as the 60/40 formula that Mario Conejo devised in Otavalo, Ecuador. The municipality also received a modest amount of funding from national development funds. Another fund, the Program for Alternative Regional Development, devised to encourage coca growers to engage in other economic activities, was inaccessible because the U.S. government refused to work with political parties allied with the coca growers' movement. The ASP municipal government compensated for the scarcity of resources by regularly convening obligatory communal labor events, as Pachakutik mayors have done in Ecuador (Cruz 1998: 29).

During this first administration Chimoré's civil society actors undertook direct relations with the mayor's office and its various technical agencies, circumventing the impotent municipal council (Lizárraga and Villarroel 1998: 15). Within the mayor's office, Lizárraga and Villarroel describe as "notorious" the extent to which public officials were subordinated to the local coca growers' federation (ibid.). Municipal officials provided quarterly written reports to the sindicatos and maintained fluid contacts with campesino communities (Cruz 1998: 31). The mayor distorted the functioning of the formal channels of power by concentrating his control over access to information (Lizárraga and Villarroel 1998: 15). Thus we can see the negative effects when mayors are unable to establish economy from their social base: Nonbase members are excluded and resentful, and government authority is captured and diminished.

In 1999 the MAS won four of five municipal council seats, electing one female councillor. Mayor Cruz was reelected and planning continued much as it had during his first term. In 2004 the MAS again won four of five seats (59.38% of the vote), this time electing a female mayor, campesino indigenous leader Juana Quispe. Quispe had served as executive secretary of the Federation of Women of Chimoré and as secretary of the executive council of the women's branch of the Six Federations (Garza 2005: 49). She was the first woman elected mayor in the Chapare. Nevertheless, a group of male campesino leaders and elected councillors linked to the former mayor refused to accept her victory and through psychological and physical pressure prevented her from taking office. Her candidacy, they argued, was imposed from national MAS leaders – no doubt to break the total male domination of government in the Chapare – and thus illegitimate (confidential interviews, La Paz, Cochabamba, 2005). The Bolivian Association of Female Councillors (Asociación de Concejalas de Bolivia, or ACOBOL) denounced this attack on a legitimately elected female mayor and accused the attackers of wishing to perpetuate a regime that had been subject to questions (*Opinión* 2005: 2.2). A spokesperson for the group concluded that "what happened with the Mayor of Chimoré is an unlucky precedent for municipal democracy in Bolivia, that adds to a series of acts through which female mayors and councillors are accosted physically, psychologically and politically within the deplorable practices of political assault by reason of gender" (my translation; ibid.).

Villa Tunari

The Villa Tunari municipal government undertook its own census in 1996 and reported a population of 81,136, significantly higher than the 2001 census estimate of 53,996 (Kohl 2001: 92). Of the population, 87% are indigenous, and the vast majority identify themselves as Quechua (80.7%); 3.8% are Aymara migrants, and the remainder belong to one of the lowland indigenous groups (Medina 2003b: 131). The canton's geographic expanse (21,700 square kilometers) makes it the largest municipality in the department (*Atlas del Trópico de Cochabamba* 2004: 64).

Economic indicators are similar to those elsewhere in the Chapare. 87.2% of the population lived in poverty in 2001, a decline from 96.8% in 1992. 91.65% of the population lives in rural areas (Censo Nacional de Población y Vivienda 2001). Because of its proximity to the capitol – a four-hour drive – Villa Tunari enjoys a lively tourist economy and is considered "the economic and social capitol of Chapare" (Colanzi 2006: 13). It contains the Isiboro Securé National Park, a legally recognized indigenous territory, which is the site of confrontation between coca growers wishing to expand their frontier and the Indians who trace their ancestry to this territory. In addition, important natural gas reserves have been discovered in the park, which by law belong to the state. A final source of conflict is the disputed frontier between Cochabamba and the department of Beni (Kohl 2001: 93).

Two coca growers' federations represent Villa Tunari: the Chapare's dominant federation, FETCTC and the Special Federation of the Yungas of the Chapare (Federación Especial de los Yungas del Chapare, or FEYCH). Together these represent 266 sindicatos and 46 centrals that report (ambiguously) to both federations (Córdova Eguivar 2004: 61). In addition, members of both federations also may belong to one of 71 producer associations (*Atlas del Trópico de Cochabamba* 2004: 39).

In 1995 the ASP won four of seven municipal council seats and elected Mayor Felipe Cáceres. The UCS, MBL, and MNR each elected one councillor. With the exception of the titular councillor representing UCS, all titular and alternate councillors elected were men (Ministerio de Desarrollo Humano 1996: 81). Under the terms of an agreement common to ASP municipalities, halfway through their term the titular councillors resigned in favor of their alternates (Lizárraga and Villarroel 1998: 34).

The ASP government hired a NGO named CIDES to undertake its first five-year municipal development plan. The NGO director, Oscar Coca, has ties to the coca growers' party and later served as a MAS municipal councillor in Cochabamba's capital. At the same time that he directed the municipal planning process, Coca served as an adviser to the coca growers' federation – an example of the lack of a clear distinction between the government and civil society organizations in the Chapare. CIDES achieved a "significant involvement" of the sindicato leaders and members, resulting in a more successful than average diagnostic process owing to "the presence of a unified and sophisticated cocalero sindicato" (Kohl 2001: 94). Kohl also attributes the relative success of the planning process to the availability of qualified professionals to assist the municipality and the funds to pay them. As elsewhere in the Chapare, noncoca growers report being excluded from the planning and budgeting process and bemoan the lack of investment of resources in urban areas (ibid.).

After the 1998 split within the ASP, Mayor Cáceres and the bulk of the coca growers switched their affiliation to Morales and his IPSP. Cáceres was reelected in 1999, when the IPSP won six of seven municipal seats, one of which went to a female campesino leader. The seventh seat went to the MNR (CNE 2005). Although Cáceres is considered one of the more successful MAS mayors, owing to the economic development he fostered, the relative political stability of his administration, and the absence of corruption charges, some criticized his authoritarian behavior. According to one informant from the NGO sector, he was not receptive to new ideas and enjoyed wielding absolute power (confidential interviews, 2005).

In 2004, with 87% of the vote the MAS elected all nine municipal councillors in an expanded district. Two councillors were female. Five other political parties competed in these elections, but the second-closest competitor (National Unity [Unidad Nacional, or UN]) won only 4.85% of the vote (CNE 2005; www.cne.org.bo). A new mayor took over from Cáceres – Feliciano Mamani. Despite a history of confrontation with the Bolivian government and U.S. agents, in 2005 Mayor Mamani welcomed international aid for development projects and called blockades that had obstructed transportation in the municipality a thing of the past. International aid – including investments by USAID – enabled the mayor to build a maternity hospital and two bridges that assist local farmers in getting products to market (*La Razón* 2005e).

Villa Tunari has smoothly implemented the popular participation regime owing to relative political unity within the coca growers' movement and their complete dominance of the government and vigilance committee. Villa Tunari has not witnessed the intense battles between coca growers and their political opponents, or within the coca-growing movement, seen elsewhere, particularly in Puerto Villarroel. It also benefits from a more dynamic and diversified economy, which has reduced conflict over state resources.

Puerto Villarroel

The 2001 census lists the population of Puerto Villarroel at 39,518, although Lizárraga and Villarroel argue that the population is closer to 50,000 if one includes the floating population that migrates seasonally between Puerto Villarroel and other areas of the tropics (1998: 18). 82.96% of residents are indigenous. Just under 80% self-identify as Quechua; 3.2% are Aymara, and the remainder belong to lowland groups (Medina 2003b: 131). The traditional capitol, also called Puerto Villarroel, is a port on the Río Ichilo that hosts a naval base (Córdova Eguivar 2004: 5). Of the population, 81.7% lived in poverty in 2001, a sharp decline from 94.9% in 1992; 83.89% of the population live in rural areas (Censo Nacional de Población y Vivienda 2001; Córdova Eguivar 2004: 6).

The coca growers' federation corresponding to Puerto Villarroel is the Syndical Federation of Colonists of Tropical Carrasco (Federación Sindical de Colonizadores de Carrasco Tropical, or FSCCT), established in 1984. It represents approximately 6790 families belonging to 365 sindicatos, which are grouped into 31 centrals (Córdova Eguivar 2004: 61, 64). Puerto Villarroel also contains 82 producers' associations, whose membership overlaps that of the federation (based on 2001 data, *Atlas del Trópico de Cochabamba* 2004: 39). In addition to the federation there are 286 recognized territorial base organizations (Organizaciónes Territoriales de Base, or OTBs) in Puerto Villarroel, including urban neighborhood juntas (17) and economic organizations (2) (Córdova Eguivar 2004: 6). The major opposition to the coca growers and affiliated peasants and transportation workers is the eastern, nonindigenous population settled around the town of Puerto Villarroel. Other important social and political actors in Puerto Villarroel are the Bolivian Navy, a state-run oil company, the urban-based Civic Committee, the Catholic Church, and the National Road Service (Córdova Eguivar 2004: 8, 196; Lizárraga and Villarroel 1998: 25).

In 1995 the ASP won 58.69% of the vote, electing the mayor and four of five municipal councillors. Previously all local officials had represented elites from the capitol. The federation chose the ASP candidates: Each central, corresponding to the four cantons in the municipality, designated its own candidates for the municipal council, all of whom had to have performed a leadership role in the federation and served in the top leadership position in their centrals (Córdova Eguivar 2004: 161). This requirement, as well as a land-ownership requirement, eliminated female candidates, as women typically are relegated to their own auxiliary organizations.[2] In

---

[2] As in Chimoré, sindicato members stand behind the candidate that they support; the candidate with the longest line behind him or her is chosen for the most prestigious position, and secondary and tertiary positions are awarded to candidates in correspondingly shorter lines. The same method is used to select the top positions in the campesino organization (interview, Eduardo Cordova 2005; Lizárraga and Villarroel 1998: 35–6).

contrast to the open, "fila" method used to choose municipal candidates and federation leaders, the executive board of the federation that dominates Puerto Villarroel is elected by secret vote among delegates from each affiliated sindicato, with the number of delegates corresponding to the number of members in each sindicato. In addition, three delegates from each central participate in the secret election. Again, the requirements that all candidates for these top positions own a parcel of land and have served as secretary general of their central exclude women (Lizárraga and Villarroel 1998: 43).

The municipal council and mayor elected in 1995 all represented the coca growers' federation, with the exception of the councillor representing the urban population of Puerto Villarroel. He represented the populist party UCS, which had won 16.89% of the vote (Herbas and Lizárraga 2001: 43). The mayor elected was Guido Tarqui, a former miner (Córdova Eguivar 2004: 4, 162–3; interview, Eduardo Córdova, 2005). Because the mayor attracted more than 50% of the vote, he was elected "directly" rather than by vote of municipal council members. Thus, *technically*, he could be removed only in the case of serious legal infractions.

As in Chimoré and Villa Tunari, the first participatory planning experience in Puerto Villarroel took place before the Bolivian government's participatory planning methodology had taken on its rigid structure. The local government worked with the federation in a series of meetings that sindicato leaders hosted in each community. At these meetings colonists formulated demands to present to the municipal government. Córdova reports that federation leaders considered this participatory planning activity to be one of the most important events in its history. Representatives of the campesino sindicatos, urban neighborhood juntas, the federation, and diverse NGOs participated in the process, primarily by presenting demands for public works in their communities. NGOs and technical advisers from the prefect's office provided technical support. The local civic committee mainly observed the process and made suggestions with regard to the plan as it was taking shape (Lizárraga and Villarroel 1998: 45–6). In practice, in response to pressure from the federation, the municipal government did not always execute the projects in the plan, as required by law. This gave the Civic Committee grounds to try to oust the mayor. But these efforts were fruitless, owing to the broad political support Mayor Tarqui enjoyed with the federation (Córdova Eguivar 2004; Lizárraga and Villarroel 1998: 46).

In implementing the plan, the municipality divided resources among its four cantons according to population. The main sources of resources are the national coparticipation funds, which are supplemented by resources within the municipality acquired through various taxes and royalties for economic activities. Beneficiaries of municipal spending also contribute a significant amount, in some cases rising to 25% of the cost of a project. The municipality did not benefit much from external resources because the requirements for access to national development funds are difficult to fulfill, and because the municipality's involvement in the illegal drug trade distanced it from many international donors (Córdova Eguivar 2004: 190–1).

The 1998 split within the national campesino movement had severe repercussions in Puerto Villarroel. Some sindicato and central leaders stayed with Alejo Véliz while others sided with Evo Morales (Córdova Eguivar 2004: 91). This was less of a problem in Villa Tunari and Chimoré because the campesino federations there overwhelmingly supported Morales (Herbas and Lizárraga 2001: 47). The ASP president of the municipal council, Valentín Gutiérrez, left in 1997 to serve as an alternate for Morales in Congress. Gutiérrez and the newly elected mayor, Tarqui, were both allies of Véliz. After the ASP expelled Morales, Mayor Tarqui remained with the ASP, while the federation supported Morales. After the split between Véliz and Morales the vigilance committee and the mayor were enemies. The committee accused the mayor of stealing from the municipality, incompetence, and favoritism (Córdova Eguivar 2004).

After the split, three municipal councillors sided with Véliz while their alternates supported Morales. Although, as elsewhere in the Chapare, those elected in 1995 had promised to resign in the middle of their term, Véliz's allies refused. During this dispute, the vigilance committee, representing the sindicatos directly, seized control of the planning process but Mayor Tarqui and the municipal council refused to approve their plan without changes (Córdova Eguivar 2004: 185–7). In March 1999 the federation decided to remove the titular councilors and to accuse the mayor of misusing municipal funds. It forced out the elected councillors by using Morales' allies on the council to convene meetings in remote locations that were impossible for the Véliz-allied councillors to attend. The latter were removed on April 5 for absenteeism and their alternates replaced them. The federation produced the letters of resignation that all the ASP councillors had signed when the federation nominated them to run for local office (interview, Córdova, August 3, 2005; Córdova Eguivar 2004; Herbas and Lizárraga 2001).

These blatant illegal maneuvers prompted national intervention in the absence of local countervailing power. Mayor Tarqui recouped his office after a March 17, 1999, Constitutional Court ruling, as did two of the other ousted council members in a separate April 27 ruling. But the federation ignored these rulings. During 1999, two parallel councils with two different mayors (Tarqui and Morales ally Rosendo Mita) convened meetings: the titular councillors in the traditional urban center of Puerto Villarroel, and the rival MAS-linked council in the coca growers' headquarters in Ivirgarzama (Córdova Eguivar 2004; Herbas and Lizárraga 2001). As the confrontation escalated, the FSCCT imposed sanctions that campesino organizations customarily employ to punish contempt for sindicato authority – physical aggression and humiliation, such as dressing the offending person in a skirt, and ritual whipping with a stick tipped with nettles – and refused to pay the ousted councillors (Córdova Eguivar 2004: 203; Herbas and Lizárraga 2001: 46).

The situation persisted until the December 1999 elections owing to the intransigence of both factions and the involvement of Morales and Véliz, who tended to radicalize the problem (Córdova Eguivar 2004: 199–203; Herbas and Lizárraga 2001: 45–9). The federation was unable to resolve the dispute and the functioning of the municipality suffered. As Herbas and Lizárraga explain, these conflicts absorbed the government's attention, in detriment to the needs of the population, whose demands went unattended. In the absence of clear government authority, the mayor's office followed the federation's demands and pressured dissident councillors to resign. Opposing politicians' dogged pursuit of political power prevented the resolution of the conflict (2001: 50). Córdova Eguivar concludes, based on his intensive study of the 1995–1999 period, that while the federation claimed to be learning to adapt to new municipal norms, they were instead adapting formal municipal norms to federation norms and procedures. The result was a mutual accommodation of cocalero/sindicato norms with the new regime of Popular Participation (2004: 12). Thus, despite the relative rigidity of the participatory planning legal framework, the manner in which the annual operating plan was formulated varied considerably from year to year as participants gained more knowledge about the process and as power shifted among the social sectors and political factions (ibid.).

In 1999 the IPSP won 41.3% of the vote and elected three of five municipal councillors, including one woman. The MIR and the MNR each won one seat, with 16.85% and 11.26% of the vote, respectively (Córdova Eguivar 2004: 203). The ASP, running under the registration of the PCB, won only 4.3% of the vote. Thereafter, the political hegemony of Morales' faction was complete, but conflict continued. In 2001, after years of political and legal maneuvers, physical attacks and threats of violence against municipal authorities based in Puerto Villarroel, and several blockades of the road between the two urban centers, the federation moved the capitol from Puerto Villarroel to Ivirgarzama, in the municipality's geographic center, near the highway linking Cochabamba and Santa Cruz. This was more convenient for coca growers, who frequently come to town on errands (Córdova Eguivar 2004: 204–17).

In 2004 the MAS won 78.66% of the vote, electing Felix Acosta Vázquez and earning the party six municipal council seats in an expanded seven-seat district. A citizens' group won the remaining seat (www.cne.org.bo). The MAS takeover of power was complete.

Improvements in Democratic Quality in the Chapare

The Chapare municipalities under MAS control underwent a dramatic shift in power away from a small economic elite and toward the majority-indigenous population. Local government was infused with cultural norms promoting solidarity and dedication to the common good. The allocation of development resources was redirected toward poor, rural communities that had seen little state attention. Indigenous citizens – mostly men – had the opportunity to serve in public office for the first time. The preexistence of strong networks of sindicatos facilitated comprehensive diagnostics of development needs and the formulation of annual and five-year budget priorities.

After a few years of adapting to the complex new regime, in Chimoré and Villa Tunari MAS municipal governments worked in harmony with civil society organizations to promote long-awaited economic and social development projects. In Puerto Villarroel, in contrast, a high degree of internal, factional conflict within the coca growers' movement, as well as urban–rural conflict, increased political instability and reduced the ability of new municipal institutions to function. The winner of the conflict monopolized political power, leaving losers excluded (Córdova Eguivar 2004).

Five problems permeate the three cases studied here, and these dramatically reduce the quality of democracy in the Chapare. First, the MAS had established a form of single-party rule that is incompatible with democracy. Coca federation leaders have prioritized group solidarity, unity, and power at the expense of equality and pluralism (Merkl 2007: 343). One result is the persistent political marginalization of groups unaffiliated with the coca growers. In Chimoré, for example, native indigenous groups, who have the added burden of being located on the border with other municipalities and far from the government center, are routinely excluded (Herbas Camacho 2000: 34). In Puerto Villarroel the Yuquí Indians complain that no spending occurs in their areas (Córdova Eguivar 2004: 213). Colonists and NGOs associated with the national government's Alternative Development Program are excluded for having accepted government assistance in the past. Even more excluded from participatory planning are private-sector interests, such as enterprises producing tea, hearts of palm, and bananas for the national and international markets (Herbas Camacho 2000: 89–91).

Second, MAS militants commonly resort to authoritarian means to assert their domination. Dissidents are routinely coerced into submission or expelled. In Puerto Villarroel, dissident factions were removed through extralegal means and beaten. Opponents also were threatened and beaten. In 2001 MAS municipal councillor Cristóbal Cáceres was accused of beating a fellow councillor representing the MIR party in the Cochabamba municipality of Morochata. Nearby residents did not dare intervene (*Los Tiempos* 2001: D2.2). This behavior extends beyond the Chapare to the department capitol. In January 2007 MAS militants, demanding the resignation of the departmental prefect, burned down his office, blocked roads into the department to prevent his return, and engaged in violent confrontations that left two dead and hundreds injured. Eighteen militants established a "revolutionary departmental government" and occupied the central plaza for more than a week (*Latin American Weekly Report* 2007: 1–2). The MAS national government has yet to hold the instigators of violence accountable.

The third major problem is the lack of balance between state and civil society actors in the new budgeting and planning institutions. Coca growers' federations dominate municipal government officials and the vigilance committees. These government representatives understand, and are often reminded, that they gained their offices with the support of the cocalero sindicatos (Córdova Eguivar 2004: 172–3). The federations are so powerful relative to municipal institutions that they can sanction municipal officials and the vigilance committee for failing to follow federation instructions or comply with promises. They can freeze municipal spending on projects that are not going according to federation guidelines and receive funding for projects not envisioned in the annual operating plan. This practice is consistent throughout the Chapare and is derived from the original intent of the movement to create a political party that would act as the movement's subservient instrument.

Thus local federations formally are in charge of party activities and, by extension, party members in office (García Linera 2004: 432). In Puerto Villarroel, interim Mayor Rosendo Mita, who served after Mayor Tarqui was expelled, exemplified the submissive attitude of public employees in the face of federation pressure. In a 1999 interview, Mita told Eduardo Córdova that the federation, which controlled 70% of council seats, had put him in office; he must therefore obey its commands and coordinate with sindicato, central, and federation leaders (Córdova Eguivar 2004: 198).

Fourth, planning was derailed in favor of "urgent" demands coming from the federation, leading to the failure to complete a number of infrastructure projects when their funding ran out. Thus municipal authorities have the choice of fulfilling the demands of the federation or complying with legal requirements (Córdova Eguivar 2004: 218). Citizens are partly to blame because they poorly understand the role of elected officials and their relationship to social-movement hierarchies. They typically expect campesino leaders to represent campesino interests exclusively after entering elected office and to exclude the movement's enemies from access to power and resources (Lizárraga and Villarroel 1998: 7).

Finally, the record of Chapare municipalities with respect to gender equity is abysmal. As in the highlands, the establishment of separate organizations effectively excludes women from municipal government. Despite the legal requirement of gender quotas on municipal council lists, male campesino leaders effectively exclude women by placing them in low positions and harass and intimidate them if they are elected.

LA PAZ

La Paz is the country's most populous department (2,350,466) and one of the two most indigenous (77.5%). Although there is economic dynamism in the capitol city, the rural areas of the department, where the MIP gained mayors' offices in 2004, are markedly more impoverished and less economically dynamic than either urban areas of the department or the rural bastions of the MAS Chapare of Cochabamba. These high-altitude plateaus are dry and poorly suited to agriculture and unintegrated into major trading networks. Although poverty in the department stood approximately at the national average in 1992, poverty has declined at a far slower rate than the national average. In some rural areas of La Paz poverty has increased. La Paz is the country's most-rural department (*Participación popular y municipio* 1996: 13). La Paz's rural municipalities

TABLE 6.2. *Party-System Fragmentation on Bolivian Municipal Councils after the 1995 and 1999 Elections*

Parties on Council		% 1995	% 1999
1.1.1.1.1	No absolute majority	15	15
2.1.1.1	No absolute majority	43	37
2.2.1	No absolute majority	17	21
3.1.1	Absolute majority versus 2	10	15
3.2	Absolute majority versus one	12	7
4.1	Absolute majority versus one	3	4
1	Absolute majority	–	1
Total 269		100	100

Source: Xavier Albó and Víctor Quispe, *Quiénes son indígenas en los gobiernos municipales,* Cuadernos de Investigación 59 (La Paz: CIPCA, 2004), 131.

face more serious socioeconomic problems and, owing to the sparse population of rural towns, have relatively fewer resources to address them.

La Paz's political terrain differs from Cochabamba's as dramatically as their distinctive geography. In contrast to the overwhelming hegemony of one party in the Chapare, in the comparably indigenous *altiplano* (highlands) of La Paz extreme partisan fragmentation marks municipal politics. After the 1995 and 1999 elections La Paz's municipal councils were the most fragmented in the country: Approximately 80% lacked a party with an absolute majority, compared with the national average of 75% in 1995 and 73% in 1999. In contrast, in Cochabamba 69.2% of municipalities lacked a majority (Albó and Quispe 2004: 131). Albó and Quispe argue that Bolivia's most fragmented departments (La Paz and Oruro) have closer ties to the large cities of La Paz and El Alto, where rural citizens migrate regularly, causing the volatile partisan competition there to influence rural politics (2004: 132). Bolivia's least-politically fragmented departments – Tarija, Beni, and Pando – have the lowest level of ethnic diversity and are furthest from the large cities. Thus moderately high levels of indigenous population combined with the proximity of a major city appear to generate higher levels of party-system fragmentation and competition (Albó and Quispe 2004: 133). Table 6.2 reproduces findings concerning party-system fragmentation on five-member municipal councils throughout Bolivia after the 1995 and 1999 elections. Five-member councils made up a significant majority of those then in existence.

Party-system fragmentation increased in 2004 after indigenous peoples were allowed to compete independently of parties – including the MAS and MIP, with which many communities had run in 1999. In La Paz in

2004 on average 9.36 distinct political vehicles – parties, citizens' groups, and indigenous peoples combined – competed in each municipal election. On average, 6.42 political vehicles earned at least 5% of the vote in those elections, whereas in Cochabamba 4.51 political vehicles exceeded the 5% threshold. My La Paz cases are particularly striking with respect to their degree of political fragmentation. In the 2004 race in Achacachi, 11 political parties and 6 citizens' groups and indigenous peoples competed for 11 council seats. In Ayo Ayo, nine political parties competed for five. Another way of appreciating the higher level of fragmentation is to look at the percentage of the vote received by the first-place party. Nationally, the hegemony of the MAS in its areas of dominance is clear. The party won more absolute majorities in the 2004 elections than any other party (21), compared with 6 for the MNR, its closest competitor. Ten of these majorities were secured in Cochabamba, and only one in La Paz. Thirteen of Cochabamba's municipalities elected mayors by absolute majority in 2005, whereas only four of La Paz's more-numerous municipalities directly elected their mayor (*La Prensa* 2004: 4).[3]

Greater political fragmentation in La Paz compared with Cochabamba implies not only weaker support for executives and greater political struggle within municipalities for access to resources and power, but also greater political instability, since councils have the power to remove the mayor every year. Competition for municipal power (as opposed to the hegemonic dominance of one vehicle) might promote political pluralism. However, under conditions of extreme fragmentation, political battles are essentially personal. In rural La Paz municipalities only a few hundred votes may be cast and politics is essentially a struggle among individuals seeking to maximize scant economic opportunities. Partisan fragmentation also reflects a long history of factionalism within the peasant and leftist movements.

In the altiplano, indigenous electoral vehicles – both parties and the social-movement organizations that have been allowed to compete since 2004 – confront what Panebianco calls a "complex" electoral arena: All of them face numerous competitors for the same indigenous electorate. The existence of numerous *competitors* presents more of a strain than the existence of electoral *opponents* representing distinct potential voters. Electoral *competitors* generate greater electoral uncertainty and result in crises of identity because indigenous parties are unable to credibly claim the legitimate right to lead the entire indigenous population. Moreover,

---

[3] Author's calculations from results published in CNE (2005).

as the party is unable to provide "collective incentives," the credibility of the leadership is placed in doubt. Disagreement within the party over how to deal with the crisis generates internal divisions and leadership instability (Panebianco 1988: 211). Complex, turbulent electoral arenas are particularly difficult for weakly institutionalized parties, such as those studied here (ibid.: 208). Despite these challenges, indigenous parties can often rely on strong networks of civil society support. In the predominantly Aymara altiplano, communities typically are organized around a campesino union or sindicato dating back more than 50 years. These are similar to the sindicatos in the Chapare and are linked to the same national campesino confederation, CSUTCB. But in the altiplano, the sindicato system overlaps a parallel authority system based on cultural traditions dating to the Inca era and tied to territories called allyus.

The basic unit of politics in the allyus is the adult couple. Only married people are considered to be full persons and thus eligible to perform leadership roles, although in the absence of a spouse, the mother/father or sister/brother may perform his or her role (Arnold 2004 35; López 2003: 88–9; Medina 2003a: 17). This principle is called *chachawarmi* (man–woman). As Arnold observes, male leaders often use this vision of gender harmony "to disguise regional or local practices" that exclude and subordinate women (2004: 35). As in other rural areas of Bolivia, women's political rights are restricted by their lower levels of literacy and access to identity documents. As in the Chapare, a system of dual organization formally recognizes women's political rights but in practice subordinates them and their organizations to auxiliary status.[4] Couples progress through a system of *cargos* of increasing responsibility and prestige, which rotate annually, except for the highest leadership positions, which may last several years. Leadership rotation coincides with the rotation of the earth and the rotation of fields to allow some to rest. It ensures that no individual or family, notwithstanding resources or prestige, can dominate others. Rotating social responsibility and the use of natural resources is meant to reinforce a link between human society and the natural world. Thus the ayllu serves a spiritual function in which religious ceremonies reinforce political authority and social ties[5] (Arnold 2004: 35; Medina 2003a: 17).

---

[4] According to the 2001 census, 55.5% of women lack identity documents, compared with 52.9% of men (Arnold 2004: 79).

[5] Aymara migrants to the megacities of La Paz and El Alto preserve the principle of leadership rotation in their urban neighborhoods. For example, the politically powerful Federation of Neighborhood Juntas (Federación de Juntas Vecinales, or FEJUVE) has employed

The most important unit of Aymara sociopolitical organization is the *allyu*, a discontinuous territory in which families related through kinship undertake productive activities at different ecological levels. Ayllus contain varying numbers of communities and are joined together in a *marka* (Arnold 2004: 48–9). Ayllu organization traditionally is rooted in the values of reciprocity, equilibrium, consensus, and complementarity, expressed through social and economic cooperation. Families earn a subsistence through their own efforts and through cooperation with neighbors in interfamily economic exchanges. This cooperation is crucial because, compared with the economically dynamic Chapare, there is little economic potential in the cold, dry altiplano. Ayllus cooperate with each other and their marka to promote integrated development across ecological zones. The prestige and dignity of an individual and his or her family depend on willing participation in community service obligations. Authorities may sanction transgressions (Medina 2003a: 17; López 2003: 86–8).

Aymara communities choose their municipal-government candidates according to local traditions for leadership selection and rotation. In some cases these have been modified to adjust to the new municipal regime and to conflicts that partisan competition generates. For example, for the 2004 elections, the municipality of Jesús de Machaca, an Aymara community of 13,535 people, divided its 24 allyus into five equal parts so that each could choose its own mayoral candidate. In grand assemblies, each community proposed a candidate and expressed his merits. Several rounds of discussion achieved consensus on a subset of candidates. Where none could be reached, participants lined up behind their preference – the same fila comunitaria used in the Chapare.

The selection process was repeated at the allyu level. In a Gran Cabildo held in the central plaza in August, prior to the December elections, the maximum leaders of each allyu assembled with their wives in the plaza. Representatives of each of the five territorial groups gave a report of their elections and introduced their candidate. After a lengthy discussion of their relative merits, the mallkus lined up behind the candidate that would be the municipality's choice for mayor and his/her alternate. Under the system agreed in August 2004, each of the five territories will have an opportunity to have their own candidate as mayor, rotating terms among them. In addition, as in the Chapare, the titular mayor and councillors

since 2002 a system of leadership rotation that regularly rotates the top offices among geographic units of the federation (Arnold 2004: 53).

agreed to exercise their elected positions for 2–1/2 years and then to resign in favor of their alternates, reinforcing the system of rotation of power. Whereas in other municipalities candidates began to campaign for the December elections, in Jesús de Machaca the preelected mayor and his alternate visited communities and consulted with leaders (Arnold 2004: 52–3; *Construyendo* 2004: 4–5).

In addition to facilitating leadership rotation and geographic and political equilibrium, the Jesús de Machaca system, which has received recognition from the National Electoral Court, ensures complete transparency because deliberations are public (Arnold 2004: 52–3; *Construyendo* 2004: 4–5). The system eliminates the role of political parties in order to preserve the unity of the municipality and the allyus and to avoid the extreme fragmentation and conflict that have convulsed other towns in the altiplano. It was specifically instituted to avoid the partisan divisions that might occur should the candidate of the MAS or the MNR gain office and exclude the losers, a possibility of great concern to indigenous authorities. In particular, the municipality's allyu organization, Markas, Ayllus and Original Communities of Jesús de Machaca (Marka, Ayllus y Comunidades Originarias de Jesús de Machaca, or MACOJMA) asserted its authority over the electoral process as a bulwark against the rising political influence of the MAS in the altiplano. MACOJMA deems the MAS political presence to be illegitimate owing to its lack of origin in cultural traditions. In contrast, in neighboring San Andrés de Machaca, 14 political parties and citizens' groups competed in 2004. The attitude of MACOJMA toward political parties reflects the point of view of the larger allyu reconstruction movement (Arnold 2004: 52–9). Rejecting political parties serves the interests of traditional authorities struggling to gain power over their rivals from Western campesino organizations and political parties – especially the MAS.

The political fragmentation, the presence of entrenched rival parties, and competition with allyu-based social organizations presents a distinct political environment for the MAS. Conflicts within municipalities in La Paz revolve less around rural–urban and indigenous–mestizo divides, as in the Chapare, and more around partisan and personal differences, reflecting divisions within the highland campesino movement. They also reflect the tension between the system of campesino organizations and the allyu organizations, which tend to overlap geographically. The intensity of conflicts may also be attributable to the greater poverty and economic stagnation of the altiplano and thus fiercer competition over scarce public resources. The two towns studied exhibit these challenges and conflicts.

They are the only two municipalities in which the MIP elected a mayor in 2004.

Achacachi

Achacachi is the bastion of MIP leader Felipe Quispe's support. When the author observed the 2002 national elections here for the Organization of American States, support for "El Mallku" was palpable. As each ballot was opened and read publicly, Quispe's honorific title was shouted in place of his name. Achacachi has a well-earned reputation for combativeness and the forced expulsion of state authorities, even apart from contemporary actions instigated by Quispe and his supporters. The canton's population of 70,503 persons is 93.11% indigenous, virtually all of whom are Aymara. Poverty levels of 93.3% were reported both in 1992 and 2001, demonstrating nil progress. Achacachi is predominantly rural (89.31%), desolate, and dry (Censo Nacional de Población y Vivienda 2001).

None of the indigenous parties studied here competed in Achacachi in 1995. That year Conscience of the Fatherland (Conciencia de Patria, or CONDEPA), a party with a large urban Aymara following, elected the mayor (Juan Pérez) and an additional municipal councillor. The MNR, Tupaj Katari Revolutionary Liberation Movement[6] (Movimiento Revolucionario Tupaj Katari de Liberación, or MRTKL), and MIR each elected an additional councillor to the five-member council. All 10 titular and alternate candidates elected were men (Ministerio de Desarrollo Humano 1996). Peasant candidates represented diverse clientelist and leftist parties. In the 1999 elections the municipality's now-nine council seats were divided among seven clientelist and leftist parties. The center–left MIR won three of the nine seats and three of the nine total seats went to women. The MIP first competed in municipal elections in 2004. It finished first with 30.22% of the vote, corresponding to five council seats and providing a rare partisan majority. Three political parties each won a single seat (including the MAS), as did a new citizens' grouping. Nine additional parties competed for seats but did not win, demonstrating continued extreme political fragmentation in Achacachi despite the emergence of a native-son party. No municipal councillor elected in 2004 was female. Men in Achacachi harassed female councillors elected in 1999,

---

[6] This campesino-movement-based party was founded by Aymara intellectual Víctor Hugo Cárdenas. It cogoverned between 1993 and 1997 with the MNR.

which discouraged women from seeking office (confidential interviews 2005).

Ayo Ayo

Ayo Ayo is a tiny canton of 6981 people, 90.79% of whom are indigenous, virtually all Aymara. In 2001, 99.3% of the population lived in poverty, representing an *increase* in the level of poverty measured in 1992 (98.9%). The entire indigenous population lives in rural areas (Censo Nacional de Población y Vivienda 2001). In fact, the urban center consists simply of a small plaza surrounded by primitive buildings.

In the 1995 elections CONDEPA finished first, and elected Mayor René Illanes. The MNR, UCS, MRTKL, and ADN-PDC (Christian Democratic Party [Partido Demócrata Cristiano]) each elected a councillor. All 10 titular and alternate candidates elected were men (Ministerio de Desarrollo Humano 1996). In 1999 four parties split five municipal seats, with the populist New Republican Force (Nueva Fuerza Republicana, or NFR) winning two seats and electing Mayor Benjamin Altamirano. Altamirano was lynched in June 2004 by a mob of residents who accused him of corruption (*La Razón* 2004a). Militants of the rival MST later were accused of instigating the crime. After the violence, the Controlaría froze the municipality's coparticipation funds. It is important to remember that opposition factions frequently use (often unfounded) accusations of corruption to destabilize opponents.

In 2004 the tradition of political fragmentation continued. Five parties gained seats contested by nine parties or citizens' groups. The MIP won 20.22% of the vote and elected Mayor Gabriel Calle Condori. The MAS won the fifth seat with 12.83% of the vote (www.cne.org.bo). When I visited in July 2005 there were two MIP council members, including one woman. The MIP mayor and councillor have formed an alliance with councillors from two other parties, leaving the MAS and another councillor in the opposition. The government had opened its offices only in July, after the Controlaría unfroze the municipality's accounts (confidential interview with councillor, Ayo Ayo, July 28, 2005).

According to Mayor Condori, assemblies are held every two weeks in which the municipal council, the mayor, and his advisors meet with civil society organizations. These consist of representatives from the two principal local organizations, one indigenous (*originario*) that corresponds to the allyu movement, and the local affiliate of the national campesino organization CSUTCB (interview, Ayo Ayo, July 28, 2005). A councillor confidentially concurs that there is a great deal of transparency with respect to how money is spent and consultation with civil society organizations:

We always see who is taking out money, how much they are taking. Each Thursday there is a session of the authorities and civil society always is informed how the money is being spent. The sessions are open to the public and civil society representatives are always there. The money is shared equitably among all of the communities. Each community gets its share. (My translation; interview, Ayo Ayo, July 28, 2005.)

Improvements in Democratic Quality in La Paz

The institutional innovations brought by the new popular participation regime have had little impact on democratic quality in the municipalities studied. These towns are so poor, rural, and predominantly indigenous that there was not much of an economic elite for indigenous communities to displace. As they did before the arrival of indigenous parties, ambitious men seek to represent whatever political party will run them for office because this is one of the only means of gaining salaried employment. Because all of these aspirants represent the same cultural and social milieu and the indigenous parties have little organizational structure or leverage to impose norms, there is no real difference among parties in terms of governance style. Indeed, many of the new MIP and MAS municipal officials previously represented other political parties. Alliances among parties are precluded by the intense competition to be the sole representative of indigenous voters and solidify the identities of new, weakly institutionalized electoral vehicles. As Panebianco observes,

a party's stability depends on its ability to defend its own identity. Identity is, however, threatened by the existence of competitors; and it is even more endangered in alliances made with them. Alliances between competing parties threaten both parties' stability, and thus increase environmental unpredictability. (1988: 218.)

With tiny budgets, scant economic development opportunities, and an enormous deficit of unmet basic needs, even the windfall provided by coparticipation resources makes little difference in citizens' daily lives. Many tiny Aymara municipalities that demanded separate status as municipalities after 1995 on cultural grounds are not economically viable. Municipal politics benefits the small elite able to gain a municipal salary, and competition for these positions is a struggle for economic survival.

Two problems are particularly vexing. First, violence against elected officials is commonplace and elected officials and civil society actors use violence to resolve political conflicts. Council women in both municipalities report being harassed and intimidated (confidential interviews August 2005). In Ayo Ayo political rivalries ended in the murder of the mayor and the incarceration of opposition militants. Contemporary political violence is rooted in centuries of conflict among allyus over territorial boundaries, some of which continue to this day, as well as generations of conflict between campesinos and the Bolivian state.

Second, women appear to be even more subjugated in the Aymara altiplano than in the Chapare owing to a dual system of subjugation. Within the campesino union structure they are relegated to an auxiliary status that forecloses the possibility of serving as candidates. Within the traditional allyu cargo system, women serve as auxiliary figures beside men. Women lack social standing apart from their husbands, and husbands prevent women from advancing in public life. As male allyu authorities increasingly challenge elected officials for power they reinforce conservative gender norms, as their legitimacy is based on defense of traditional culture. Moreover, women in the Chapare benefited from the efforts of national MAS leaders to impose norms of gender equity as they forge alliances with nonindigenous popular and middle-class organizations. In the case of Villa Tunari, local male leaders resisted these efforts, but elsewhere campesina women are advancing. In contrast, in La Paz the MIP is not seeking these alliances and thus has no incentive to grant political power to women, whereas the MAS has no influence over La Paz communities that run under its banner. In both Ayo Ayo and Achacachi women report being afraid to hold office and risk humiliation and violence if they do (confidential interviews July 2005).

CONCLUSION

In Bolivia cultural practices promoting annual leadership rotation and the instability of mayoral terms impeded the development of durable leaders who could unite constituents and employment institutional innovation over a period of several years. On rare occasions in which leaders served more than one term in office they were unable to act autonomously of political-party–social-movement authority structures. On occasion, national party authorities intervened in local political conflicts, most notably in Puerto Villarroel. Although indigenous parties enjoy a great advantage owing to their origin in dense, dynamic civil society networks and strong collective identities, the fusion of parties and movements into single leadership structures restricted the ability of one to hold the other accountable.

The LPP, which directly resulted in the formation of the MAS, enabled indigenous social-movement organizations to enter local politics in great numbers. Both indigenous parties immediately transferred cultural and organizational traditions to municipal institutions, adjusting liberal–Western political institutions to the people they serve. This is most clearly seen in the use of traditional methods of proposing, selecting, and rotating leaders. It also is evident in the transfer of various aspects of public decision making to indigenous–campesino assemblies. As in Ecuador, elected officials incorporated the tradition of collective work into the construction of public works in order to stretch scarce resources, increase community involvement, and collectively monitor public spending. Elected officials provided regular, public reports to civil society organizations, just as civil society leaders are required to do (García Linera 2004: 432). From the point of view of indigenous citizens, capturing these local political and economic processes constitutes an enormous achievement. Although, as in Ecuador, measurable improvements in socioeconomic indicators such as literacy and poverty are not yet visible, it is clear to all that more money is being invested in services and projects targeted to poor, indigenous communities. These enjoy a greater sense of empowerment and control over their collective destiny.

These achievements have come at a high cost that radical democrats may be unwilling to pay. Governance in the cases studied is permeated by undemocratic norms: the legitimate use of violence and intimidation against adversaries; the monopolization of power and expulsion of adversaries; the subjugation and humiliation of women; social pressure to conform to the "consensus" cultivated by leadership cupulas; and disregard for minority rights. Indigenous communities' desire to seize absolute power is understandable given the long history of state repression, social exclusion, and economic exploitation. That legacy has resulted in one of the highest rates of street protest in Latin America (Red Interamericana para la Democracia 2005: 14). Bolivians' high propensity to participate in protests is accompanied by a comparably high propensity to participate in deliberative assemblies and PB processes: the highest propensity of eight countries surveyed in 2005. The country even ranks first with respect to PB, with 54.1% wanting to participate, compared with 44.8% in Brazil, where the institution was developed (ibid.: 17–18). But by exaggerating the legitimacy and authority of civil society organizations, coca growers' federations and traditional authorities reduce the ability of weak state institutions to cultivate rational–legal authority and democratic legitimacy.

From a design standpoint, the institutional model that the Bolivian state imposed in the mid-1990s, notwithstanding helpful revisions in the last decade, remains flawed. A lack of resources to support its functions, particularly for travel to far-flung areas to oversee public works, has impeded the effective and independent operation of vigilance committees. In the Chapare, this partly was addressed by having leaders of the sindicato in the area of project activity undertake the monitoring function and report back to the committee. In Chimoré, the municipality provided some rooms and furniture and other technical support for the committee within the municipal offices (Lizárraga and Villarroel 1998: 16). This reflects the cozy relationship between the federation-controlled vigilance committee and the municipal government. To function properly, both should have independent authority and resources.

A more profound problem is that the communities do not understand the benefits or legal necessity of planning; they are accustomed to fulfilling demands as needs arise. Tensions persist between the complicated, modern municipal regime and the inexperienced, poorly educated subjects of the LPP (Medina 2003a; Vilaseca 2003: 93). In 2003 only 35 of 73 indigenous planning districts had produced their plans and a minority of these conformed to existing development plans. Owing to these and other technical hurdles, the number of municipalities having their coparticipation revenues frozen by the national government has been increasing steadily [7] (Galindo Soza 2003: 119).

---

[7] In some cases norms of reciprocity regarding the maintenance of family and ritual family relations led public officials to violate strict rules regarding public spending that left officials in jail charged with corruption. For example, Galindo describes a Capitán Grande of the Guaraní who thought it was legitimate to use municipal resources to purchase clothing and homes for his family members because they would be participating in the exercise of his leadership duties and had to look presentable, and he had to have a place to undertake his responsibilities in various parts of the territory when he visited distant communities (Galindo Soza 2003: 119).

7

Conclusion: An Interaction Model of Democratic Institutional Innovation

Some observers – anthropologists, philosophers, human rights' activists, development professionals – were horrified when indigenous peoples shed their political innocence and entered formal politics in significant numbers in the mid-1990s. Would this be the end of "pure" native cultures uncorrupted by Western politics? Would we no longer have living, morally superior models of prepolitical human relations to juxtapose to modern, complex, failing states?

For the most part indigenous citizens (and not a few political scientists) were thrilled with the prospect of empowering Latin America's most-excluded groups and with the possible implications for democracy of this promising and unexpected turn of events. As a Pachakutik militant explained to me one afternoon in Quito in July 2005,

This is the reality today. Now, what happens is that the indigenous peoples have become politicized. We have maintained and we have ratified that we are a political organization, because politics is a science, no?, that seeks the common good. Given that the society in its entirety – not just the indigenous – is assuming a political attitude, the rich that run the country don't have to be *políticos*. And many people assume this, as if politics were bad and, thus, they should stay away from it. And we say that no, we are political. Our organizations are political. All of our actions, all of our activities are political actions. (My translation; interview, Alberto Yumbay, July 7, 2005.)

Three weeks later in La Paz I spoke with Apolinar Baltazar, the MAS mayor of the rural, Aymara town of Umala, flanked by his advisers. After the mayor guardedly answered my questions about governing practices in Umala, his associate, an agronomist who worked in the municipality, was eager to share his thoughts concerning the implications of the rapid shift in power relations that was overtaking Bolivia:

We are entering the ministries. We are capable, we are more prepared than those who are now managing us, and still with discrimination they manage us. So Aymara, Quechua, people of the Andean world are climbing little by little. And there is going to be a moment in which we are going to have the majority in the Congress, people who are well prepared and with a well-formed ideology and identity, *estimada hermana*. (My translation; interview, Ponciano Quispe, July 26, 2005.)

He told me how the Bolivian Constitution soon would be changed to reflect the culture and identity of the indigenous majority. I nodded respectfully. Six months later Evo Morales was president and the MAS controlled an unprecedented absolute majority in the Chamber of Deputies. Two years later a MAS-dominated constituent assembly approved a new Constitution. Clearly Bolivia's indigenous people had mastered the science of politics. It remains to be seen whether they have mastered the art of democracy.

In the preceding chapters I have shown how three factors are most likely to foster local-level democratic institutional innovation: a legal and political context that facilitates bottom-driven decentralization and allows local actors some flexibility to design their own institutions; effective mayoral leadership; and support from a cohesive, organic political party rooted in civil society. These findings hold up across 10 diverse political contexts in two distinct countries where indigenous peoples' movements formed electoral vehicles and sought to capture local power. They also complement and confirm findings from studies of participatory–deliberative practices in Brazil, Guatemala, Mexico, and elsewhere in Latin America. As they build on our growing understanding of the contribution of indigenous peoples' cultures to participatory–deliberative technologies, my findings call greater attention to factors and conditions that had previously received insufficient attention from social scientists and development professionals.

In this concluding chapter I summarize my arguments concerning how each of the three facilitating factors may promote radically democratic institutional innovations and show how the impact of these factors may be stunted or magnified by the political environment in which they operate. The crucial interaction of conditions and context underscores the importance of undertaking the comparative study of multiple cases within their rich, complex environments. Giving diverse contexts their rightful attention is not a barrier to theoretical generalization but, rather, a more solid basis for constructing generalizable theories because context reveals important information about the operation of key variables. To show how decentralization dynamics, mayoral leadership, and organic parties interact within favorable political contexts to produce favorable outcomes, I first present an interactive model of democratic institutional innovation. The remainder of the chapter is devoted to examining the distinct imprint that indigenous peoples' movements have left on local governance in the Andes in light of the stated goals of radical democrats and to suggesting implications for democratic theory and development policy.

BOTTOM-DRIVEN, FLEXIBLE, LEGAL CONTEXT FOR DECENTRALIZATION

Institutional innovation is more likely to serve local needs when local actors initiate the process and must design their own mechanisms to suit the sociocultural, political, and geographic context. As Daubón and Saunders eloquently conclude, "while these institutions can be created by fiat and enacted by edict, they will in fact not achieve a level of trust comparable to when they are created and implemented by those who will be governed by them" (2002: 187; see also Bebbington and Carroll 2000: 39). Creating trust in government is imperative in contexts like the rural Andes, where most citizens view government as the enemy. Divergent dynamics of decentralization partly explain why the Ecuadorian cases are on the whole more appealing than the Bolivian ones. The homogenizing logic of Bolivia's popular participation regime is the law's "greatest virtue and worst defect" because it creates constant tensions between distinct political cultures (my translation; Galindo Soza 2003: 110). In contrast, institutional designs in Ecuador are more adapted to their local context and rooted in civil society networks, creating a greater sense of pride and ownership. Leaders succeed when they have sufficient flexibility to innovate and where civil society organizations that brought them to office feel invested in the outcomes of institutional change.

The following four conditions favorable to democratic institutional innovation were derived from observations of variation in outcomes in the Bolivian and Ecuadorian cases as well as studies from elsewhere in the region:

- Local actors must have the power to petition the government to transfer responsibilities and resources so that they feel ownership of the decentralization process and a sense of empowerment.

- Central-government actors must respond quickly and cooperatively to decentralization requests and counter central bureaucrats' efforts to resist transferring authority.
- Central governments must transfer substantial resources to local authorities to support their new responsibilities, particularly in impoverished, rural areas. PB was effective in Brazil because significant sums were disbursed to local governments. According to Goldfrank, most Brazilian cities spend between $250 and $400 per capita, whereas his survey of demand-driven PB in 14 towns in Bolivia, Peru, Nicaragua, and Guatemala found that they invested on average between $5 and $50 per capita (2007a: 101, 111–12).
- Local actors should be provided considerable flexibility in designing institutions provided that they protect constitutional rights and freedoms, that all individuals and groups have a way to participate in deliberative institutions, and that new local institutions conform to national standards of accountability and transparency (see UNDP 2006: 65).

The Andean examples support conclusions from studies of PB in other Latin American countries. Based on his review of PB experiences in eight municipalities in Brazil, Wampler concludes that the institution of participatory–democratic institutions succeeds best when there is a *convergence of interests* on the part of higher government officials and civil society activists representing popular organizations. In contrast, top-down models, or those driven solely by civil society organizations, produce inferior results (Wampler 2008: 32). Similarly, Goldfrank concludes that locally driven participatory institutions are more deliberative than centrally imposed models because they typically respond to societal demands for more deliberation (2007a: 103).

Predominantly indigenous municipalities may best counter the negative impact of top-down models. Ackerman found, based on his study of Brazil, Mexico, the United States, and India, that top-down, centrally imposed designs produced only positive results when they were appropriated by indigenous communities in the Mexican state of Oaxaca, owing to their high degree of social capital and collective identity and long-term exercise of autonomous self-government (2004: 12–13; see also Fox 1996: 1091; Grindle 2007: 126–39). Based on his study of Guatemala, Goldfrank also finds that participatory processes undertaken in predominantly indigenous municipalities produce the most admired results and evince a strong commitment to participatory mechanisms (2007a: 107). Beyond indigenous enclaves, Baiocchi, Heller, and Silva identified a similar phenomenon in Brazil, where top-down reforms were imposed on a variety of municipalities. They conclude that where civil society organizations already are well established at the time that top-down, rigid state institutions are imposed they are better positioned to capture them and to maximize their potential for gaining access to the state (2008: 12).

MAYORAL LEADERSHIP

To secure an optimal democratizing outcome, mayors must accomplish six tasks as they undertake institutional innovation:

- Mayors must have sufficient personal charisma to establish a rapport with diverse actors and attract and maintain support from constituents in the face of meager social welfare improvements.
- Mayors must secure reelection in order to lengthen the time they have to implement institutional innovations and to codify their principles in municipal law. Formal codification signifies to citizens that new institutions are not beholden to individuals. In Weberian terms, their authority is transferred from traditional–charismatic to rational–legal sources. If legal codification is not achieved – it is, in fact, unusual – reelection provides time to convene annual iterations of deliberative–participatory processes that inculcate ownership by citizens and civil society organizations, who can oppose subsequent governments' efforts to dismantle them.
- Mayors must maintain the support of civil society groups that elected them as a defense against conflicts that are likely to arise among the mayor, party leaders, and partisan opponents. Civil society support gives mayors leverage to manage opposition. Civil society support has proven to be a more powerful tool for innovating mayors than a majority on the municipal council, since the council enjoys less legitimacy and authority than a popular mayor backed by institutionalized civil associations. Mayoral–civil society partnerships constitute a type of "countervailing power" that helps to neutralize extreme preexisting disparities in access to power (Fung and Wright 2003a: 261).
- Mayors must maintain a continuous, visible presence in the community through frequent interaction with constituents in order to build trust and to obtain feedback with respect to the progress of institutional innovations. *Present* mayors foster and maintain existing social capital and enable communities to resolve collective action problems

that ethnic divisions and structural inequality generate (Krishna 2007).

- Mayors must communicate effectively across ethnic lines, especially with national and international donors. Securing external donations enables mayors to provide early, substantive benefits that maintain public enthusiasm while they maintain resource transfers to erstwhile elites, who otherwise might sabotage new institutions (Bebbington and Carroll 2000; Cameron 2003b: 299–303; Grindle 2007).
- Mayors must maintain sufficient autonomy from sponsoring organizations to avoid being perceived as captive to particular interest groups. This makes mayors more credible negotiators when dealing with higher-tier governments, external donors, and opposition political actors.

The capacity of mayors to perform these six tasks varied among the 10 cases. Even among the more promising cases mayors varied in their emphasis of particular tasks, owing to variations among the cases with respect to particular obstacles to institutional reform. For example, Mayor Tituaña of Cotacachi had no prior connection to the dominant indigenous organization in the canton and enjoyed support from other key local and external actors. Thus he did not need to assert his autonomy from sponsoring organizations, unlike mayors in Bolivia's Chapare who serve as instruments of coca-federation will. In Otavalo, given the minority status of indigenous voters, Mayor Conejo had to emphasize cross-ethnic collaboration, whereas in predominantly indigenous Guamote, Mayor Curicama did not have to please mestizo voters to secure reelection.

ORGANIC PARTIES

Organic parties – electoral vehicles formed as the political arms of civil society organizations and networks – are the ideal partners for innovating mayors. They channel the energy, enthusiasm, and ideas of diverse civil society groups, which have been necessary to inaugurate participatory-deliberative institutions in Latin America. Organic parties are less susceptible to professional incentives and bureaucratic rigidity than professional parties (Panebianco 1988) and thus are more likely to favor institutional change. However, organic parties are typically weakly institutionalized, and they must continually resist pressures to split them apart, disperse their energy, or transform them into the professional political parties their sponsoring organizations sought to replace. Organic parties must surmount the following four challenges when they enter the electoral arena:

- Organic parties must minimize the confusion that coexisting party and movement organizational structures and leadership hierarchies generate. Party and movement leaders must cooperate with respect to important steering decisions and avoid dissolving into two or more factions struggling for absolute control.
- Organic parties must reduce the resentment generated by competition for scarce candidacies and salaried positions by offering other meaningful ways for militants to participate.
- Organic parties must avoid diverting resources and energy away from the social movement activities that earned them their strength. Neglecting movement goals and activities alienates their base and creates distance between movement and party leaders as the former feel left behind.
- Party leaders must adopt the principles of democracy, pluralism, and peaceful negotiation and discourage the use of violence against opponents. Norms enforcing movement discipline that were necessary for them to seize political power must be relaxed in order to create a more tolerant and pluralistic political environment.

After organic parties gain office they face four additional challenges:

- Parties must respect the local governance norms and cultural values of the indigenous communities that elected them while they learn and obey state governance norms. They must encourage constituents to put faith in government and to support the rule of law.
- Parties must choose candidates who have some educational training and experience so that they will succeed in complex government offices. They must seek special training and education programs from the state and NGOs in order to improve the skills of municipal managers. Turnover in these positions should be limited to allow staff to gain experience and to reduce the need and the cost of repeated retraining.
- The party should assist the mayor in attracting economic assistance from NGOs and international donors without letting militants become coopted by access to financial resources.

- The party must plan for and survive the inevitable disillusionment of voters – particularly militants of sponsoring organizations – when radical changes in power relations do not quickly produce social welfare benefits.

Whereas mayors and civil society organizations are typically directly involved in institutional innovation, parties more commonly act indirectly as the political arm of both and the formal representative of the mayor and sponsoring organizations on the municipal council. Here, organic parties can use their legislative authority and access to resources to facilitate and promote institutional innovation. Or, as occurred in both countries, party representatives may obstruct change as a means to retain control over patronage resources and thus institutional innovation. Political parties also are important to the success of institutional innovation because they can contribute to the construction of "collaborative countervailing power." As Fung and Wright argue, party leaders are more likely than social-movement leaders to perceive a political advantage in collaborating with opponents in order to provide benefits to constituents and thus secure political support (2003a: 284).

Focusing on parties enables us to combine analyses of representation and participation, which have tended to be treated in separate literatures as distinct problems for democratic theory. This tendency mirrors the bifurcation of literatures covering social movements and political parties. Participatory democrats need to better take into consideration the important role of representation because even ideal models require some people standing in for others (Fung 2007: 453). Participatory mechanisms should be seen as a supplement to representative institutions, particularly in municipalities that are highly unequal, in which many individuals and groups otherwise would suffer complete political exclusion (Baiocchi et al. forthcoming: 2; see also Nylen 2003: 150–1). As Cohen and Fung argue, participatory and representative institutions can be "transformed and linked" such that they are mutually reinforcing and supportive (2004: 31). They can then serve as problem-solving mechanisms and schools of citizenship that hold government officials serving in representational and administrative agencies accountable to the public (ibid.: 31–2). It is the dialectic between participatory-deliberative and representative public spheres that ultimately improves the quality of democratic life and establishes durable links between state and society. Thus, whereas the performance of mayors was found to be more critical to the outcome of democratic innovations, for such innovations to fulfill their potential municipal councils must contribute to the process by more effectively representing diverse constituencies, particularly those less favored by the mayor's base of support.

THE IMPORTANCE OF CONTEXT

Even when there is an institutional environment that favors bottom-driven innovation, mayors are effective leaders, and they represent cohesive organic parties, the political context – particularly the nature of parties and party systems – influences the outcome of institutional innovation. Moderate pluralism in the political party and social environment – with neither a hegemonic political force nor extreme fragmentation among competitive parties – proved to be the most important contextual variable. Indigenous-party leaders learned from the exclusionary model that mestizo politicians provided. Where indigenous peoples' parties had to compete for mestizo votes in order to win office, and where they needed at least noninterference from mestizo economic elites in order to promote their programmatic agendas, effective mayors designed and instituted admirable participatory-deliberative institutions. In Cotacachi, Guaranda, and Otavalo the need to win support from some mestizo elites motivated cross-ethnic negotiation. It also helped to promote solidarity and reduce factionalism within each municipality's indigenous movement because the threat of a return to mestizo rule was real. Similarly, in Bolivia, in areas outside its base in tropical Cochabamba, MAS leaders must negotiate with other popular political forces and middle-class notables and groups in order to win office or to form a majority on the municipal council (interviews, Rafael Archondo, La Paz, and Fernando Mayorga, Cochabamba, 2005).

However, under conditions of indigenous-party hegemony, in which indigenous voters constitute an overwhelming majority, there is less incentive to design institutions that facilitate deliberation and participation across ethnic and class lines. In Bolivia's Chapare, more than a decade of fighting state coca-eradication policy forged a disciplined, highly mobilized movement that inculcated a strong sense of collective identity and a desire to seize power and eject the state. When that force monopolized political power there was no need to negotiate with mestizo elites, ejected sectors of the campesino movement, or indigenous groups native to the region. There was no electorally competitive political organization to challenge the coca growers' party and motivate negotiation and deliberation within the municipal government. There was no social force able to act as a counterweight to the coca growers' monopoly. The LPP could not operate as designed because coca growers' federations dominated seats on vigilance committees and dictated policy to captive municipal authorities. State and society were not linked: They were fused.

Similarly, in the altiplano, traditional Aymara self-government systems imbued with spiritual and cultural meanings resolve many of the most important decisions affecting local citizens. Where they are stronger than competing campesino or political-party organizations, traditional authorities have taken advantage of a 2004 law that allows them to compete for political office. In this way, the hegemonic sociocultural and informal political force in the municipality also comes to dominate formal political authority. As in the Chapare, there is no civil society counterweight to state power and, as a result, little opportunity for the expression of democratic pluralism or the institutionalization of autonomous state–society partnerships or deliberative spheres. In O'Donnell's terms, there is vertical, but not horizontal, democratic accountability (1994). Moreover, as in the Chapare, there is no pressure to conform to modern norms of gender equality. Although this is troubling from a liberal–democratic perspective, such governments enjoy extraordinarily high public approval and have reduced or eliminated intense and often violent struggles derived from partisan political competition that have plagued the area for generations.

Extreme party-system fragmentation, and the conflict and violence it may generate, also reduces democratic quality. This is most clearly seen in Bolivia in impoverished, predominantly Aymara, municipalities like Achacachi and Ayo Ayo, where indigenous municipal authorities traditionally have represented numerous mestizo political parties offering access to power and resources in exchange for wearing the party insignia. The emergence of indigenous political parties has intensified political conflict here as indigenous–campesino leaders representing mestizo parties now compete against MAS and MIP candidates. Competition between the two indigenous parties is particularly intense because both have wagered their organizational legitimacy on establishing an identity as the sole, authentic indigenous party. Complicating the field of conflict, which ebbs and flows with electoral seasons, are struggles for exclusive authority among traditional Aymara leadership hierarchies favoring, alternatively, elders, campesino unions, and the newer MST. Open conflict within national umbrella organizations with which local organizations are affiliated further intensifies these struggles. In a context of extreme political fragmentation and bitter interpersonal and factional conflict, it is difficult for any political force that captures the mayor's office to form a working majority and advance a political project. Without an absolute majority, mayors cannot even rely on serving out their terms and politics is absorbed by struggles over patronage and group esteem. Neither state nor society is sufficiently cohesive to participate in durable state–society partnerships.

Other contextual conditions also influence the democratic quality of outcomes. The existence of higher-tier governments (regional, national) from the same party or an allied party provides more auspicious conditions for innovation because higher-tier allies can channel additional resources to affiliated municipalities (see Andersson and Van Laerhoven 2007: 1102). Because my research ended in 2005 before MAS leader Evo Morales assumed Bolivia's presidency, I cannot say whether MAS municipalities have received preferential treatment, but it is likely that a MAS national government would be less likely to scrutinize and punish MAS governments' divergence from municipal norms. In addition, a moderately high level of local economic growth and development ensures that substantive improvements in the quality of life for the poor are not impossible. A larger macroeconomic environment that promotes participatory–deliberative local governance initiatives also should be helpful.

AN INTERACTION MODEL OF DEMOCRATIC
INSTITUTIONAL INNOVATION

The three facilitating conditions previously described are important on their own but even more decisive when they act together to promote democratic institutional innovation. Their mutually reinforcing interactions are delineated in Figure 7.1. The model takes us beyond the mere listing of conditions by specifying mechanisms through which conditions interact to contribute to variation in the democratic effects of institutional innovation (Strauss and Corbin 1999: 166–8).

Beginning at the top of the model, mayors who perform all or most of the functions described in Chapter 3 can best take advantage of favorable decentralization dynamics. Mayors use popular legitimacy, personal charisma, and deep roots in civil society to negotiate effectively for the transfer of policy and spending powers with higher-tier actors. They use their technical and professional training and experience, and their contacts with technocrats from NGOs and international institutions, to design innovative solutions for local problems. The fact that mayors have

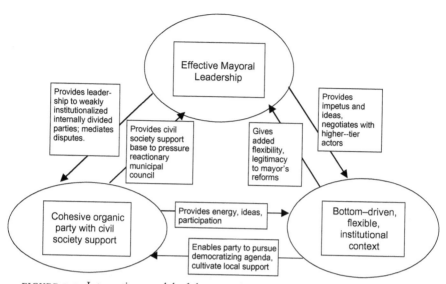

FIGURE 7.1. Interaction model of democratic institutional innovation.

the flexibility to initiate and guide institutional innovation that suits local needs lends their projects greater legitimacy, as opposed to projects that the center imposes to serve other goals. Effective mayors serve as crucial partners for cohesive organic parties rooted in civil society organizations and networks that seek more deliberative–participatory opportunities. Mayors provide the leadership to corral disparate associations with diverse goals and leaders. These often are weakly institutionalized and internally divided over strategy and mission. A skillful mayor can focus the attention of diverse groups, harness their energy and ideas to a common project, and speak as an authoritative representative to external donors and higher-tier government officials. In turn, mayors depend on their civil society base to provide political support when their political party sponsors are weak or recalcitrant and are poorly able to perform this function.

At the bottom of the model the mutually supportive relationship between an organic party and a legal regime that promotes bottom-driven, flexible, institutional innovations is depicted. The flexibility of the legal regime and its preference for local initiative enables local actors to pursue their democratizing, empowering agenda through the design of new local institutions. These are likely to gain popular support through their association with legitimate social organizations. The availability of civil society actors that are now formally engaged in the political system provides a channel for new ideas to revive the standard repertoire of local governance mechanisms.

All three conditions depicted in the model are necessary for democratic institutional innovation. Working together in synergy, mayoral leadership, socially rooted organic parties, and flexible, bottom-driven decentralization regimes magnify each other's facilitative properties. Conversely, the absence of any one condition presents great obstacles to improving democratic quality that the presence of the other two conditions may not overcome. For example, in Guaranda and Guamote, even with organic, cohesive parties and the existence of locally designed state–society linkages, in the absence of mayoral leadership promising institutions collapsed. The virtuous interaction of the three conditions also is affected by the political context in which they operate at the local level. They will operate most beneficially under conditions of moderate political pluralism, as previously described. Democratic institutional innovation in all five Bolivian cases was constrained both by the rigid, top-down decentralization scheme and by the scarcity of municipalities where moderate pluralism prevails.

THE "VALUE-ADDED" (AND SUBTRACTED) OF INDIGENOUS PARTIES

Are indigenous parties improving democracy in local governance? What unique values and practices do they bring to democratic institutional innovation? These questions inspired this research. Given the diversity of indigenous cultures and local settings, and the relatively small number of cases studied, it is impossible to give a definitive answer. One way to begin to assess the quality of indigenous-party-led governance is to apply the Canadian Centre for Policy Alternatives' four-tier continuum. The continuum measures the deliberative–participatory nature of PB institutions around the world. At the lowest level, citizens participate indirectly through voting and writing letters to the media. At the next level citizens enjoy "low direct participation" that adds "lobbying, letter writing, and deputations" to the previous activities. At the third "consultative" level, they add additional activities to the preceding list: "community outreach, commissions, surveys, community advisory boards" (Alternative Federal Budget 2003: 5). At the highest level they place "direct deliberative" citizen participation, which entails all of the preceding activities in addition to the involvement of common citizens in some budgetary decision making (2003: 5). By this measure we can place even the most problematic cases from Bolivia and Ecuador toward the most-beneficial, most-deliberative–participatory end of the spectrum. Indigenous parties have significantly increased the extent to which excluded, disadvantaged groups participate in local budgeting decisions and the execution of public policy. Even when their decisions affect only a small percentage of the budget, the provision of space for participation of the excluded makes a normative contribution to democracy by providing a place for silent and excluded voices to speak (Sen 1999: 291). Participation, thus, is an *end* of political development and not just a means toward better decision making (ibid.).

Another way to answer these questions is to assess our cases in terms of goals associated with radical democracy. Cohen and Fung (2004) identify four: (1) expanded opportunities to participate in public decision making, (2) greater accountability and transparency, (3) increased equality, and (4) autonomy and self-government. I add an additional governance goal: establishing government authority, which is necessary for weak democratic institutions to achieve these goals in ethnically divided, impoverished countries.

Participation

The number of citizens involved in public policy debates that affect government decisions is a common measure of the participatory quality of democracy. All of my cases revealed a consistently greater propensity of indigenous-governed communities to involve a large number of community members in spheres in which public policy decisions are made. All citizens need not be involved in every decision for a deepening of democracy to have taken place (Goldfrank 2007b: 148–9). The presence of a cross section of a community – even when many community members, particularly women, are not able to affect the decision-making process – gives government decisions greater legitimacy while constructing and maintaining community solidarity. In the Andes, indigenous parties bring to local governance an ethic of reciprocity, intragroup trust, and an orientation toward the common good, while discouraging self-interest and disengagement. A habit of regular community assemblies has facilitated a smooth transition to deliberative planning and decision-making sessions involving community representatives. In these assemblies indigenous cultures and associations adapt traditional practices of seeking consensus or, in its absence, mutual accommodation and the balancing of conflicting interests. Assemblies serve as spaces for the habituation and formalization of consensus-seeking and negotiation where political opponents are pressured to reach agreement and reduce open conflict.

Accountability and Transparency

Accountability and transparency improve when government decision–making processes are opened to public scrutiny. In both countries indigenous communities and social-movement organizations continue long-standing practices of reviewing government decisions and holding their leaders accountable – a value called "social control." Communities observe leaders' behavior on a daily basis and question them in open assemblies (Ticona Alejo 2003: 143). These practices have been transferred to state–society partnerships to monitor local government performance. Municipal officials in indigenous-led municipalities typically provide annual, oral reports to the community with respect to their accomplishments and provide a detailed accounting of how money has been spent. Some, such as Mario Conejo, Pachakutik mayor of Otavalo, have been pioneers in promoting more transparent government contracting practices. Conejo rewrote the contracting law such that engineers are referred for public works from a list provided by professional associations. Conejo and others have created websites or posted documents listing public spending as it occurs. In Bolivia accountability is facilitated through vigilance committees that the LPP established to monitor public spending. In the Chapare the MAS has enhanced this function by incorporating campesino assemblies into the process. In the highlands, mayors typically consult with ayllu and sindicato authorities, as well as provide oral reports to assemblies.

Equality

Where indigenous parties have taken power, the weight of money and social status in the allocation of local government resources has been dramatically reduced, whereas investment in projects that aim to meet the basic needs of impoverished and excluded groups has been prioritized. In Bolivia regular rotation of elected leaders – accelerated above elected terms – promotes equality and reduces competition for access to paid employment. Because the sums distributed to local governments are so small, the measurable impact on well-being has been negligible. Nevertheless, disadvantaged groups are more empowered than under previous governments because they have a much greater impact on how the small sums are spent. Moreover, as Cohen and Fung argue, empowering the most disadvantaged has beneficial effects on the quality of democratic participation: by counteracting biases that tend to give wealthier, more-educated individuals greater advantages in nominally equal participatory processes (2004: 31).

Autonomy and Self-Government

Indigenous-led local governments have made their greatest advances toward radical democratic goals in the areas of autonomy and self-government. This is where Andean indigenous political agendas and radical democracy are most in tune. But radical democrats require that autonomy and self-government be achieved under conditions of democratic pluralism in which diverse views are expressed and decisions result from reasoned arguments based on universal values, such as fairness and equality (Cohen and Fung 2004: 26). Such conditions exist in the Andes only when competing and opposing political organizations and hostile ethnic groups perceive an incentive to cooperate. Elsewhere, indigenous parties often pursue self-government at the expense of democratic principles, such as minority rights, gender equality, free expression, and political pluralism.

Authority

The UN Permanent Forum on Indigenous Issues emphasized the participatory nature of indigenous governance and its support for establishing state authority in a 2006 report on "Indigenous Participation and Good Governance":

At the local level, indigenous peoples see good governance as meaning a stronger focus on processes rather than structures, implying support to evolving participatory forms of governance rather than imposed and static models. Governance models that recognize the diversity of world views and that are based on cultural values and traditions lead to genuine decision–making authority and local control. (Permanent Forum on Indigenous Issues 2006: 6.)

In the Andes, institutional innovations incorporating indigenous cultural norms and practices are helping to generate new sources of authority for weak local political institutions. As Mason argues, nonstate actors can contribute their often-superior problem-solving abilities to government processes that have failed to address local needs (2005: 47). In some cases (e.g., the Chapare) indigenous parties have ignored and challenged rational–legal authority and local government authority is derived from its association with valued civil society practices. In others (e.g., Cota-cachi, Otavalo), establishing connections to traditional, authoritative practices enhances the legitimacy of Western institutions.

The Value Subtracted

Indigenous parties' contributions to local governance have not come with-out serious challenges and, in the Bolivian cases, troubling consequences. The main problem stems from the fact that the values facilitating radical democracy that are identified with indigenous culture in the Andes (i.e., reciprocity, trust, equality, consensus-seeking) are mostly observed *within* indigenous communities and only rarely extend *across* social, ethnic, and geographical boundaries. In some cases they do not even extend through-out the same ethnolinguistic identity. These values may be prevalent only within particular sociopolitical organizations – as in the Ecuadorian com-munities of Guamote, where the overwhelmingly indigenous population is divided by religion, or Guaranda, where the indigenous–campesino movement is divided by competing political factions. Multiple sources of internal friction and faction impede the construction and maintenance of trust and reciprocity within indigenous communities in a context of extreme economic scarcity, in which access to municipal government is a means to economic survival. In short, it is difficult to build trust and feel-ings of reciprocity across cultures, and more difficult still when one has dominated the other for centuries. But it is necessary for the realization of radical democratic goals (Perczynski 2000: 167).

This problematic is better understood if we consider the driving goal for the formation of indigenous-movement-based parties in the 1990s. All four indigenous political parties studied here were formed to seize the state and secure self-government for the excluded indigenous-poor majority. This is a power-taking, not a power-sharing, agenda. MIP leader Felipe Quispe, for example, has advocated dismantling the Western, liberal–democratic state and replacing it with a socialist, communitarian utopia in which the indigenous majority rules without interference. Coca growers' leader Evo Morales has asserted that the movement seeks "to recuperate political power as Quechuas, Aymaras, Guaranies; absolute owners" (my translation, interview cited in García Linera 2004: 449). As Morales' vice president, Alvaro García Linera, concluded more than a year before accepting an invitation to join the party, the most important external model for the MAS is Cuba, not ancient Athens or the New England village (2004: 450). This project is radically egalitarian, but it is not radically democratic.

In terms of the model of empowered participatory governance that Fung and Wright advance, the type of countervailing power that the coca growers – and indigenous–campesino movements formed to lead protracted agrarian struggles – possess is of the "adversarial" rather than the "participatory–collaborative" variety and thus is less beneficial for promoting participatory–deliberative institutions. As they argue, adversarial groups develop particular skills, forms of organization, and collective identities "that depend upon victory in conflict." Participatory collaboration, in contrast, is facilitated by a different set of "skills, sources of support, and bases of solidarity" (2003a: 266). It is difficult to convert adversarial into participatory–collaborative forms of power or to make organizations that are adversaries into willing collaborators because negotiating with others, especially adversaries, defeats the purpose the organization was designed to serve (ibid.: 267–82). As a result of these dynamics, the democratizing contribution of indigenous parties may be limited in the following ways.

Extremism. The parochial and isolated nature of political life in the rural Andes appears to provide all the criteria necessary for what Sunstein calls the "law of group polarization" (2003). Sunstein argues that all deliberating groups tend to shift their position toward an extreme as they engage in iterated deliberations owing to the lack of exposure to contrary arguments and to group members' desire to gain prestige and defeat rivals by adopting what they perceive to be the group's most-dominant view (2003:85). He concludes that groups are likely to become more radicalized under certain conditions, all of which tend to converge in the rural Andes: (1) a practice of regular, frequent deliberations, which continually push the group toward further extremes; (2) deliberation within enclaves that exclude those with divergent interests and identities; (3) the existence of strong shared identities and affective ties among group members, which intensify social pressure to conform; and (4) the existence of at least one "rival 'outgroup,'" which strengthens feelings of obligation to support the group (Sunstein 2003: 81–5). Although Sunstein concedes that a certain degree of enclave deliberation facilitates the formulation of critical views of the status quo and the strategies to challenge it, isolated deliberations are likely to lead to "widespread error and social fragmentation" as well as social instability (2003: 90).

Social Conformism and Disregard for Individual Rights. Equally problematic from a (radically) democratic perspective is the strong ethic of conformity that indigenous parties bring to governance. This is exemplified by the Quichua indigenous principles of "one heart, one thought, one single force" (*shuk shukulla, shuk yayalla, shuk makilla*) (UNDP 2006:61). Disciplinary practices that enabled indigenous peoples to survive as distinct cultures and to construct dense networks of loyal social-movement organizations constrict the ability of community members to exercise individual autonomy by expressing preferences that diverge from the majority or from opposing authority structures that older men tend to dominate. Indigenous political parties and social movements routinely expel dissidents. For example, leaders of the indigenous–campesino organization FECAB–RUNARI, which controls the Guaranda Pachakutik affiliate, expelled Mayor Alberto Coles and Vice-Mayor Washington Bazante for refusing to follow their directives, and MAS leaders in Puerto Villarroel expelled supporters of Alejo Véliz after his split with Evo Morales. Indigenous leaders often denounce dissent as "individualism," which they perceive to be one of the greatest threats to achieving the movement's goal of self-determination (see, e.g., Macas 2005). The exclusion of certain community members from indigenous, customary decision-making practices is common throughout the Americas. Durand Ponte observes that, in communities in Oaxaca, Mexico, older men who have served in all of the authority positions in the community monopolize decision making, although other members who participate in the reciprocal system of community service may be invited to participate in assemblies to legitimate decisions already made (2007: 11–12).

Unexamined Inequalities. An additional challenge for indigenous-party-led local government in the Andes is the persistence of inequalities within indigenous societies. Inequalities based on gender, geographic location, age, and access to external financial and information resources are not sufficiently scrutinized. As Yashar warns, increasing the autonomy of local cultures and authorities runs the risk of giving power to individuals and factions who use such power in illiberal ways, unchecked by horizontal and vertical accountability (2005: 299). And, as Morrison and Singer found in their study of Bolivia's 2000 National Dialogue, "structures of inequality" within a society can affect the outcome and impact of deliberations and delegitimize deliberative processes (2007: 724–6). Such inequalities need not be based, as might be expected, on income or social status. They find that the capacity of social groups to mobilize for participation and deliberation is more critical.

Gender inequality and men's intimidation and harassment of female indigenous elected officials are particularly troubling (Yashar 2005: 299–300). Mandatory gender quotas in both countries have increased the participation of women at all levels of government, but indigenous men still restrict women to the least-influential positions, rarely nominate or elect them mayor, and, when women do take office, may physically and emotionally abuse them. The problem is worse in Bolivia, and it is not confined to the indigenous population. In 2000 5.4% of mayors and 4.9% of vigilance committee presidents were female (Morrison and Singer 2007: 729n7). Female mayors also have been scarce in Ecuador. The evangelical indigenous party has elected no female mayors and only two women were serving as Pachakutik mayors in 2004 (Proyecto Formia 2004). The continued political exclusion and subordination of indigenous women is a concern in its own right. It also threatens the improvement of well-being in indigenous-party-governed municipalities because development experts elsewhere have found that, when they are involved in deliberations over public spending, female leaders are more likely to channel public resources to projects that address local communities' basic needs (Humphreys et al. 2006: 607). Moreover, deliberations moderated by women may be more likely to result in consensus, as a recent study in Africa demonstrated (ibid.: 608).

In short, we must examine critically the claims of *all* civil society groups that they offer models of democracy that are superior to existing democratic political institutions. Such groups bring new practices, ideas, and energy to governance, but these are not always supportive of democracy, especially when they represent particular identity groups or interests (Armony 2004: 4; Szasz 1995: 150; Warren 2001:18). We should be particularly suspicious of claims that the models they offer are "nonpolitical." Such claims capitalize on citizens' generally low view of politicians but fail to acknowledge that it is impossible to "take the politics out of democratic politics" and that civil society is permeated by inequalities and efforts by individuals and groups to dominate others (Budge 2000: 200). On the other hand, we must recognize that the Western, liberal–democratic regimes indigenous parties seek to replace suffer from serious deficits of democratic quality. Inequality is commonplace, whether owing to formal exclusion or to profound socioeconomic disparities. Existing deliberative spheres tend to favor certain groups and individuals at the expense of others while representational spheres overprivilege better-organized and financed community sectors. In both spheres citizenship is partial and poorly constructed. Both are marked by sexism, authoritarian tendencies, and violence as a means to express and accumulate political power. Neither political parties nor indigenous systems of customary self-government guarantee a full measure of citizenship to all community members.

PRACTICAL IMPLICATIONS

Even "least-likely cases" for the establishment of radical democratic models can produce positive changes in relations among hostile ethnic groups, shift resources toward underserved populations, and create spaces for citizens and civil society groups to deliberate public-spending priorities. But for deliberative–participatory institutions to endure and to improve democratic quality, certain conditions must prevail. External actors – international policymakers, national governments, multilateral donors, and nongovernmental organizations – can promote some of these conditions and, thus, increase the likelihood of beneficial outcomes for society.

First, where democratic institutions are young and weak, effective innovative mayors should be targets of political, technical, and financial support. In their absence, innovative experiments are likely to fail, no matter how well intentioned or designed. Assistance also should be provided to municipal councils to enable them to fulfill representational functions and to restrain the power-concentrating tendency of popular mayors. The exaggerated importance of mayors' leadership styles and capacities to the outcomes of institutional innovation underscores the problem of weak democratic institutions in Latin America. Municipal-government structures, political parties, and the links between local and national governments all are mired in partisan, clientelist, and personalist relations and are subject to too little institutionalized scrutiny. Indeed, weak democratic institutions are the hallmark of Andean governments at all levels (Drake and Hershberg 2006; Mainwaring et al. 2006). More must be done to strengthen political institutions in order to provide auspicious conditions for improving democratic quality in local governance. To start, institutional innovations should be codified in municipal law and consolidated in politically independent institutions so that they will survive the fall of innovating mayors and the whims of their successors. External actors also can facilitate the dissemination of information about these innovations by the mayors themselves. The World Bank has found mayors to be the most effective source of dissemination to other mayors (Campbell and Fuhr 2004).

Second, international donors should identify and fund promising institutional innovations so that they have the resources to fulfill their potential. This entails financial support for infrastructure (i.e., offices, equipment), social spending, and economic development, as well as training programs to enable local people to run their own governments. Bolivia's Ministry of Finance estimates that Bolivian municipalities annually spend on average only 62% of poverty alleviation funds available owing to a lack of technical capacity for writing and implementing project proposals and to the excessive complexity of government regulations relative to human capital at the local level (Morrison and Singer 2007: 733). Moreover, external financial support that improves education levels in communities may have an indirect positive impact on democratic quality by improving the availability and quality of local leaders and reducing levels of inequality that frustrate the formation of social capital (Krishna 2007: 954).

International funding is particularly important in cases in which unmet basic needs are great. This is one reason that the Porto Alegre case succeeded in advancing living conditions whereas the Andean cases did not. Most residents of Porto Alegre already had access to education, electricity, and water, but desired "street paving, trash collection, public transportation, and lighting," and only a minority lived in poverty (Goldfrank 2007b: 153). As a budget councillor that Goldfrank interviewed explained, without money, political will is not sufficient (2007b: 165). Financial and technical resources from international donors, the national government, and domestic NGOs improve democratic quality by facilitating substantive results that maintain citizen interest in and support of new deliberative–participatory institutions. Without sufficient resources to enable local governments to respond to societal demands, state–society linkages may "create more disenchantment than hope" (Ackerman 2004: 11).

Third, development professionals and social scientists should pay more attention to the role of political parties as the architects and engines of innovative democracy-improving institutions. There has been a great deal of attention paid to civil society but relatively less to the role of parties (Baiocchi 2005: 149; Fung and Wright 2003a: 285; Wampler 2008). Parties are in a unique position to serve as transmission belts of ideas and methods between and within geographic levels of government once they have earned public support and have established effective means of communication and coordination. To harness this potential, proposals to improve the region's low democratic quality must not seek to circumvent the region's ailing parties but, rather, to make them a central focus of reform. Nevertheless, the diffusion of innovative democratic institutions will require a strategy that transcends the ambit of any one party or set of parties.

Fourth, social scientists and development professionals should focus on ways to diffuse successful models. I concur with Fung and Wright that local spaces of empowered participatory governance should not serve as "autonomous, atomized sites of decision-making" (2003b: 21). Rather, their lessons should be diffused horizontally to parallel spaces and verti-cally to higher scales of governance. They observed that, in Porto Alegre, Brazil, and Kerala, India, decentralized units coordinate their actions in order to find practical solutions to common problems and they transmit their decisions to higher government levels. In all four cases they stud-ied local units are linked to central coordinating bodies that promote the norms of empowered participatory governance, resolve problems within the units, hold units accountable to common standards, distribute resources, and promote learning (ibid.).

A lack of coordination among and within geographic levels and the resistance of local indigenous organizations to mandates from the center (and vice versa) have prevented indigenous parties from disseminating successful models. Pachakutik and MAS, which control supramunicipal levels of government and cover a broad geographical area, often are characterized by strained relations between municipal-government offi-cials and local party leaders, and between local and national party lead-ers. Local leaders resist national and provincial leaders' efforts to limit the autonomy of local organizations by imposing candidates and pro-grammatic agendas and prioritize managing local relationships ahead of alliances and strategies originating from higher levels. Barriers to hori-zontal coordination among municipalities also exist.

Pachakutik and MAS have tried to meet the challenge of diffusing successful models. In Bolivia, an effort began in 2005 to create a sup-port network among MAS municipalities to diffuse what are considered to be successful models in the Chapare to other parts of the country. Pursuant to this initiative, some municipal officials traveled to Cuba to study the Cuban example in health and education (interview, Rafael Archondo, La Paz, August 1, 2005). Efforts to diffuse successful mod-els are more advanced in Ecuador but they have produced few results. In 1998 the CONAIE-led government agency, Council for the Develop-ment of the Nationalities and Peoples of Ecuador (Consejo de Desar-rollo de las Nacionalidades y Pueblos del Ecuador, or CODENPE), with support from international agencies, established an office for a Coordi-nator of Local Alternative Governments, housed in Pachakutik's Quito headquarters. It is linked to CODENPE's project, Strengthening of Indigenous Alternative Municipalities (Fortalecimiento a Municipios Indígenas Alternativas, or FORMIA). Originally all 29 member governments were Pachakutik-controlled municipalities but by 2005 there were a handful of non-Pachakutik affiliates, representing cases in which Pachakutik lost control of the municipality but technical cooperation continues.[1] Alternative municipalities are defined as those that go beyond their legal obligations to incorporate social participation into public decision making (my translation, Esquel Foundation, cited in UNDP 2006:41). Affiliated local authorities elect the coordinator's leadership, and a technical secretariat provides technical assistance, facilitates exchanges of experiences, articulates the overall philosophy of the alternative municipal government, and organizes conferences and publications that facilitate the exchange of experiences among their members. But the coordinator does not design, impose, or execute particular institutional models or practices. Critics assert that the coordinator has had scant real impact, and some prominent alternative indigenous governments have distanced themselves and criticized it.[2] Muñoz concludes that, "the common project toward the intercultural democratization of local powers" depends mainly on the motivation and capacities of individual mayors and civil society rather than the leadership of CONAIE or Pachakutik (my translation; 1999: 48).

CONCLUSION

This book reflects on what happened when indigenous-party leaders incorporated indigenous political and cultural institutions and values, as well as ideas offered by NGOs, such as PB, into existing liberal–democratic institutions in the Andes in the late 20th century. The

---

[1] In August 2006 the coordinator's website listed 32 alternative municipal governments participating in the second phase of the project, which was to have been completed in February 2005, but was running late when the author interviewed staff in June 2005. Members include all five of the municipalities studied here (www.codenpe.gov.ec/formia.htm) (*Hoy* 2004; interviews in Quito, Gilberto Talahua, June 23, 2005; Julio Yuquilema, June 16, 2005).

[2] Cotacachi Mayor Auki Tituaña has criticized the coordinator for failing to offer its successful model to other Pachakutik-led municipalities, while delegations visit from nonindigenous parties to seek advice – a practice that the mayor attributes to the jealousy of other indigenous officials and party leaders. He also faults the coordinator for trying to impose top-down decisions on the indigenous political movement, without sufficient consulting with the bases, and for being too submissive to government ministries. He views the coordinator as a "little association of municipalities with ponchos" (Tituaña 2004: 9, 21–2).

convergence of diverse governance approaches and ideas created a uniqu
laboratory for mixing distinct governing logics. The marked difference
between the Bolivian and Ecuadorian processes and their outcomes fore
ground the importance of the national context in which decentralization
and institutional innovation take place. Although it is difficult to modif
long-standing historical and cultural conditions and their impact on loca
processes, national actors can make a significant difference to the outcom
of institutional innovation. In Ecuador we saw how President Gutiérrez'
attacks against his former coalition partner Pachakutik ended promising
radically democratic experiments by pushing their main sponsor out o
office in Chimborazo and splitting the indigenous electorate along con
fessional lines. Elsewhere, ironically, Pachakutik's prior association with
Gutiérrez severely restricted the party's achievements in the 2004 loca
and 2006 national elections, curtailing the geographic extension of long
standing successful models elsewhere. In Bolivia, by imposing a rigid
complex, model of local governance, the Sánchez de Lozada governmen
reduced the potential for experimentation at the local level. As nationa
politics became increasingly polarized and violent after 2000, intense
partisan competition permeated local spaces perceived as battleground
in the struggle between "systemic" and "antisystemic" (i.e., indigenous
parties. Intense competition impeded collaboration across parties in loca
government.

The influence of national actors need not always be negative. Although
the intervention of the Bolivian National Controlaría in the fiscal affair
of MAS municipalities irritated the coca federations, it prevented them
from illegally diverting funds away from underrepresented social group
and enforced a new ethic of annual and long-term planning. In circum
stances of overwhelming political hegemony and the fusion of state and
civil society actors, national government representatives provided bal
ance and oversight. Since research for this study ended in 2005, left
leaning governments with strong support in the indigenous population
have gained power in both countries. In 2006–2007 President Morales
led a controversial constitutional reform that may give greater flexibil
ity to indigenous municipalities to design their own institutions. It is
unclear, however, whether the new Constitution will make progress in
this area, owing to the ambiguity of the text, the questionable legitimacy
of a process that Morales skillfully manipulated, and the necessity for
passage of the Constitution by referendum in 2008. Moreover, given the
authoritarian tendencies in rural indigenous culture – and Bolivian pol
itics, more generally – it is uncertain whether greater flexibility would

result in more radically democratic outcomes. In Ecuador, with a mestizo president leading the constitutional reform and a severely weakened indigenous movement far in the background, there is no evidence that the process will result in greater autonomy or more resources for indigenous-party-led municipalities. Indeed, it is likely that President Correa will follow in the footsteps of Morales and Venezuela's Chávez by using the constituent assembly to centralize power and weaken political rivals. With European donors withdrawing from Ecuador, even long-standing Pachakutik alternative governments may be nearing an end. These possibilities underscore the importance of national, and even international, support for local innovative processes.

Notwithstanding the unique settings studied, the findings presented here can be transported to other societies and cultures marked by high levels of poverty and inequality, weak democratic institutions, low public opinion of the law and government, and a lack of experienced politicians and policymakers. As new sectors of society gain access to local elected office in developing areas, their mayors will encounter many of the difficult challenges that indigenous-party mayors encountered in the Andes. And they are unlikely to live in a country like Brazil, where mayors have exaggerated executive powers and access to significant funding resources (Wampler 2007).

The Andean experiences offer an array of self-governing practices that may prove useful in impoverished towns: collective work; incorporating local cultural and religious symbols to enhance the authority of new governance institutions; incorporating traditional methods of leader selection into formal election rituals; and providing mechanisms for community leaders to exercise "social control" over elected authorities. Although these institutions are endemic to Andean indigenous cultures, they can be introduced elsewhere by accommodating local needs and practices, just as Bolivian and Ecuadorian indigenous leaders embraced and transformed Brazil's model of participatory budgeting. Whether or not they represent indigenous peoples or even ethnic minorities, social movements now have another model to follow as they make the leap toward formal representation and electoral politics – in addition to the prior models of the Brazilian Workers' Party and other leftist parties in South American megacities. Because most of the world's municipalities are smaller than Latin America's urban centers, the Andean cases offer more transportable lessons for social movements and civil society networks to manage the expansion of movement activities into electoral campaigns and local government.

These findings shatter the idealized, romantic visions that many social scientists and philosophers promote of indigenous communities. But they are not offered as a critique of indigenous peoples, their cultures, or political institutions. There is much that we can learn and admire – as citizens and social scientists – about indigenous political values and practices by studying them closely. Doing so should broaden our conception of the possibilities we have for radically improving democratic institutions in the global south and north.

References

Abers, Rebecca. 2000. *Inventing Local Democracy: Grassroots Politics in Brazil.* Boulder, CO: Lynne Rienner.

Ackerman, Bruce, and James S. Fishkin. 2002. "Deliberation Day." *The Journal of Political Philosophy* 10, 2: 129–52.

Ackerman, John. 2004. "Co-Governance for Accountability: Beyond 'Exit' and 'Voice.'" *World Development* 32, 3: 447–63.

Aguirre, Consuelo. 2003. "Visita de Presidente provocó división en Guamote." *El Universo*, Aug. 11.

Albó, Xavier. 2002. "Bolivia: From Indian and Campesino Leaders to Councillors and Parliamentary Deputies." In Rachel Sieder, ed. *Multiculturalism in Latin America: Indigenous Rights, Diversity and Democracy.* 74–102. London: Palgrave Macmillan.

———. 1997. "Alcaldes y concejales campesinos/indígenas: La lógica tras las cifras." In *Indígenas en el Poder Local.* La Paz: Ministerio de Desarrollo Humano.

———. 1985. *Desafíos de la solidaridad Aymara.* La Paz: CIPCA.

Albó, Xavier, and Víctor Quispe. 2004. *Quiénes son indígenas en los gobiernos municipales.* Cuadernos de Investigación 59. La Paz: CIPCA.

Albó, Xavier, et al. 1995. *Votos y wiphalas: Campesinos y pueblos originarios en democracia.* La Paz: CIPCA-Fundación Milenio.

Albro, Robert. 2006. "Bolivia's 'Evo Phenomenon': From Identity to What?" *Journal of Latin American Anthropology* 11, 2: 408–28.

Alcántara, Manuel, and Flavia Freidenberg. 2001. "Los Partidos Políticos en América Latina. *América Latina Hoy* 27 (April): 17–35.

Alternative Federal Budget. 2003. *Democracy Counts! Participatory Budgeting In Canada and Abroad.* Technical Paper #4. February 17. Ottawa: Canadian Centre for Policy Alternatives. Available online at http://www.policyalternatives.ca.

Altman, David, and Anibal Pérez-Liñan. 2002. "Assessing the Quality of Democracy: Freedom, Competitiveness and Participation in 18 Countries." *Democratization* 9, 2 (Summer): 85–100.

Andersson, Krister, and Frank Van Laerhoven. 2007. "From Local Strongman to Facilitator: Institutional Incentives for Participatory Municipal Governance in Latin America." *Comparative Political Studies* 40, 9 (Sep.): 1085–111.

Andolina, Robert. 1999. "Colonial Legacies and Plurinational Imaginaries: Indigenous Movement Politics in Ecuador and Bolivia." Ph.D. dissertation. Department of Political Science, University of Minnesota.

Andrade, Susana. 2005. "El despertar político de los indígenas evangélicos en Ecuador." *Iconos. Revista de Ciencias Sociales* (Quito) 22 (May): 49–69.

———. 2004. *Protestantismo Indígena: Procesos de conversión religiosa en la provincia de Chimborazo, Ecuador.* Quito: FLACSO Ecuador.

———. 2003. "Gobiernos locales indígenas en el Ecuador." *Revista Andina* 37: 115–36.

Andrango, Alberto. 1986. "Como indígenas tenemos nuestros planteamientos políticos." *Ecuador Debate* 12 (Dec.): 247–58.

Anrango Ch., Rumiñahui. 2004. "La incursión de la UNORCAC en los procesos del Canton Cotacachi para lograr el poder local." Tesis de Grado, licenciatura. Quito: Universidad Politécnica Salesiana, Facultad de Ciencias Humanas y Educación, Escuela de Gestión para el Desarrollo Local Sostenible.

Aramayo, Fernando. 2003. "Autoidentificación según el Censo Nacional de Población y Vivienda, 2001." In Javier Medina, comp. *Municipio Indígena: La profundización de la descentralización en un Estado multicultural.* 35–43. La Paz: Ministerio de Participación Popular.

Archondo, Rafael. 2004. "Usos Políticos de la Etnicidad en Bolivia." Paper presented at Foro Político: "Líderes y Partidos Indígenas: El Factor Étnico En El Sistema Político Boliviano," La Paz, Bolivian Association of Political Science, Konrad Adenauer Foundation, International Republican Institute, October 6.

———. N.d.a "'Distribuir proporcionalmente', he ahí la discrepancia." Mimeo.

———. N.d.b. "Quién le arrebató al MAS un tercio de sus dominios?" Mimeo.

Arévalo, Segundo Gonzalo, and Ninfa Chela Amangandi. 2001. "*Gestión Indigena en los Poderes Locales: Estudio del caso municipio del Canton Guaranda.*" Monografía del grado. Escuela de Gestión para el Desarrollo Sostenible. Quito: Universidad Politecnica Salesiana.

Armony, Ariel C. 2004. *The Dubious Link: Civic Engagement and Democratization.* Stanford, CA: Stanford University Press.

Armony, Ariel C., and Hector E. Schamis. 2005. "Babel in Democratization Studies." *Journal of Democracy* 16, 4 (Oct.): 113–28.

Arnold, Denise Y. 2004. *Pueblos Indígenas y Originarios de Bolivia: Hacia su soberanía y legitimidad electoral.* La Paz: Corte Nacional Electoral.

Arnson, Cynthia, ed. 2001. *The Crisis of Democratic Governance in the Andes.* Washington, DC: Woodrow Wilson International Center for Scholars.

Atlas del Trópico de Cochabamba. 2004. Cochabamba: Universidad Mayor San Simón.

Avritzer, Leonardo. 2002. *Democracy and the Public Space in Latin America.* Princeton, NJ: Princeton University Press.

Ayo, Diego. 2004. *El Control Social en Bolivia: Una reflexión sobre el Comité de Vigilancia, el Mecanismo de Control Social y demás formas de control social.* Santa Cruz: Editorial El País.

———. 1999. *Los desafíos de la participación popular.* La Paz: CEBEM.

Baéz, Sara, Mary García, Fernando Guerrero, and Ana María Larrea. 1999. *Cotacachi: Capitales comunitarios y propuestas de desarrollo local.* Quito: Ediciones Abya Yala.

Baiocchi, Gianpaolo. 2005. *Militants and Citizens: The Politics of Participatory Democracy in Porto Alegre.* Stanford, CA: Stanford University Press.

———. 2003. "Participation, Activism, and Politics: The Porto Alegre Experiment." In Archon Fung and Erik Olin Wright, eds. *Deepening Democracy: Institutional Innovations in Empowered Participatory Governance.* 45–69. London: Verso.

———. 2001. "Participation, Activism, and Politics: The Porto Alegre Experiment and Deliberative Democratic Theory." *Politics & Society* 29, 1 (March): 43–72.

Baiocchi, Gianpaolo, Patrick Heller, and Marcelo Kunrath Silva. Forthcoming. "Making Space for Civil Society: Institutional Reforms and Local Democracy in Brazil." *Social Forces.*

Barber, Benjamin. 1984. *Strong Democracy: Participatory Politics for a New Age.* Berkeley, CA: University of California Press.

Barona, Jorge. 2003. "Municipios de Pachakutik: Administración con participación local." *El Universo,* Feb. 27, 225–6.

Bartholdson, Orjan, Anders Rudquist, and Charlotta Widmark. 2002. *Popular Participation in Bolivia, Colombia and Peru.* Stockholm: Swedish International Development Agency. Available at www.kus.uu.se/sadelstudie.pdf.

Bass, Bernard M. 1997. "Concepts of Leadership." In Robert P. Vecchio, ed. *Leadership: Understanding the Dynamics of Power and Influence in Organizations.* 3–23. Notre Dame, IN: University of Notre Dame Press.

Bebbington, Anthony. 2005. "Los espacios públicos de concertación local y sus límites en un municipio indígena: Guamote, Ecuador." From the website "Innovación Pública Local en América Latina." Available at http://www.innovacionciudadana.cl/latinoamerica/espacios.asp, retrieved Jan. 15, 2007.

Bebbington, Anthony, and Thomas Carroll. 2000. "Induced Social Capital and Federations of the Rural Poor." Working Paper No. 19 (Feb.). World Bank Social Capital Initiative. Available at www.irisprojects.umd.edu/socat/papers/papers.htm.

Bebbington, Anthony, Gonzalo Delamaza, and Rodrigo Villar. 2005. "El desarrollo de base y los espacios públicos de concertación local en América Latina." From the website "Innovación Pública Local en América Latina." Available at http://www.innovacionciudadana.cl/latinoamerica/espacios.asp, retrieved Jan. 15, 2007.

Beck, Scott H., and Kenneth J. Mijeski. 2001. "Barricades and Ballots: Ecuador's Indians and the Pachakutik Political Movement." *Ecuadorian Studies* 1 (Sep.). Available at http://www.yachana.org/ecuatorianistas/journal/journal.html.

———. 2000. "The Electoral Performance of Ecuador's Pachakutik Political Movement, 1996–1998." Unpublished manuscript.

Becker, Marc. 2007. "Continental Summit of Indigenous Peoples Meets i
Guatemala." April 4, 2007. Available at http://upsidedownworld.org/main
content/view/687/1/.
———. 1999. "Comunas and Indigenous Protest in Cayambe, Ecuador." *Th*
Americas 55, 4: 531–59.
Bernhard, Michael. 1998. "Charismatic Leadership and Democratization: *A*
Weberian Perspective." Working Paper, Penn State University, Center for Euro
pean Studies. Available at http://www.ciaonet.org/wps/bem01.
Birnir, Jóhanna Kristín. 2007. *Ethnicity and Electoral Politics.* New York: Cam
bridge University Press.
———. 2004. "Stabilizing Party Systems and Excluding Segments of Society
The Effects of Formation Costs on New Parties in Latin America." *Studies i*
Comparative International Development 39, 3: 3–28.
Birnir, Jóhanna Kristín, and Donna Lee Van Cott. 2007. "Disunity in Diversity
Party System Fragmentation and the Dynamic Effect of Ethnic Heterogeneit
in Latin America." *Latin American Research Review* 42, 1 (Feb.): 97–123.
Blair, Harry. 2000. "Participation and Accountability at the Periphery: Demo
cratic Local Governments in Six Countries." *World Development* 28, 1: 21–39
Blanes, José. 2003. "La descentralización en Bolivia: Avances y retos actuales." I*
Fernando Carrión, ed. *Procesos de descentralización en la Comunidad Andina*
177–219. Quito: FLACSO.
———. 2000. *Mallkus y Alcaldes: La Ley de Participación Popular en Comu*
nidades Rurales del Altiplano Paceño. La Paz: PIEB, CEBEM.
Boletín ICCI–Rimay. 2002. "Evaluación política del movimiento indígena ecua
toriano." *Boletín ICCI–Rimay* 4, 34 (Jan.). Available at http://icci.nativeweb
org.
Booth, David, Suzanne Clisby, and Charlotta Widmark. 1996. "Empowering th
Poor Through Bold Institutional Reform? An Initial Appraisal of the Bolivia
Experience." Working Paper No. 32. Development Studies Unit, Departmen
of Social Anthropology, Stockholm University.
Booth, David, with Laure-Hélène Piron. 2004. "Politics and the PRSP Approach
Bolivia Case Study." Working Paper No. 238. London: Overseas Developmen
Institute.
Bretón, Víctor. 2005. *Capital Social y etnodesarrollo en los Andes.* Quito: CAAP
———. 2001. *Cooperación al desarrollo y demandas étnicas en los Andes ecua*
torianos. Quito: FLACSO Ecuador.
Bruce, Iain. 2004. "From First Steps to Final Strategies." In Iain Bruce, ed. an
trans. *The Porto Alegre Alternative: Direct Democracy in Action.* 38–53. Lon
don: Pluto Press.
Bruhn, Kathleen. 1997. *Taking on Goliath: The Emergence of a New Left Part*
and the Struggle for Democracy in Mexico. University Park, PA: Penn State
Press.
Budge, Ian. 2000. "Deliberative Democracy Versus Direct Democracy – Plu
Political Parties!" In Michael Saward, ed. *Democratic Innovation: Delibera*
tion, representation and association. 195–209. New York: Routledge.
Bustillo, Raúl. 2003. "Marco Legal." In Javier Medina, comp. *Municipi*
Indígena: La profundización de la descentralización en un Estado multicul
tural. 32–4. La Paz: Ministerio de Participación Popular.

Calla, Ricardo. 2001. "Indigenous Peoples, the Law of Popular Participation and Changes in Government: Bolivia, 1994–1998." In Willem Assies, Gemma van der Haar, and André Hoekema, eds. *The Challenge of Diversity: Indigenous Peoples and Reform of the State in Latin America*. 77–94. Amsterdam: Thela Thesis.

Cameron, John D. 2003a. "Municipal Democratization and Rural Development in Highland Ecuador." In Liisa L. North and John D. Cameron, eds. *Rural Progress, Rural Decay: Neoliberal Adjustment Policies and Local Initiatives*. 164–85. Bloomfield, CT: Kumarian Press.

———. 2003b. "The Social Origins of Municipal Democracy in Rural Ecuador: Agrarian Structures, Indigenous–Peasant Movements, and Non–Governmental Organizations." Ph.D. dissertation. Department of Political Science, York University, Canada.

———. 2000. "Municipal Decentralization and Peasant Organization in Ecuador: A Political Opportunity for Democracy and Development?" Paper prepared for delivery at the 2000 meeting of the Latin American Studies Association. Miami, FL, March 16–18.

Campbell, Tim. 2003. *The Quiet Revolution: Decentralization and the Rise of Political Participation in Latin American Cities*. Pittsburgh, PA: University of Pittsburgh Press.

Campbell, Tim, and Harald Fuhr, eds. 2004. *Leadership and Innovation in Subnational Government: Case Studies from Latin America*. Washington, DC: World Bank Institute.

Carrión M., Fernando. 2003. *Procesos de descentralización en la Comunidad Andina*. Quito: FLACSO.

Censo Nacional de Población y Vivienda. 2001. La Paz: República de Bolivia.

Centro de Desarrollo Integral de la Mujer Aymara. 2000. *Construyendo el camino hacia la toma del Poder local de las comunidades indígenas–originarias*. La Paz: CDIMA.

Chambers, Simone. 2004. "Behind Closed Doors: Publicity, Secrecy, and the Quality of Deliberation." *The Journal of Political Philosophy* 12, 4: 389–410.

Chavez, Daniel, and Benjamin Goldfrank, eds. 2004. *The Left in the City: Participatory Local Governments in Latin America*. London: Latin America Bureau.

Chávez, Walter. 2005. "El MAS avanza en la conformación de un frente social." *El juguete rabioso* (La Paz) (July 24), 8.

CNE. 2005. *Elecciones Municipales 2004: Mayor participación, mayor democracia*. Resultados. Documento de Información Pública No. 5. La Paz: Corte Nacional Electoral, República de Bolivia (Jan.).

Cohen, Jean, and Andrew Arato. 1992. *Civil Society and Political Theory*. Cambridge, MA: MIT Press.

Cohen, Joshua. 1998. "Democracy and Liberty." In Jon Elster, ed. *Deliberative Democracy*. 185–231. Cambridge: Cambridge University Press.

———. 1989. "Deliberation and Democratic Legitimacy." In Alan Hamlin and Philip Pettit, eds. *The Good Polity: Normative Analysis of the State*. 17–34. New York: Blackwell.

Cohen, Joshua, and Archon Fung. 2004. "Radical Democracy." *Swiss Journal of Political Science* 10, 4 (Winter): 23–34.

Cohen, Joshua, and Joel Rogers. 2003. "Power and Reason." In Archon Fung and Erik Olin Wright, eds. *Deepening Democracy: Institutional Innovations in Empowered Participatory Governance.* 237–55. London: Verso.

———, eds. 1995a. *Associations and Democracy.* London: Verso.

———. 1995b. "Solidarity, Democracy, Association." In Joshua Cohen and Joel Rogers, eds. *Associations and Democracy.* 236–67. London: Verso.

Colanzi, Liliana. 2006. "From Social Activists to Political Powerhouse: Evo Morales and the Cocalero Movement in Bolivian Politics." Dissertation submitted for the degree of Master of Philosophy, Wolfson College, Oxford University.

Collins, Jennifer. 2001. "Opening Electoral Politics: Political Crisis and the Rise of Pachakutik." Prepared for delivery at the 2001 meeting of the Latin American Studies Association. Washington, DC, September 6–8.

———. 2000. "A Sense of Responsibility: Ecuador's Indigenous Movement Takes Center Stage." *NACLA Report on the Americas* 33 (March–April): 40–9.

Construyendo. 2004. "Cómo es una elección por usos y costumbres?" *Construyendo* 8 (Dec.): 4–5.

Coordinadora de Gobiernos Locales Alternativos. 2004. *Gobiernos Locales Alternativos* 2 (Dec.).

Coppedge, Michael. 1998. "The Evolution of Latin American Party Systems." In Scott Mainwaring and Arturo Valenzuela, eds. *Politics, Society and Democracy: Latin America.* 171–206. Boulder, CO: Westview Press.

Coppedge, Michael, Angel Alvarez, and Claudia Maldonado. 2008. "Two Persistent Dimensions of Democracy: Contestation and Inclusiveness." *Journal of Politics* 70, 3 (July).

Córdova Eguivar, Gustavo Eduardo. 2004. "Movimientos Sociales y Gestión Municipal: Campesinos cocaleros en el gobierno local del municipio de Puerto Villarroel, Cochabamba, Bolivia (1996–1999)." Tesis para obtener el grado de Maestro en Estudios Políticos y Sociales, Universidad Nacional Autónoma de México. Mexico City.

Cruz, Epifanio. 1998. "Gobiernos municipales y participación popular en el trópico boliviano." In Ana María Larrea and Juan Pablo Muñoz, eds. *Organizaciones Campesinos e Indígenas y Poderes Locales: Propuestas para la Gestión Participativa del Desarrollo Local.* 24–32. Quito: Abya Yala.

CSUTCB. 1996. *VII Congreso CSUTCB: Documentos y Resoluciones.* La Paz: CSUTCB.

Cullel, Jorge Vargas. 2004. "Democracy and the Quality of Democracy." In Guillermo O'Donnell, Jorge Vargas Cullel, and Osvaldo M. Iazzetta, eds. *The Quality of Democracy: Theory and Applications.* 93–162. Notre Dame, IN: University of Notre Dame Press.

Dahl, Robert. 1971. *Polyarchy: Participation and Opposition.* New Haven, CT: Yale University Press.

Daubón, Ramón E., and Harold H. Saunders. 2002. "Operationalizing Social Capital: A Strategy to Enhance Communities' 'Capacity to Concert.'" *International Studies Perspectives* 3: 176–91.

De la Cadena, Marisol. 2000. *Indigenous Mestizos: The Politics of Race and Culture in Cuzco, Peru, 1919–1991.* Durham, NC: Duke University.

De la Fuente, Manuel. 2001. "Introducción." In Manuel de la Fuente, comp. *Participación Popular y Desarrollo Local: La situación de los municipios rurales de Cochabamba y Chuquisaca.* 13–35. Cochabamba: Universidad Mayor de San Simón.

———. 1999. "Desafíos de los municipios innovadores." *Pachakutik: Revista de Debate Político* 1 (July): 66–7.

Desai, Manali. 2003. "From Movement to Party to Government: Why Social Policies in Kerala and West Bengal Are so Different." In Jack A. Goldstone, ed. *States, Parties, and Social Movements.* 170–96. New York: Cambridge University Press.

Domínguez, Jorge I., ed. 1997. *Technopols: Freeing Politics and Markets in Latin America in the 1990s.* University Park, PA: Penn State University Press.

Drake, Paul, and Eric Hershberg, eds. 2006. *State and Society in Conflict: Comparative Perspectives on Andean Crises.* Pittsburgh, PA: University of Pittsburgh Press.

Dryzek, John S. 2005. "Deliberative Democracy in Divided Societies: Alternatives to Agonism and Analgesia." *Political Theory* 33, 2 (April): 218–42.

———. 1990. *Discursive Democracy.* Cambridge: Cambridge University Press.

Durand Ponte, Víctor Manuel. 2007. "Prólogo." In Jorge Hernández–Díaz, coord. *Ciudadanías diferenciadas en un estado multicultural: los usos y costumbres en Oaxaca.* 11–34. México: Siglo XXI.

Eaton, Kent. 2004. *Politics Beyond the Capital: The Design of Subnational Institutions in South America.* Stanford, CA: Stanford University Press.

Eckstein, Susan. 2001. "Where Have All the Movements Gone: Latin American Social Movements at the Millennium." In Susan Eckstein, ed. *Power and Popular Protest: Latin American Social Movements.* 351–406. Berkeley, CA: University of California Press.

Eid, Claudia. 2007. "Arden Punata y Villa Rivero y ya van 5 alcaldes vetados." *Los Tiempos,* March 3, online.

Eisenstadt, S. N. 1968. "Introduction." In Max Weber. *On Charisma and Institution Building. Selected Papers.* Edited and with an introduction by S. N. Eisenstadt. ix–lvi. Chicago, IL: University of Chicago Press.

Eisenstadt, Todd. 2004. *Courting Democracy in Mexico: Party Strategies and Electoral Institutions.* New York: Cambridge University Press.

———. 2008. "Surveying the Silence: Liberal and Communal Identities in Southern Mexico's Indigenous Rights Movement." Unpublished book manuscript.

Eisenstadt, Todd, and Viridiana Rios Contreras. 2007. "The Manipulation of Indigenous Electoral Traditions in Mexico?" Paper prepared for presentation at the 2007 International Conference of the Latin American Studies Association. Montréal, Québec. September 6–8.

El Comercio. 2004a. "El Gobierno sabe manejar a la fe indígena." *El Comercio,* Dec. 6, no page number.

———. 2004b. "Las comunidades evangélicas minaron." *El Comercio,* Aug. 28, no page number.

———. 2003a. "El Gobierno distribruría sus fundas de arroz a los pobres." *El Comercio,* March 1, no page number.

————. 2003b. "La otra lectura de las visitas de Gutiérrez a Chimborazo." *El Comercio*, March 19, no page number.

El Diario. 2005. "MAS inició 'masacre blanca' con despidos en región de Quillacollo." *El Diario* [La Paz], March 11, no page number.

Elster, Jon. 1998. "Introduction." In Jon Elster, ed. *Deliberative Democracy*. Cambridge: Cambridge University Press.

Enlared Municipal. 2005. "Más de 100 concejales indígenas gobernarán en 60 municipios." Enlared Municipal. Online at www.enlared.org.bo/2004.

Evans, Peter. 1997. "Government Action, Social Capital, and Development: Reviewing the Evidence on Synergy." In Peter Evans, ed. *State-Society Synergy: Government and Social Capital in Development*. 178–209. Berkeley, CA: University of California Press.

Faust, Jorg, and Imke Harbers. 2007. "Political Parties and the Politics of Administrative Decentralization: Exploring Subnational Variants in Ecuador." Paper prepared for presentation at the 27 Annual Meeting of the Southern Political Science Association. New Orleans, Louisiana, January 10–13.

Febres Cordero, Francisco. 2004. "Campaña en cantones pobres." *El Universo*, Sep. 19.

Fearon, James D. 1998. "Deliberation as Discussion." In Jon Elster, ed. *Deliberative Democracy*. 44–68. Cambridge: Cambridge University Press.

Fishman, Robert M. 2004. *Democracy's Voices: Social Ties and the Quality of Public Life in Spain*. Ithaca, NY: Cornell University Press.

Flor, Eulalia. 2001. "Interculturalidad al fronterizar poder, política y representación en Ecuador: Experiencias en algunos municipios." Prepared for presentation at the International Congress of the Latin American Studies Association. Washington, DC, September 6–8.

Foweraker, Joe. 1995. *Theorizing Social Movements*. London: Pluto Press.

Foweraker, Joe, Todd Landman, and Neil Harvey. 2003. *Governing Latin America*. Cambridge: Polity Press.

Fox, Jonathan. 1996. "How Does Civil Society Thicken? The Political Construction of Social Capital in Rural Mexico." *World Development* 24, 6: 1089–103.

Fung, Archon. 2007. "Democratic Theory and Political Science: A Pragmatic Method of Constructive Engagement." *American Political Science Review* 101, 3 (Aug.): 443–58.

————. 2005. "Deliberation Before the Revolution: Toward an Ethics of Deliberative Democracy in an Unjust World." *Political Theory* 33, 2 (June): 397–419.

Fung, Archon, and Erik Olin Wright, 2003a. "Countervailing Power in Empowered Participatory Governance." In Archon Fung and Erik Olin Wright, eds. *Deepening Democracy: Institutional Innovations in Empowered Participatory Governance*. 259–89. London: Verso.

————. 2003b. "Thinking about Empowered Participatory Governance." In Archon Fung and Erik Olin Wright, eds. *Deepening Democracy: Institutional Innovations in Empowered Participatory Governance*. 3–42. London: Verso.

Galindo Soza, Mario. 2003. "Municipio Indígena: Análisis político de la profundización de la descentralización en un Estado multicultural." In Javier Medina, comp. *Municipio Indígena: La profundización de la descentralización en un Estado multicultural*. 103–20. La Paz: Ministerio de Participación Popular.

García, Édgar. 2005. "Transición e inexperiencia: Pocas obras en municipios." *Los Tiempos*, July 31, 12.

García Linera, Alvaro, coord. 2004. "La Coordinadora de las seis federaciones del Trópico de Cochabamba." In *Sociología de los Movimientos Sociales en Bolivia: Estructuras de movilización, repertorios culturales y acción política.* 383–457. La Paz: Diakonia Acción Ecumenica Sueca, Oxfam.

Garman, Christopher, Stephan Haggard, and Eliza Willis. 2001. "Fiscal Decentralization: A Political Theory with Latin American Cases." *World Politics* 53 (Jan.): 205–36.

Garza, Michelle. 2005. "Coca Politics: Women's Leadership in the Chapare." Bachelor's thesis, Departments of Anthropology, Women, Gender, and Sexuality. Harvard University, Cambridge, MA.

Gente. 2005. "MAS impone 'masacre blanca.'" *Gente* [Cochabamba], March 10, no page number.

Gerth, H.H., and C. Wright Mills. 1946. *From Max Weber: Essays in Sociology.* 77–128. New York: Oxford University Press.

Glenn, John K. 2003. "Parties out of Movements: Party Emergence in Post-Communist Eastern Europe." In Jack A. Goldstone, ed. *States, Parties, and Social Movements.* 147–69. New York: Cambridge University Press.

Goldfrank, Benjamin. 2007a "Lessons from Latin America's Experience with Participatory Budgeting." In Anwar Shah, ed. *Participatory Budgeting.* 91–126. Washington, DC: World Bank.

———. 2007b. "The Politics of Deepening Local Democracy: Decentralization, Party Institutionalization, and Participation." *Comparative Politics* 39, 2: 147–68.

———. 2006. "Los procesos de "presupuesto participativo" en América Latina: éxito, fracaso y cambio." *Revista de Ciencia Política* 26, 2: 3–28.

———. 2004. "Conclusion: The End of Politics or a New Beginning for the Left?" In Daniel Chavez and Benjamin Goldfrank, eds. *The Left in the City: Participatory Local Governments in Latin America.* 193–211. London: Latin America Bureau.

Goldstone, Jack A., 2003. "Introduction: Bridging Institutionalized and Noninstitutionalized Politics." In Jack A. Goldstone, ed. *State, Parties, and Social Movements.* 1–24. New York: Cambridge University Press.

Gootaert, Christian, and T. Van Bastelaer. 2001. *"Understanding and Measuring Social Capital: A Synthesis of Findings and Recommendations from the Social Capital Initiative."* Working Paper No. 24. Washington, DC: World Bank.

Gray Molina, George. 2003. "The Offspring of 1952: Poverty, Exclusion and the Promise of Popular Participation." In Merilee S. Grindle and Pilar Domingo, eds. *Proclaiming Revolution: Bolivia in Comparative Perspective.* 345–63. London: Institute of Latin American Studies.

———. 2001. "Exclusion, Participation and Democratic State–Building." In John Crabtree and Laurence Whitehead, eds. *Towards Democratic Viability: The Bolivian Experience.* 63–82. Oxford: Palgrave.

Gray Molina, George, and Carlos Hugo Molina Saucedo. 1997. "Popular Participation and Decentralization in Bolivia: Building Accountability from the Grassroots." Paper prepared for a seminar to evaluate the Bolivian reforms organized by the Harvard Institute for International Development, Cambridge MA, April 30.

Grinde, Donald A. 1992. "Iroquois Political Theory and the Roots of American Democracy." In Oren Lyons and John C. Mohawk, eds. *Exiled in the Land of the Free: Democracy, Indian Nations, and the U.S. Constitution.* Santa Fe NM: Clear Light.

Grindle, Merilee S. 2000. *Audacious Reforms: Institutional Invention and Democracy in Latin America.* Baltimore, MD: Johns Hopkins University Press.

———. 2007. *Going Local: Decentralization, Democratization, and the Promise of Good Governance.* Princeton, NJ: Princeton University Press.

Guerrero C., Fernando. 1999. "La experiencia de participación y gestión local en Cotacachi." In *Ciudadanias Emergentes: Experiencias democráticas de desarrollo local.* 113–28. Quito: Ediciones Abya Yala.

Guss, David M. 2006. "Introduction: Indigenous Peoples and New Urbanisms." *Journal of Latin American Anthropology* 11, 2: 259–66.

Habermas, Jurgen. 1984. *The Theory of Communicative Action.* Boston: Beacon Press.

Hagopian, Frances. 2005. "Conclusions." In Frances Hagopian and Scott P. Mainwaring, eds. *The Third Wave of Democratization in Latin America: Advances and Setbacks.* 319–62. New York: Cambridge University Press.

Hagopian, Frances and Scott P. Mainwaring, eds. 2005. *The Third Wave of Democratization in Latin America: Advances and Setbacks.* New York: Cambridge University Press.

Hambleton, Robin. 2004. "Leading localities in a partnership era." *Local Governance* 30, 1: 4–13.

Healy, Kevin. 1991. "Political Ascent of Bolivia's Peasant Coca Leaf Producers." *Journal of Inter–American Studies and World Affairs* 33, 1 (Spring): 87–121.

Heller, Patrick. 2001. "Moving the State: The Politics of Democratic Decentralization in Kerala, South Africa, and Porto Alegre." *Politics & Society* 29, 1: 131–63.

Herbas, Mónica, and Alberto Lizárraga. 2001. "Conflicto político en el municipio de Puerto Villarroel." In *Crisis en el desarrollo local: Conflictos políticos, desastres y protestas sociales en municipios de Cochabamba.* 41–57. Cochabamba: Centro de Estudios de la Realidad Económica y Social.

Herbas Camacho, Gabriel. 2000. "El Desarrollo Local y la articulación de sus factores en el Municipio del Chimoré." Tesis de Maestría en Estudios de Desarrollo. Cochabamba: CESU–UMSS.

Hernández-Díaz, Jorge. 2007a. "Dilemas en la construcción de ciudadanías diferenciadas en un espacio multicultural: el caso de Oaxaca." In Jorge Hernández Díaz, coord. *Ciudadanías diferenciadas en un estado multicultural: los usos costumbres en Oaxaca.* 35–86. México: Siglo XXI.

———. 2007b. "Presentación." In Jorge Hernández-Díaz, coord. *Ciudadanías diferenciadas en un estado multicultural: los usos y costumbres en Oaxaca.* 7–10. México: Siglo XXI.

Hernández-Díaz, Jorge, and Víctor Leonel Juan Martínez. 2007. *Dilemas de la institución municipal. Una incursión en la experiencia oaxaqueña.* México City: Miguel Angel Porrúa.

Hirst, Paul Q. 1995. "Can Secondary Associations Enhance Democratic Governance?" In Joshua Cohen and Joel Rogers, eds. *Associations and Democracy.* 101–13. London: Verso.

———. 1994. *Associative Democracy: New Forms of Economic and Social Governance.* Amherst, MA: University of Massachusetts Press.

Hiskey, Jonathan T., and Mitchell A. Seligson. 2003. "Pitfalls of Power to the People: Decentralization, Local Government Performance, and System Support in Bolivia." *Studies in Comparative International Development* 37, 4 (Winter): 64–88.

Hoy. 2004. "Voz del pueblo es ley en 27 zonas." *Hoy*, Aug. 3, no page number.

———. 2003. "Indios ven afán político de PSP en entrega de palas." *Hoy*, May 13, no page number.

Humphreys, Macartan, William A. Masters, and Martin E. Sandbu. 2006. "The Role of Leaders in Democratic Deliberations: Results from a Field Experiment in São Tomé and Príncipe." *World Politics* 58 (July): 583–622.

Hurtado, Edison A. 2002. "Una participación en busca de actors: Otavalo 2000–2002." Paper presented at the First Conference of Ecuadorianists. Available at www.ecuatorianistas.org/encuentro/2002/ponencias/hurtado.pdf.

Immergut, Ellen M. 1995. "An Institutional Critique of Associative Democracy." In Joshua Cohen and Joel Rogers, eds. *Associations and Democracy.* 201–6. London: Verso.

Instituto Nacional de Estadística y Censos. 2001. *Censo Nacional de Población y Vivienda.* Available at www.inec.gov.ec.

Inter-American Development Bank. 2002. *Making Decentralization Work in Latin America and the Caribbean: A Background Paper for the Subnational Development Strategy.* Washington, DC: Inter-American Development Bank.

International Crisis Group. 2006. *Bolivia's Rocky Road to Reform.* Latin America Report No. 18. Bogotá/Brussels: International Crisis Group (July 3).

James, Michael Rabinder. 2004. *Deliberative Democracy and the Plural Polity.* Lawrence, KS: University Press of Kansas.

Johnson, James. 1998. "Arguing for Deliberation: Skeptical Consideration." In Jon Elster, ed. *Deliberative Democracy.* 161–84. Cambridge: Cambridge University Press.

Keck, Margaret E. 1992. *The Workers' Party and Democratization in Brazil.* New Haven, CT: Yale University Press.

Kitschelt, Herbert. 2000. "Linkages Between Citizens and Politicians in Democratic Polities." *Comparative Political Studies* 33, 6/7 (Aug./Sep.): 845–79.

———. 1989. *The Logics of Party Formation: Ecological Politics in Belgium and West Germany.* Ithaca, NY: Cornell University Press.

Kohl, Benjamin. 2001. "ONGs y Participación Popular en las Areas Rurales de Bolivia." In Manuel de la Fuente, comp. *Participación Popular y Desarrollo Local: La situación de los municipios rurales de Cochabamba y Chuquisaca.* 75–107. Cochabamba: Universidad Mayor de San Simón.

Korovkin, Tanya. 2003. "Agrarian Capitalism and Communal Institutional Spaces: Chimborazo after the Land Reform." In Liisa L. North and John D. Cameron, eds. *Rural Progress, Rural Decay: Neoliberal Adjustment Policies and Local Initiatives.* 127–42. Bloomfield, CT: Kumarian Press.

Krishna, Anirudh. 2007. "How Does Social Capital Grow? A Seven–Year Study of Villages in India." *Journal of Politics* 69, 4 (Nov.): 941–56.

Kymlicka, Will. 1999. "Citizenship in an Era of Globalization: Commentary on Held." In Ian Shapiro and Casiano Hacker-Cordon, eds. *Democracy's Edges.* 112–26. New York: Cambridge University Press.

Kymlicka, Will, and Wayne Norman. 2000. "Citizenship in Culturally Diverse Societies: Issues, Contexts, Concepts." In Will Kymlicka and Wayne Norman, eds. *Citizenship in Diverse Societies.* 1–41. New York: Oxford University Press.

Lalander, Rickard. 2005. "Movimiento indígena, participación política y buen gobierno municipal en Ecuador: El Alcalde Mario Conejo de Otavalo." *Ecuador Debate* 66 (Dec.): 153–82.

La Prensa. 2004. "Provincias: de 720 candidatos 603 postulan por los partidos." *La Prensa* [La Paz], Oct. 12, 4.

———. 2002. "Ud. Elige," special supplement. *La Razón*, June 28, 8.

La Razón. 2006a. "Alcaldías recibirán más de Bs mil millones." *La Razón*, Oct. 17, online.

———. 2006b. "La censura todavía es una costumbre municipal." *La Razón*, Dec. 26, online.

———. 2006c. "Las petroleras se convierten en operadoras de Yacimientos." *La Razón*, Oct. 30, online.

———. 2006d. "Los municipios ya deben elaborar su POA y Presupuesto del 2007." *La Razón*, Oct. 17, online.

———. 2005a. "El MAS confía en el voto rural y apunta a la clase media." *La Razón*, Sep. 12, online.

———. 2005b. "El MAS tiene alianzas con 50 sectores." *La Razón*, Sep. 11, online.

———. 2005c. "Evo negocia e hipoteca curules con sus aliados." *La Razón*, Sep. 2, online.

———. 2005d. "Los tres principales partidos prevén cambios en sus listas." *La Razón*, Sep. 14, online.

———. 2005e. "Villa Tunari y Chimoré se benefician con ocho obras." *La Razón*, March 4, D2.2.

———. 2004a. "Los líderes del altiplano destapan su disputa por lograr hegemonía." *La Razón*. June 28, A6.

———. 2004b. "Los resultados no muestran tendencias a nivel nacional." *La Razón*. Dec. 16, online.

———. 1998. "Congreso de ASP expulsó a Alejo Véliz y eligió a Evo Morales." *La Razón*, Oct. 7, 22–23.

Larrea, Ana María, and Fernando Larrea. 1999. "Participación ciudadana, relaciones interétnicas y construcción del poder local en Saquisilí." In *Ciudadanías Emergentes: Experiencias democráticas de desarrollo local.* 129–52. Quito: Ediciones Abya Yala.

Latin American Weekly Report. 2007. "Bolivia succumbs to social conflict as Morales loses control." *Latin American Weekly Report*, Jan. 18, 1–2.

Lauer, Matthew. 2006. "State–led Democratic Politics and Emerging Forms of Indigenous Leadership Among the Ye'kwana of the Upper Orinoco." *Journal of Latin American Anthropology* 11, 1: 51–86.

Levi, Ron, Will Kymlicka, and Peter Evans. 2007. "Transnational Transfer and Societal Success: Examining the Transnational Construction of Institutions Aimed at Expanding Rights and Enhancing Capacities." Unpublished draft manuscript.

Levitsky, Steven. 2001. "Inside the Black Box: Recent Studies of Latin American Party Organizations." *Studies in Comparative International Development* 36, 2 (Summer): 92–110.

Levitsky, Steven, and Maxwell A. Cameron. 2001. "Democracy Without Parties? Political Parties and Regime Collapse in Fujimori's Peru." Paper Prepared for presentation at the Congress of the Latin American Studies Association, Washington, DC, September 6–8.

Lizárraga, Alberto. 1998. "Sindicalismo campesino en el trópico cochabambino y participación local." In Ana María Larrea and Juan Pablo Muñoz, eds. *Organizaciones Campesinos e Indígenas y Poderes Locales: Propuestas para la Gestión Participativa del Desarrollo Local.* 54–62. Quito: Red Interamericana Agricultura y Democracia.

Lizárraga, Alberto, and Héctor Villarroel. 1998. *Organizaciones Sindicales Agrarias y Gobierno Local: El Caso de los Municipios de Puerto Villarroel y Chimoré.* Cochabamba: CERES.

López, Félix. 2003. "Modelo de estructura política andina. Insumos para una propuesta de gestión pública para Municipios Indígenas en Tierras Altas." In Javier Medina, comp. *Municipio Indígena: La profundización de la descentralización en un Estado multicultural.* 83–92. La Paz: Ministerio de Participación Popular.

Los Tiempos. 2007. "Hubo tráfico de avales del MAS en la gestión Alvarado en YPFB." *Los Tiempos,* March 6, online.

———. 2004. "MAS arrasó con alcaldías cochabambinas." *Los Tiempos,* Dec. 9, 4.

———. 2001. "Conflicto municipal deriva en agresiones," *Los Tiempos,* May 22, D2.2.

———. 1999a. "Evo Morales y los cocaleros fundan su partido político." *Los Tiempos,* Jan. 15, 2A.

———. 1999b. "Morales y Véliz tienen sectores contrarios." *Los Tiempos,* Jan. 15, 2A.

———. N.d. Special edition. "Bolivia en Transición." *Los Tiempos,* 12–13.

Loughlin, John. 2005. "The 'Transformation' of Governance: New Directions in Policy and Politics." In Ramon Maiz and Ferran Requejo, eds. *Democracy, Nationalism and Multiculturalism.* 144–59. New York: Routledge.

Lowndes, Vivien, and Steve Leach. 2004. "Understanding Local Political Leadership: Constitutions, Contexts and Capabilities." *Local Government Studies* 30, 4 (Winter): 557–75.

Lucero, José Antonio. 2008. *Struggles of Voice: The Politics of Indigenous Representation in the Andes.* University of Pittsburgh Press.

———. 2006. "Representing 'Real Indians': The Challenges of Indigenous Authenticity and Strategic Constructivism in Ecuador and Bolivia." *Latin American Research Review* 41, 2 (June): 31–56.

Macas, Luis. 2005. "Reflexiones sobre el sujeto comunitario, la democracia y el Estado." Entrevista realizada por Daniel Mato en Quito, el 25/07/2003; editada y revisada por Luis Macas y Pablo Dávalos, en marzo de 2005. *Colección Entrevistas a Intelectuales Indígenas* No. 3. Caracas: Programa Globalización, Cultura y Transformaciones Sociales, CIPOST, FaCES, Universidad Central de Venezuela. Available at http://www.globalcult.org.ve/entrevistas.html.

Machado Puertas, Juan Carlos. 2007. "Ecuador: El Derrumbe de los partidos tradicionales." *Revista de Ciencia Política*. Volúmen Especial, Anuario Político de América Latina, 129–47.

Madrid, Raúl. 2005. "Ethnic Cleavages and Electoral Volatility in Latin America." *Comparative Politics* 38, 1 (Oct.): 1-20.

Maguire, Diarmuid. 1995. "Opposition Movements and Opposition Parties: Equal Partners or Dependent Relations in the Struggle for Power and Reform." In Craig J. Jenkins and Bert Klandermans, eds. *The Politics of Social Protest: Comparative Perspectives on States and Social Movements*. 199–228. Minneapolis, MN: University of Minnesota.

Mainwaring, Scott. 1999. *Rethinking Party Systems in the Third Wave of Democratization: The Case of Brazil*. Stanford, CA: Stanford University Press.

Mainwaring, Scott, Ana María Bejarano, and Eduardo Pizarro Leongómez. 2006. *The Crisis of Democratic Representation in the Andes*. Stanford, CA: Stanford University Press.

Mainwaring, Scott, and Frances Hagopian. 2005. "Introduction: The Third Wave of Democratization in Latin America." In Frances Hagopian and Scott P. Mainwaring, eds. *The Third Wave of Democratization in Latin America: Advances and Setbacks*. 1–13. New York: Cambridge University Press.

Mainwaring, Scott, and Anibal Pérez-Liñan. 2005. "Latin American Democratization Since 1978: Democratic Transitions, Breakdowns, and Erosions." In Frances Hagopian and Scott P. Mainwaring, eds. *The Third Wave of Democratization in Latin America: Advances and Setbacks*. 14–62. New York: Cambridge University Press.

Mainwaring, Scott, and Timothy Scully, eds. 1995. *Building Democratic Institutions: Party Systems in Latin America*. Stanford, CA: Stanford University Press.

Mansbridge, Jane J. 2000. "What Does a Representative Do? Descriptive Representation in Communicative Settings of Distrust, Uncrystallized Interests, and Historically Denigrated Status." In Will Kymlicka and Wayne Norman, eds. *Citizenship in Diverse Societies*. 99–123. New York: Oxford University Press.

———. 1995. "A Deliberative Perspective on Neocorporatism." In Joshua Cohen and Joel Rogers, eds. *Associations and Democracy*. 133–47. London: Verso.

———. 1983. *Beyond Adversary Democracy*. Chicago, IL: University of Chicago Press.

Mason, Ann C. 2005. "Constructing Authority Alternatives on the Periphery: Vignettes from Colombia." *International Political Science Review* 26, 1: 37-54.

Mauceri, Philip and Jo-Marie Burt, eds. 2004. *Politics in the Andes: Identity, Conflict, Reform*. Pittsburgh, PA: University of Pittsburgh Press.

Mayer, Margit, and John Ely. 1998. *The German Greens: Paradox between Movement and Party*. Philadelphia, PA: Temple University Press.

Medina, Javier. 2003a. "Municipio Indígena: Historia de un concepto." In Javier Medina, comp. *Municipio Indígena: La profundización de la descentralización en un Estado multicultural*. 13–31. La Paz: Ministerio de Participación Popular.

———. 2003b. "Una sugerencia." In Javier Medina, comp. *Municipio Indígena: La profundización de la descentralización en un Estado multicultural*. 123–5. La Paz: Ministerio de Participación Popular.

Meisch, Lynn. 2002. *Andean Entrepreneurs: Otavalo Merchants and Musicians in the Global Arena*. Austin, TX: University of Texas Press.

Merkl, Peter H. 2007. "Becoming the Party of Government." In Peter H. Merkl and Kay Lawson, eds. *When Parties Prosper: The Uses of Electoral Success*. 331–51. Boulder, CO: Lynne Rienner.

Ministerio de Desarrollo Humano. 1996. *Las Primeras Elecciones: Directorio de Alcaldes y Concejales de la Participación Popular*. La Paz: Ministerio de Desarrollo Humano, Secretaría Nacional de Participación Popular.

Ministerio de Desarrollo Municipal. 2002. *Estudio de Evaluación de Capacidades Institucionales y de Gestión de los Gobiernos Municipales*. La Paz: Ministerio de Desarrollo Municipal, República de Bolivia.

Ministerio de Desarrollo Sustenible y Planificación. 2000. "El proceso de Participación Popular a seis años de su vigencia." Advertisement in *Presencia* (La Paz), April 20, 1.

Miranda, Jorge. 2003. "Problemática territorial indígena." In Javier Medina, comp. *Municipio Indígena: La profundización de la descentralización en un Estado multicultural*. 75–82. La Paz: Ministerio de Participación Popular.

Montero, Alfred P., and David J. Samuels. 2004. "The Political Determinants of Decentralization in Latin America: Causes and Consequences." In Alfred P. Montero and David J. Samuels, eds. *Decentralization and Democracy in Latin America*. 3–32. Notre Dame, IN: University of Notre Dame Press.

Molina Monasterios, Fernando. 1997. *Historia de la participación popular*. La Paz: Ministerio de Desarrollo Humano.

Morlino, Leonardo. 2004. "What is a 'Good' Democracy?" *Democratization* 11, 5 (Dec.): 10–32.

Morrison, Kevin M., and Matthew M. Singer. 2007. "Inequality and Deliberative Development: Revisiting Bolivia's Experience with the PRSP." *Development Policy Review* 25, 6: 721–40.

Mouffe, Chantal and Ernesto Laclau. 1985. *Hegemony and Socialist Strategy: Towards a Radical Democratic Politics*. London: Verso.

Movimiento al Socialismo. 2004a. "Complementación al documento fundamental "Nuestros Principios Ideológicos," antes redactado, aprobado por el Movimiento al Socialismo, en su V Congreso Nacional Ordinario, llevado adelante en la Ciudad de Oruro los Días 13, 14 Y 15 de diciembre de 2003. In *Movimiento al Socialismo. MAS–IPSP, Poder, Territorio, Sabiduría*. La Paz: Imprenta Editorial Grafival.

———. 2004b. *Poder, Territorio, Sabiduría*. La Paz: Imprenta Editorial Gráfica.

Movimiento al Socialismo–IPSP. 2004c. *Propuesta Integral para el Municipio de Puerto Villarroel, Gestión 2005–2010*. Mimeo.

Munck, Gerardo L., and Jay Verkuilen. 2002. "Conceptualizing and Measuring Democracy: Evaluating Alternative Indices." *Comparative Political Studies* 35, 1 (Feb.): 5–34.

Muñoz, Juan Pablo. 1999. "Indígenas y gobiernos locales: Entre la plurinacionalidad y la ciudadanía cantonal." In *Ciudadanías Emergentes: Experiencias democráticas de desarrollo local*. 39–62. Quito: Ediciones Abya Yala.

Naula Yangol, Hilario. 2003. "Mecanismos de participación democrática en el gobierno local del canton de Guamote." Tesis de Grado, licenciatura. Quito: Universidad Politécnica Salesiana, Facultad de Ciencias Humanas y Educación, Escuela de Gestión para el Desarrollo Local Sostenible.

Nylen, William R. 2003. *Participatory Democracy versus Elitist Democracy: Lessons from Brazil*. London: Palgrave Macmillan.

O'Donnell, Guillermo. 2004. "Human Development, Human Rights and Democracy." In Guillermo O'Donnell, Jorge Vargas Cullel, and Osvaldo M. Iazzetta, eds. *The Quality of Democracy: Theory and Applications*. 9–92. Notre Dame, IN: University of Notre Dame Press.

———. 1997. "Illusions about Consolidation." In Larry Diamond, Mark F. Plattner, Y. Chu, and H. Tien, eds. *Consolidating the Third Wave Democracies: Themes and Perspectives*. Baltimore, MD: Johns Hopkins University Press.

———. 1994. "The State, Democratization, and Some Conceptual Problems: (A Latin American View with Glances at Some Post–Communist Countries)." In William C. Smith, Carlos H. Acuña, and Eduardo A. Gamarra, eds. *Latin American Political Economy in the Age of Neoliberal Reform: Theoretical and Comparative Perspectives for the 1990s*. 157–80. New Brunswick, NJ: Transaction Publishers.

Offe, Claus. 1984. *Contradictions of the Welfare State*. John Keane, ed. Cambridge, MA: MIT Press.

Ojeda Segovia, Lautaro. 2004. "Por qué la descentralización no avanza?" *Ecuador Debate* 61 (April): 95–116.

O'Neill, Kathleen. 2005. *Decentralizing the State: Elections, Parties, and Local Power in the Andes*. New York: Cambridge University Press.

———. 2004. "Decentralization in Bolivia: Electoral Incentives and Outcomes." In Alfred P. Montero and David J. Samuels, eds. *Decentralization and Democracy in Latin America*. 35–66. Notre Dame, IN: University of Notre Dame Press.

Opinión. 2005. "Exigen respeto al triunfo de la alcaldesa de Chimoré." *Opinión* [Cochabamba], Jan. 13, D 2.2.

———. 2004. No title. *Opinión*, Dec. 9, no page number.

Orellana Halkyer, René. 2001. "Municipalization and Indigenous Peoples in Bolivia: Impacts and Perspectives." In Willem Assies, Gemma van der Haar, and André Hoekema, eds. *The Challenge of Diversity: Indigenous Peoples and Reform of the State in Latin America*. 181–94. Amsterdam: Thela Thesis.

Ortiz Crespo, Santiago. 2004. *Cotacachi: una apuesta por la democracia participativa*. Quito: FLACSO.

———. 1999. "Participación ciudadana y desarrollo local: Algunas pistas de reflexión." In *Ciudadanías Emergentes: Experiencias democráticas de desarrollo local*. 68–86. Quito: Ediciones Abya Yala.

Ospina, Pablo. 2005. "Movimiento Indígena y democracia local en Cotacachi y Cotopaxi: apuntes sobre el desarrollo rural." Ponencia presentada en el Primer Encuentro de Investigacíon sobre la Sociedad Rural, Quito, October 26–27.

Pachano, Simón. 2006. *The Elections in Ecuador*. Real Instituto Eleano, ARI 101/2006. Sep. 29, 1–6.

Panebianco, Angelo. 1988. *Political Parties: Organization and Power*. Cambridge: Cambridge University Press.

Pallares, Amalia. 2002. *From Peasant Struggles to Indian Resistance. The Ecuadorian Andes in the Late Twentieth Century*. Norman, OK: University of Oklahoma Press.

Participación popular y municipio. 1996. Debate Regional 24. Cochabamba, La Paz: ILDIS, CERES.

Perczynski, Piotr. 2000. "Active Citizenship and Associative Democracy." In Michael Saward, ed. *Democratic Innovation: Deliberation, Representation and Association*. 161–71. New York: Routledge.

Permanent Forum on Indigenous Issues. 2006. *Report of the International Expert Group Meeting On the Millennium Development Goals, Indigenous Participation and Good Governance*. 5th session. New York: United Nations Economic and Social Council. Document E/C.19/2006/7.

Posner, Paul W. 2003. "Local Democracy and Popular Participation: Chile and Brazil in Comparative Perspective." *Democratization* 10, 3 (Autumn): 39–67.

Proyecto Formia. 2004. *Gestión local alternativa, gobernabilidad y democracia... diálogo directo con los actores*. Quito: Proyecto Formia, Agencia España de Cooperación Internacional, CODENPE.

Przeworski, Adam. 1998. "Deliberation and Ideological Domination." In Jon Elster, ed. *Deliberative Democracy*. 140–60. Cambridge: Cambridge University Press.

Putnam, Robert. 1993. *Making Democracy Work*. Princeton, NJ: Princeton University Press.

Quispe, Juana. 1998. "De la organización sindical al poder local." In Ana María Larrea and Juan Pablo Muñoz, eds. *Organizaciones Campesinos e Indígenas y Poderes Locales: Propuestas para la Gestión Participativa del Desarrollo Local*. 115–20. Quito: Red Interamericana Agricultura y Democracia.

Radcliffe, Sarah A. 2001. "Indigenous Municipalities in Ecuador and Bolivia: Transnational Connections and Exclusionary Political Cultures." Paper prepared for the workshop "Beyond the Lost Decade: Indigenous Movements and the Transformation of Development and Democracy in Latin America." Princeton University, Princeton, NJ, March 2–3.

Red Interamericana para la Democracia. 2005. *Indice de participación ciudadana. Informe 3 Bolivia*. Nov. Available at www.redinter.org.

Rice, Roberta. 2006. "From Peasants to Politicians: The Politicization of Ethnic Cleavages in Latin America." Ph.D. dissertation in Political Science. University of New Mexico.

Roberts, Andrew. 2005. "The Quality of Democracy." *Comparative Politics* 37, 3 (April): 357–76.

Roberts, Kenneth M. 2002. "Party–Society Linkages and Democratic Represen-
tation in Latin America." *Canadian Journal of Latin American and Caribbean
Studies* 27, 53: 9–34.
————. 1998. *Deepening Democracy? The Modern Left and Social Movements
in Chile and Peru.* Stanford, CA: Stanford University Press.
Roberts, Kenneth M. and Erik Wibbels. 1999. "Party Systems and Electoral
Volatility in Latin America: A Test of Economic, Institutional, and Structural
Explanations." *American Political Science Review* 93, 3 (Sep.): 575–90.
Rojas Ortuste, Gonzalo. 1998. *Censura constructiva, inestabilidad y democracia
municipal.* Descentralización y Participación No. 1. La Paz: Friedrich Ebert
Stiftung/ILDIS.
Ronquillo, Gisella. 2003. "Fedepicne fragmentó a indígenas." *El Universo*, Aug.
8.
Sánchez, Jeannette. 2004. "Descentralización, macroeconomía y desarrollo
local." *Ecuador Debate* 61 (April): 77–94.
Santana, Roberto. 2004. "Cuando las élites dirigentes giran en redondo: El caso
de los liderazgos indígenas en Ecuador." *Ecuador Debate* 61 (April): 235–58.
Santos, Boaventura de Sousa. 1998. "Participatory Budgeting in Porto Alegre:
Towards a Redistributive Justice." *Politics and Society* 26, 4: 461–510.
Sarango Macas, Luis Fernando. 1997. "Movimiento Indígena Frente a los Esta-
dos Nacionales. El Caso de Ecuador." In Magdalena Gómez, coord. *Derecho
Indígena.* 318–9. Mexico City: Instituto Nacional Indigenista.
Saward, Michael. 2000a. "Democratic Innovation." In Michael Saward, ed.
Democratic Innovation: Deliberation, Representation and Association. 3–13.
New York: Routledge.
————. 2000b. "Variation, Innovation and Democratic Renewal." In Michael
Saward, ed. *Democratic Innovation: Deliberation, Representation and Associ-
ation.* 3–220. New York: Routledge.
Schmitter, Philippe, and Terry Lynn Karl. 1991. "What Democracy Is... and
What It Is Not." *Journal of Democracy* 2: 75–80.
Schönwälder, Gerd. 1997. "New Democratic Spaces at the Grassroots? Popu-
lar Participation in Latin American Local Governments." *Development and
Change* 28: 753–70.
Schumpeter, Joseph A. 1996. *Capitalism, Socialism, and Democracy.* London:
Routledge.
Scott, James C. 1990. *Domination and the Arts of Resistance: Hidden Transcripts.*
New Haven, CT: Yale University Press.
Selverston-Scher, Melina. 2001. *Ethnopolitics in Ecuador: Indigenous Rights and
the Strengthening of Democracy.* Miami, FL: North–South Center Press.
Sen, Amartya. 1999. *Development as Freedom.* New York: Knopf.
Shin, Doh Chull, Chong–Min Park, and Jiho Jang. 2005. "Assessing the Shifting
Qualities of Democratic Citizenship: The Case of South Korea." *Democratiza-
tion* 12, 2 (April): 202–22.
SIISE. 2003. *Sistema Integrado de Indicadores Sociales del Ecuador.* Version 3.5.
CD ROM.
Simmel, Georg. 1955. *Conflict and the Web of Group Affiliations.* New York:
Free Press.

Sisk, Timothy D., ed. 2001. *Democracy at the Local Level: The International IDEA Handbook on Participation, Representation, Conflict Management and Governance.* Stockholm: International IDEA.

Smith, Kevin B., Christopher W. Larimer, Levente Littvay, and John R. Hibbing. 2007. "Evolutionary Theory and Political Leadership: Why Certain People Do Not Trust Decision Makers." *Journal of Politics* 69, 2 (May): 285–99.

Snyder, Richard. 2001. "Scaling Down: The Subnational Comparative Method." *Studies in Comparative International Development* 36, 1 (Spring): 93–110.

Soberanía. 2003. "Ningún diputado y senador del MAS será candidato a alcalde y concejal el 2004." *Soberanía* [La Paz], July.

Sogliano H., Oscar y Alvar Cusicanqui M. 2006. "Experiencia edil boliviana es reconocida en el exterior." *La Razón*, Oct. 17, online.

Stokes, Susan C. 1998. "Pathologies of Deliberation." In Jon Elster, ed. *Deliberative Democracy.* 123–39. Cambridge: Cambridge University Press.

Strauss, Anselm, and Juliet Corbin. 1999. *Basics of Qualitative Research: Grounded Theory Procedures and Techniques.* Newbury Park, CA: Sage.

Sunstein, Cass R. 2003. "The Law of Group Polarization." In James S. Fishkin and Peter Laslett, eds. *Debating Deliberative Democracy.* 80–101. Malden, MA: Blackwell.

Szasz, Andrew. 1995. "Progress Through Mischief: The Social Movement Alternative to Secondary Associations." In Joshua Cohen and Joel Rogers, eds. *Associations and Democracy.* 148–56. London: Verso.

Tendler, Judith. 1997. *Good Government in the Tropics.* Baltimore, MD: Johns Hopkins University Press.

Thomas, Clive S., ed. 2001. *Political Parties and Interest Groups: Shaping Democratic Governance.* Boulder, CO: Lynne Rienner.

Ticona Alejo, Esteban. 2003. "El Thakhi entre los Aimara y los Quechua o la Democracia en los Gobiernos Comunales." In Esteban Ticona Alejo, ed. *Los Andes desde los Andes.* 125–46. La Paz: Ediciones Yachawasi.

Ticona Alejo, Esteban, and Xavier Albó. 1997. *Jesús de Machaqa: La Marka Rebelde. 3. La Lucha por el poder comunal.* Cuadernos de investigación 47. La Paz: CEDOIN, CIPCA.

Tituaña, Auki. 2004. "El Estado y Los Municipios Indígenas Alternativos." In *Taller de Gestión Local y Experiencias en los Municipios Indígenas y Alternativos.* 8–23. Quito: Proyecto de Fortalecimiento a Municipios Indígenas Alternativos, Presidencia de la República.

———. 1998. "Participación ciudadana y desarrollo local en Cotacachi." In Ana María Larrea and Juan Pablo Muñoz, eds. *Organizaciones Campesinos e Indígenas y Poderes Locales: Propuestas para la Gestión Participativa del Desarrollo Local.* 13–14. Quito: Red Interamericana Agricultura y Democracia.

Tola B., Betty. 1999. "Buscando Nuevas relaciones entre la población y el municipio: El caso del canton Chordeleg, Azuay." In *Ciudadanías Emergentes: Experiencias democráticas de desarrollo local.* 153–68. Quito: Ediciones Abya Yala.

Torres, Víctor Hugo. 1999. "El desarrollo local en el Ecuador: Discursos, tendencias y desafíos." In *Ciudadanías Emergentes: Experiencias democráticas de desarrollo local.* 15–38. Quito: Ediciones Abya Yala.

Tribunal Supremo Electoral. 1996. *Resultados Electorales 1996.* Quito: República de Ecuador.

UNDP. 2006. *Elementos para un modelo de gestión municipal transparente.* Quito: United Nations Development Programme. Available at http://www. UNDP.org.bo.

———. 2004. *Democracy in Latin America: Towards a Citizens' Democracy.* New York: United Nations Development Programme.

Valadez, Jorge M. 2001. *Deliberative Democracy, Political Legitimacy, and Self-Determination in Multicultural Societies.* Boulder, CO: Westview.

Van Cott, Donna Lee. 2006a. "Dispensing Justice at the Margins of Formality: The Informal Rule of Law in Latin America." In Gretchen Helmke and Steven Levitsky, eds. *Informal Institutions and Democracy: Lessons from Latin America.* 249–73. Baltimore, MD: Johns Hopkins University Press.

———. 2006b. "Radical Democracy in the Andes: Indigenous Parties and the Quality of Democracy in Latin America." Kellogg Institute Working Paper No. 333. Notre Dame, IN.

———. 2005. *From Movements to Parties in Latin America: The Evolution of Ethnic Politics.* New York: Cambridge University Press.

———. 2003. "Andean Indigenous Movements and Constitutional Transformation: Venezuela in Comparative Perspective." *Latin American Perspectives* 30, 1 (Jan.): 49–70.

———. 2000. *The Friendly Liquidation of the Past: The Politics of Diversity in Latin America.* Pittsburgh, PA: University of Pittsburgh Press.

Vargas Cullel, Jorge. 2004. "Democracy and the Quality of Democracy." In Guillermo O'Donnell, Jorge Vargas Cullel, and Osvaldo M. Iazzetta, eds. *The Quality of Democracy: Theory and Applications.* Notre Dame, IN: University of Notre Dame.

Vargas, Leónida Zurita, and Melissa C. Draper. 2004. "Women's Voices Rise from the Chapare." *Cultural Survival Quarterly* 27, 4 (Winter): 67–9.

Vecchio, Robert P. 1997. "Power, Politics, and Influence." In Robert P. Vecchio, ed. *Leadership: Understanding the Dynamics of Power and Influence in Organizations.* 71–99. Notre Dame, IN: University of Notre Dame Press.

Velásquez C., Fabio E. 2005. "Los Diseños de Planeación y Participación, Las Organizaciones de Base y la Construcción de Espacios Públicos de Concertación Local. Una Mirada a Partir del Caso Colombiano." From the website "Innovación Pública Local en América Latina." Available at http://www.innovacionciudadana.cl/latinoamerica/espacios.asp, retrieved Jan. 15, 2007.

Vilaseca, Fernando. 2003. "Tierra–Territorio y Municipio Indígena." In Javier Medina, comp. *Municipio Indígena: La profundización de la descentralización en un Estado multicultural.* 93–102. La Paz: Ministerio de Participación Popular.

Vroom, Victor H. 1997. "Can Leaders Learn to Lead?" In Robert P. Vecchio, ed. *Leadership: Understanding the Dynamics of Power and Influence in Organizations.* 278–91. Notre Dame, IN: University of Notre Dame Press.

Wade, Peter. 1997. *Race and Ethnicity in Latin America.* London: Pluto Press.

Wampler, Brian. 2008. "When Does Participatory Democracy Deepen the Quality of Democracy?" *Comparative Politics* 40, 3 (Oct.).
———. 2007. *Participatory Budgeting in Brazil: Contestation, Cooperation, and Accountability.* University Park, PA: Penn State Press.
———. 2004. "Expanding Accountability Through Participatory Institutions: Mayors, Citizens, and Budgeting in Three Brazilian Municipalities." *Latin American Politics and Society* 46, 3: 73–99.
Wampler, Brian, and Leonardo Avritzer. 2004. "Participatory Publics: Civil Society and New Institutions in Democratic Brazil." *Comparative Politics* 36, 3: 291–312.
Warren, Mark E. 2001. *Democracy and Association.* Princeton, NJ: Princeton University Press.
Weber, Max. 1968. *On Charisma and Institution Building. Selected Papers.* Edited and with an introduction by S. N. Eisenstadt. Chicago, IL: University of Chicago Press.
———. 1947. *Theory of Social and Economic Organization.* Translated by A. M. Henderson and Talcott Parsons. New York: Oxford University Press.
———. 1946a. "Politics as a Vocation." Translated, edited, and with an introduction by H.H. Gerth and C. Wright Mills. *From Max Weber: Essays in Sociology.* 77–128. New York: Oxford University Press.
———. 1946b. "The Social Psychology of the World Religions." Translated, edited, and with an introduction by H.H. Gerth and C. Wright Mills. *From Max Weber: Essays in Sociology.* 267–301. New York: Oxford University Press.
Wilkins, David E. 2007. *American Indian Politics and the American Political System.* 2nd edition. Lanham, MD: Rowman and Littlefield.
Willis, Eliza, Christopher Garman, and Stephan Haggard. 1999. "The Politics of Decentralization in Latin America." *Latin American Research Review* 34: 7–56.
Yashar, Deborah J. 2005. *Contesting Citizenship in Latin America: Indigenous Movements and the Postliberal Challenge.* New York: Cambridge University Press.
———. 2006. "Indigenous Politics in the Andes: Changing Patterns of Recognition, Reform, and Representation." In Scott Mainwaring, Ana Maria Bejarano, and Eduardo Pizarro Leongómez, eds. *The Crisis of Democratic Representation in the Andes.* 257–91. Stanford, CA: Stanford University Press.
Yin, Robert K. 2003. *Case Study Research: Design and Methods,* 3rd edition. Thousand Oaks, CA: Sage.
Young, Iris Marion. 2003. "Activist Challenges to Deliberative Democracy." In James S. Fishkin and Peter Laslett, eds. *Debating Deliberative Democracy.* 102–20. Malden, MA: Blackwell.
———. 1990. *Justice and the Politics of Difference.* Princeton, NJ: Princeton University Press.
Zubieta, Javier. 2000. *Estudio de caso a nivel local: Elementos para el desarrollo municipal de Irupana.* Santiago, Chile: Proyecto CEPAL/GTZ.

Index